RADICAL CONSTITUTIONAL PLURALISM IN EUROPE

This book explains the challenge of constitutional pluralism and its importance, showing its theoretical and practical relevance, and giving a sense of why the existing scholarship on the matter is unsatisfactory. The work explores how legal practitioners and theorists have faced the challenge of a society living under two constitutions at the same time. This comes as the European Union, which legally and politically integrates Europe and seems to challenge the view that no State can simultaneously abide by both the venerable national constitutions and the ever-developing EU constitutional law, is increasingly torn between calls for closer integration to face collective challenges and mounting Euroscepticism and nationalism. This work employs a strongly pluralist perspective and a comparative methodology, and looks at constitutional crises outside the EU to ground the claim that pluralism and conflicts are essential elements of modern constitutions. It shows how the challenge of constitutional pluralism depends on a mistaken interpretation of positivist theory and how the latter, reinterpreted in a manner close to legal realism, has the resources to explain pluralism. Finally, the book addresses the issue of constitutional conflicts within the EU: it examines in detail recent cases of open disobedience to EU law by national courts and distinguishes physiological conflict from constitutional pathology. This work will be of particular interest to students and academics in Law and Political Science. It will also be compelling reading for scholars in general jurisprudence, EU law, constitutional and comparative constitutional law, and the history of European integration.

Orlando Scarcello is Postdoctoral Fellow in Law at the University of Leuven, Belgium.

RADICAL CONSTITUTIONAL PLURALISM IN EUROPE

Orlando Scarcello

Routledge
Taylor & Francis Group
LONDON AND NEW YORK

Designed cover image: ermess

First published 2023
by Routledge
4 Park Square, Milton Park, Abingdon, Oxon OX14 4RN

and by Routledge
605 Third Avenue, New York, NY 10158

Routledge is an imprint of the Taylor & Francis Group, an informa business

British Library Cataloguing-in-Publication Data
A catalogue record for this book is available from the British Library

ISBN: 978-1-032-27147-7 (hbk)
ISBN: 978-1-032-27148-4 (pbk)
ISBN: 978-1-003-29157-2 (ebk)

DOI: 10.4324/9781003291572

Typeset in Bembo
by Newgen Publishing UK

To my parents, to my brother

CONTENTS

ACKNOWLEDGEMENTS

This work is the redrafting and update of my doctoral dissertation, discussed at Sant'Anna School of Advanced Studies in 2020. Whether or not the results are satisfactory is not for me to tell. However, during these years I have received the support and careful help of several people. Although every mistake or imperfection only belongs to me, much of the credit for every good inch of the work is theirs.

First, I must thank Professor Gianluigi Palombella and Professor David Dyzenhaus for their supervision and help in developing the dissertation. I would also like to thank Professor Giuseppe Martinico for his advice and encouragement throughout the years. Professor Pavlos Eleftheriadis and Professor Josep Joan Moreso kindly acted as reviewers of the thesis and provided several comments of great value.

The work also benefitted from the participation to various workshops and conferences during my PhD. I must therefore show gratitude to all the participants to the STALS Doctoral Workshop 2017, the European University Institute Legal and Political Theory Working Group, the 2018 Yale Law School Doctoral Conference, the 2019 Postgraduate Conference at the University of Glasgow, and the 2019 IVR Special Workshop on Globalization and Legal Philosophy at the University of Luzern.

After the viva, I had the opportunity to refine the dissertation as a postdoctoral fellow in the ERC RESHUFFLE (European Union's Horizon 2020 Research and Innovation Programme, grant agreement No. 851621) at KU Leuven, and especially update it in the light of recent and momentous events analysed in the last substantive chapter of the book. I can only be grateful to Professor Elise Muir and to all members of the RESHUFFLE team for their support.

A thought also goes to all those who throughout the years commented on previous drafts or engaged in discussions extremely useful to the topic of my research. I would like to thank at least Marcin Baranski, Sara Canduzzi, Giacomo Delledonne, Cosimo Gabbani, Nicola Lupo, Serena Menzione, Matteo Monti, Silvia Nuzzo, Giovanni Piccirilli, and the two anonymous referees on behalf of Routledge.

1

INTRODUCTION

The Riddle of Constitutional Pluralism

1.1 Legal Pluralism

The growing interconnection between legal systems is one of the great trends of contemporary law, especially when involving State and non-state actors. The State has certainly not disappeared and remains in a sense the paradigm of law,[1] but non-state legal orders have now grown to include global or regional organizations unimaginable in the past.[2] Lawyers are today perfectly used to talk, for instance, about the World Trade Organization, the World Health Organization, or the Council of Europe as prominent legal actors. They are even used to recognize the distinctive normative character of non-institutionalized nor treaty based, yet well-functioning standards as the *lex mercatoria* governing international trade.[3] Notions as intra-state, trans-state, and super-state legalities have been developed to denote such diverse regimes[4] and ever new theories are proposed to disentangle the law from the State.[5] Among the various options, probably the theory of 'legal pluralism' has

1 Joseph Raz, *The Authority of Law* (Oxford University Press 1979) 105; Jean d'Aspremont, 'International Law-Making by Non-State Actors: Changing the Model or Putting the Phenomenon into Perspective?' in Cedric Ryngaert and Noortmann Math (eds), *Non-State Actor Dynamics in International Law: From Law-Takers to Law-Makers* (Routledge 2010) 178–180; Marco Goldoni and Michael A Wilkinson, 'The Material Constitution' (2018) 81 The Modern Law Review 567, 581–582.

2 Here I use the wordings 'legal system', 'legal order', and 'law' in a loose, interchangeable manner. Others distinguish between 'system' and 'order'. See Keith Culver and Michael Giudice, 'Not a System but an Order: An Inter-Institutional View of European Union Law' in Keith Culver and Michael Giudice (eds), *Philosophical Foundations of European Union Law* (Oxford University Press 2012).

3 Gunther Teubner, 'Breaking Frames: Economic Globalization and the Emergence of Lex Mercatoria' (2002) 5 European Journal of Social Theory 199.

4 Keith Culver and Michael Giudice, *Legality's Borders* (Oxford University Press 2010) 149–171.

5 E.g., recently Nico Krisch (ed), *Entangled Legalities Beyond the State* (Cambridge University Press 2021); Jan Klabbers and Gianluigi Palombella (eds), *The Challenge of Inter-Legality* (Cambridge University Press 2019).

DOI: 10.4324/9781003291572-1

become the most diffuse conceptualization of the interconnection between distinct legal regimes.[6]

What these conceptualizations have in common is a focus on the incompatibility between this new legal world, crowded by non-state actors, and the classic explanation to which lawyers are used, something that we may define the 'standard theory' and that was developed by thinking about States in the first place. Any norm must be directly or indirectly reduced to a single, unifying norm on top of the pyramid. Lower administrative decisions, for instance, may be validated by, say, executive regulations, while norms on marriage may be part of a country's civil code. Higher norms must be respected for the lower provisions to be valid. Higher 'sources' of law must be themselves consistent with the formal and substantive limits enshrined in even-higher sources, such as the constitutional norms on *iter legis*, until a basic, ultimate norm is reached.

The ultimate norm is unique in its self-validation: there can be only one norm that validates itself, that is *autonomous*. Here autonomy means unfoundedness or, better, 'self-foundedness'.[7] While it makes sense to ask why administrative decisions are valid law, there is one norm with a special and self-standing foundation. Only norms reducible to the one ultimate norm are binding and valid, while what is outside will not be considered part of the law. As the standard theory goes, the ultimate norm performs a twofold function: unifying the system and providing a criterion of identity (two norms belongs to a certain system, i.e. are valid within it, if it can be tracked back to the same basic norm).[8] These views were expressed with some nuances by prominent scholars: for instance, by Joseph Raz through the idea supremacy of legal system,[9] by Norberto Bobbio when explaining the 'unity' of law,[10] and most famously by Hans Kelsen when introducing the idea of *grundnorm*, the presupposed norm which validates the entire legal system.[11]

Here is the reason why legal pluralism and other theories of the complexity of contemporary law were and are so much debated: they insist that this salient aspect of the standard picture is incorrect. As a matter of fact, they claim, we experience a variety of legal systems that de facto coexist and that are not ultimately validated by the same and single basic norm. These legal systems are autonomous and simultaneously claiming authority over the same territory or population. This is the

6 Inter alia, see John Griffiths, 'What Is Legal Pluralism?' (1986) 18 The Journal of Legal Pluralism and Unofficial Law 1; Sally Engle Merry, 'Legal Pluralism' (1988) 22 Law & Society Review 869; Paul Schiff Berman, 'Global Legal Pluralism' (2007) 80 Southern California Law Review 1155.

7 Giulio Itzcovich, 'Legal Order, Legal Pluralism, Fundamental Principles. Europe and Its Law in Three Concepts' (2012) 18 European Law Journal 358, 361–362.

8 Julie Dickson, 'Towards a Theory of European Union Legal Systems' in Julie Dickson and Pavlos Eleftheriadis (eds), *Philosophical Foundations of European Union Law* (Oxford University Press 2012) 37.

9 Joseph Raz, *The Authority of Law: Essays on Law and Morality* (Oxford University Press 1979) 118–119.

10 Norberto Bobbio, *Teoria dell'ordinamento giuridico* (Giappichelli 1960) chapter 2.

11 Hans Kelsen, *General Theory of Law and State* (Transaction Publishers 2005) 115–122. Kelsen's theory is analysed in more detail in Chapter 3. So is H.L.A. Hart's rule of recognition, discussed in Chapters 3 and 4.

riddle or challenge of legal pluralism to the standard theory: the pyramid seems to have *two* or *more* autonomous tops, not one as illustrated by the theory. Given this uncomfortable bifurcation, was the traditional, one-top view mistaken, then? Or are perhaps the claims of autonomy of the various systems mistaken?

The problem is a theoretical one, of course, as it regards our understanding of what a legal system is, but it also has immediate practical implications. In the standard theory, the single ultimate norm also has the function of providing a solution to cases of antinomies. This may happen, for instance, by empowering a last resort authority, such as a supreme court, in charge of solving conflicts of competence. Yet, in a pluralist scenario, when no such ultimate norm is available, norms to solve antinomies may be various and not adequately ordered. This, in turn, brings about uncertainty on the norm prevailing in the specific case at stake. Pluralism turns out to be practical as much as theoretical.

1.2 Constitutional Pluralism in Europe

When thinking about the connection between various legal orders, the example that most people would immediately think about probably is the one that was not mentioned already and that will be the case study of this book, namely the European Union (EU). Born as a series of international associations between European States in the 1950s (the Communities), it has developed into the most articulated non-state legal order currently existing.[12] The extreme level of development of the EU can be perceived by looking at the complexity of the institutional structure, the intricacy of the sources of law, and the extension and diversity of its competences. There is also another reason why the case of the EU is especially challenging, though. Indeed, the EU does not only claim to be an autonomous legal order, but also to have constitutional nature: in Přibáň's words, 'EU constitutional pluralism thus primarily signifies *the plurality of constitutional authorities*'.[13] Here is the riddle of *constitutional* pluralism, the question to which this book attempts answering: how can it be that a legal system, specifically the composite order made of the EU and of the Member States, has *two* constitutions on top?

Although the notion of 'constitutionalism' is an essentially contested one,[14] so that one may more appropriately speak of several 'constitutionalisms',[15] still there is a liberal-democratic meaning of constitutionalism that probably is the paradigm, the most diffuse meaning of modern constitutionalism. In its liberal component, it coincides with the normative view that a constitution ought to separate

12 Briefly on the history of European integration, see Robert Schütze, *European Union Law* (Oxford University Press 2021) 4–39.

13 Jiří Přibáň, *Constitutional Imaginaries: A Theory of European Societal Constitutionalism* (Routledge 2022) 138.

14 Walter B Gallie, 'Essentially Contested Concepts' (1955) 56 Proceedings of the Aristotelian Society 167.

15 Robert Schütze, 'Constitutionalism(s)' in Roger Masterman and Robert Schütze (eds), *The Cambridge Companion to Comparative Constitutional Law* (Cambridge University Press 2019).

powers to guarantee rights.[16] Since the advent during the Enlightenment of the idea of 'human being', a radical intellectual break with the past occurred as individuals and their rights became the centre of political philosophy.[17] The need to grant such prerogatives against arbitrary actions by public authorities is the main motive beneath the separation of powers: ambition must limit ambition, power must limit power, paraphrasing James Madison's famous motto.[18] As for the democratic element, it asserts that in modern constitutionalism the identification of the rights and of the powers, as well as the specification of their meaning through regulation, must ultimately happen according to the popular will. Following a line of thinking tracing back to Sieyès, the authority of the constitution itself depends on the people, the only legitimate *pouvoir constituant*.[19] Although the very idea of 'people' has been criticized as ideological and flimsy,[20] it remains the main source of democratic legitimation of modern constitutions.[21]

The liberal and democratic components are inextricably merged in the ordinary narrative on modern constitutionalism.[22] Starting with the late 18th-century revolutions in America and France, liberal-democratic constitutionalism in its various forms has progressively become the backbone of the legitimacy of European States. The constitution has been understood as the ultimate foundation of modern legal systems, the only acceptable *grundnorm*.[23]

Within this framework, it was simply natural that the law of the EU growingly committed itself to the principles of modern constitutionalism and attempted to legitimize its authority by relying on them. Such transformation is visible both in the liberal and (to a lesser extent) in the democratic side of modern constitutionalism.

Starting from the liberal component, the initial absence of a catalogue of EU rights has been progressively filled by the main judicial institution of the Union, the Court of Justice, by elaborating a series of general principles inspired by common constitutional traditions and by the European Convention on Human Rights

16 Quoting from the famous Article XVI of the *Déclaration des droits de l'homme et du citoyen de 1789*: 'Toute Société dans laquelle la garantie des Droits n'est pas assurée, ni la séparation des Pouvoirs déterminée, n'a point de Constitution'.

17 For a history of such process, see Vincenzo Ferrone, *The Enlightenment and the Rights of Man* (Liverpool University Press 2019) part 2.

18 See the Federalist Paper n. 51 in Alexander Hamilton, James Madison and John Jay, *The Federalist Papers* (Michael A Genovese ed, Palgrave Macmillan 2010) 120.

19 Emmanuel J Sieyès, 'What Is the Third Estate?' in Oliver W Lembcke and Florian Weber (eds), *Emmanuel Joseph Sieyès: The Essential Political Writings* (Brill 2014) 43–117; Lucia Rubinelli, *Constituent Power: A History* (Cambridge University Press 2020) 33–73.

20 Hans Kelsen, *The Essence and Value of Democracy* (Rowman & Littlefield 2013) 35–46.

21 Martin Loughlin, 'The Concept of Constituent Power' (2014) 13 European Journal of Political Theory 218.

22 Schütze, 'Constitutionalism(s)' (n 15) 54–60.

23 Leonard Besselink, *A Composite European Constitution* (Europa Law Publishing 2007) 10: 'In the vast majority of Member States – at least those within continental Europe which take their basis in the ideas of the French Revolution – the national constitution claims to be the ultimate source of State law i.e., the ultimate legitimation for the exercise of public authority over citizens.'

(ECHR).[24] Since the 1980s, the Court of Justice has envisaged in the Treaties a 'constitutional charter' (*charte constitutionnelle*)[25] and has progressively refined this narrative by identifying a series of documents, principles, and rights that constitute the 'higher law' of the Union.[26] The political bodies of the Union have confirmed this narrative by first codifying most of the general principles into a Charter of Fundamental Rights of the EU (2000) and then by engaging into a process of revision that established a Constitutional Treaty. Despite the failure of such Treaty in 2005 and the abandon of its constitutional symbolism, the following Lisbon Treaty confirmed most innovations, especially the binding value of the Charter (after which, the Court made of it the preferential standard of review, often replacing general principles[27]). In the following years, the EU legislator has specified the content of EU rights through legislative instruments, granting protection to rights that are at times unknown, embryonic, or unharmonized at the State level. The regulation of the right to data protection, implementing Articles 7 and 8 of the Charter, is a case in point.[28] Moreover, the Commission, the Council, and the European Parliament arranged internal procedures to try ensuring the compatibility of EU regulation with the Charter.[29]

Even more tellingly, when facing the internal backslide on the rule of law,[30] judges of the involved Member States have looked at the Court of Justice to re-establish the right to effective judicial protection dismantled by illiberal national regimes. Specifically, after the *Associação Sindical dos Juízes Portugueses* (*ASJP*) case, a string of judgments has bolstered the right to effective judicial protection under EU law,[31] using Article 47 of the Charter to specify the meaning of Articles 2 and

24 C-11/70 Internationale Handelsgesellschaft mbH v Einfuhr- und Vorratsstelle für Getreide und Futtermittel EU:C:1970:114; C-4/73 J. Nold, Kohlen- und Baustoffgroßhandlung v Commission of the European Communities EU:C:1974:5; C-36/75 Rutili v Ministre de l'intérieur, ECLI:EU:C:1975:137; C-44/79 Hauer vs. Land Rheinland Pfalz ECLI:EU:C:1979:290.

25 C-294/83 Parti écologiste 'Les Verts' v European Parliament ECLI:EU:C:1986:166.

26 Opinion 2/13 ECLI:EU:C:2014:2454, para. 169. The Opinion will be examined in detail in Chapter 2.

27 Although general principles have not been fully displaced. See Emily Hancox, 'The Relationship Between the Charter and General Principles: Looking Back and Looking Forward' (2020) 22 Cambridge Yearbook of European Legal Studies 233.

28 Thomas Streinz, 'The Evolution of European Data Law' in Paul Craig and Gráinne de Búrca (eds), *The Evolution of EU Law* (Oxford University Press 2021) 904–914.

29 Šejla Imamovic, *The Architecture of Fundamental Rights in the European Union* (Hart Publishing 2022) 27–31.

30 Laurent Pech and Kim Lane Scheppele, 'Illiberalism Within: Rule of Law Backsliding in the EU' (2017) 19 Cambridge Yearbook of European Legal Studies 3; Laurent Pech, Patryk Wachowiec and Dariusz Mazur, 'Poland's Rule of Law Breakdown: A Five-Year Assessment of EU's (In)Action' (2021) 13 Hague Journal on the Rule of Law 1.

31 See C-64/16 Associação Sindical dos Juízes Portugueses v Tribunal de Contas (*ASJP*) EU:C:2018:117, paras. 29–37; C-284/16 Slowakische Republik v Achmea BV EU:C:2018:158, paras. 32–33; Case C-216/18 PPU LM EU:C:2018:586, para. 53; C-824/18 A.B. and Others v Krajowa Rada Sądownictwa and Others (A.B.) EU:C:2021:153, paras. 115 and 143–146; C-896/19 Repubblika v Il-Prim Ministru (Repubblika) EU:C:2021:311, paras. 47–65; C-156/21 Hungary v European Parliament and Council of the European Union ECLI:EU:C:2022:97 paras. 160–162.

19(1) of the Treaty on the EU (TEU) and attempting to impose a higher standard on the right to judicial protection to reluctant Member States.[32] Thus, although the Court has at times been criticized for not being sufficiently committed to the liberties entrenched in the Charter,[33] its role as an EU 'constitutional court' seems to be expanding. Its intervention to fill in the gaps left by declining domestic commitment to constitutionalism resembles a transposition to the European context of the 'compensatory' constitutionalism already described by international lawyers.[34] Such change in the role of EU law marks a significant overturn of what was originally conceived as a 'defensive' and 'low intensity' constitutionalism, mainly aimed at reassuring Member States against the rising *government des fonctionnaires*:[35] the EU is now an actor that intervenes visibly when States fail in their commitment to rights. Thus, on the side of fundamental rights, EU constitutionalism is alive and well.[36]

When considering the second element of liberal constitutionalism, namely separation of powers, the classic tripartite *functional* separation of powers, in which each branch is conferred the function to legislate, execute, or adjudicate, does not fit well the institutional structure of the Union.[37] The Council of the EU, for instance, is close to a 'senate' of the Union, representing States in the legislative, yet also performs executive functions, especially in the field of the common foreign and security policy (CFSP).[38] However, alternative versions of the separation of powers take a more relaxed attitude and deem the sharing of powers between institutions belonging to different branches as possible. An *institutional* version of the separation of powers accepts that the same institution may exercise functions belonging to more than one branch simultaneously. If this is the notion of separation of powers we accept, then the second tenet of liberal constitutionalism is broadly compatible with the EU as well.[39] Moreover, and most importantly,

32 Matteo Bonelli and Monica Claes, 'Judicial Serendipity: How Portuguese Judges Came to the Rescue of the Polish Judiciary: ECJ 27 February 2018, Case C-64/16, *Associação Sindical Dos Juízes Portugueses*' (2018) 14 European Constitutional Law Review 622; Aida Torres Pérez, 'From Portugal to Poland: The Court of Justice of the European Union as Watchdog of Judicial Independence' (2020) 27 Maastricht Journal of European and Comparative Law 105.

33 Dorota Leczykiewicz, 'The Charter of Fundamental Rights and the EU's Shallow Constitutionalism' in Nicholas Barber, Maria Cahill and Richard Ekins (eds), *The Rise and Fall of the European Constitution* (Hart Publishing 2019).

34 Anne Peters, 'Compensatory Constitutionalism: The Function and Potential of Fundamental International Norms and Structures' (2006) 19 Leiden Journal of International Law 579.

35 Joseph HH Weiler, 'Eurocracy and Distrust: Some Questions Concerning the Role of the European Court of Justice in the Protection of Fundamental Human Rights Within the Legal Order of the European Communities' (1986) 61 Washington Law Review 41, 1115–1116.

36 Gráinne de Búrca, 'The Evolution of EU Human Rights Law' in Paul Craig and Gráinne de Búrca (eds), *The Evolution of EU Law* (Oxford University Press 2021); Imamovic (n 29) 16–23.

37 On the difficulties of applying the separation of powers scheme to the EU, see Christoph Moellers, *The Three Branches: A Comparative Model of Separation of Powers* (Oxford University Press 2013) 167–195.

38 Schütze, *European Union Law* (n 12) 287–300.

39 Robert Schütze, 'Constitutionalism and the European Union' in Catherine Barnard and Steve Peers (eds), *European Union Law* (Oxford University Press 2020) 90–96.

if in the context of modern constitutionalism the function of the separation of powers is to divide legal authority to preserve rights against potential abuse, then the EU probably developed a functional equivalent of such division through the so-called principle of institutional balance. The principle's meaning is not always clear, but it broadly limits the role of each institution to the boundaries defined in the Treaties and prevents actions de facto depriving other institutions of their lawful prerogatives. Such delimitation of institutional prerogatives and pre-emption of *ultra vires* acts by EU institutions performs a function quite close to the classical tripartite separation, although imperfectly.[40] Finally, the separation of powers in the EU is strengthened by the 'federal' balance between the EU and the Member States, a vertical separation that must be taken into account when evaluating the EU's adherence to the model of modern constitutionalism.[41] Whether and to what extent it is appropriate to define the EU as a federal or quasi-federal structure are questions to be answered later in the book (Chapter 4) but suffice here to remember that the Member States' attributions effectively balance the powers conferred to the EU. The division of powers between the EU and the States, envisaged in Article 2 of the Treaty on the Functioning of the EU (TFEU), together with the principle of conferral as in Article 5 of the TEU, restricts the Union to the powers conferred by the Treaties. At the institutional level, the Council is clearly identified as the representative of the Member States in the Union, ready to preserve their interests and attributions. Similarly, Protocol n. 2 on the principles of subsidiarity and proportionality effectively provides national parliaments with an instrument to prevent and tame *ultra vires* actions by the EU legislator.[42] Thus, although the Union does not perfectly match the classic tripartition of powers in the tradition of Montesquieu, the function of power limitation through separation is to a certain extent fulfilled in the Union.

While the guarantee of rights and the separation of powers certify compliance with liberal constitutionalism, the EU's adherence to democratic constitutionalism is more problematic.[43] The Union is still often perceived as insufficiently democratic, at least when it comes to the so-called *input* democratic legitimacy, the possibility to attribute choices of EU institutions to the will of the people.[44] To name some of the most well-known problems, the Parliament's centre-left/centre-right supermajorities seem too far from the usual dynamic between majority and opposition typical of national assemblies; special legislative procedures in which the last

40 Gerard Conway, 'Recovering a Separation of Powers in the European Union: Separation of Powers in the EU' (2011) 17 European Law Journal 304, 319–321.

41 Thomas O Hueglin and Alan Fenna, *Comparative Federalism: A Systematic Inquiry* (University of Toronto Press 2015) 90–92.

42 For an overview of the mechanism and of the first years of its application, see Tomasz Jaroszyński, 'National Parliaments' Scrutiny of the Principle of Subsidiarity: Reasoned Opinions 2014–2019' (2020) 16 European Constitutional Law Review 91.

43 David Marquand, *Parliament for Europe* (J Cape 1979).

44 Vivien A Schmidt, 'Democracy and Legitimacy in the European Union Revisited: Input, Output and "Throughput"' (2013) 61 Political Studies 2, 4–5.

word belongs to the Council are too frequent; legislative initiative is in the hands of the Commission, not the Parliament; crucial decisions are often taken by Member States through inter-governmental agreements that barely involve the European Parliament (EP).[45] More radically, the very existence of a European *demos* on which a democracy may be based has been questioned.[46] However, especially after Lisbon, the EU commitment to democracy was strengthened and codified, as testified by Articles 2 and 10 TEU.[47] The generalization of the co-decision procedure into an ordinary one, the involvement of the EP in many of the most important moments of the life of the EU (for instance, the treaty-revision procedure as in Article 48 TEU), the political rights of EU citizens enshrined into Article 20 TEU, the several attempts of the EP to move the reluctant Commission in the wake of the rule of law crisis,[48] and the dialogue between national parliaments and EU institutions via the already quoted Protocol n. 2, are all signs of a stronger (albeit probably still insufficient) commitment of the EU to the standards of modern democracy.

Briefly, based on the high standards of rights protection, on a vertical and a horizontal balance (if not properly a separation) of powers, and on a clearer commitment to internal democracy, the case for some form of European constitutionalism seems overall stronger today.

The question remains whether the EU's level of commitment to constitutionalism is enough to pass a minimum threshold. Modern constitutionalism is in fact an ideal of government that can only be approximated, even by States. Is the EU close enough to the threshold? A series of key legal actors seem to answer positively.

The EU institutions are, of course, the most obvious cases in point, if only to achieve the surplus of legitimacy that such qualification entails.[49] The Court of Justice, as already mentioned, considers the Treaties as the constitutional charter of the Union. The Conventions that drafted the Charter and the Constitutional Treaty used a powerful constitutional symbolism. When recently launching a series of actions for infringement against Poland after *ASJP*, the Commission has attempted to perform not only the mundane function of guardian of the Treaties, but that of guardian of the constitutional values of the Union enshrined in Article 2 TEU.[50]

45 Cristina Fasone, Daniele Gallo and Jan Wouters, 'Re-Connecting Authority and Democratic Legitimacy in the EU: Introductory Remarks' (2020) 5 *European Papers* 175, 175–186.

46 Dieter Grimm, *Constitutionalism: Past, Present, and Future* (Oxford University Press 2016) chapter 14.

47 A certain commitment to democracy existed even in foundational cases as *Van Gend en Loos* and *Costa v Enel*. Quoting Miguel, Poiares Maduro: '[w]hen the ECJ, in its path-breaking decisions, took EC law to be an autonomous legal order, it did so on the basis of a presumed direct relations with the peoples of Europe'. Miguel Poiares Maduro, 'The Importance of Being Called a Constitution: Constitutional Authority and the Authority of Constitutionalism' (2005) 3 International Journal of Constitutional Law 332, 336.

48 Melanie Smith, 'Staring into the Abyss: A Crisis of the Rule of Law in the EU' (2019) 25 European Law Journal 561, 573–574.

49 On the role of constitutionalism in fostering the legitimacy of EU's authority, see again Poiares Maduro (n 47).

50 Laurent Pech and Dimitry Kochenov, *Respect for the Rule of Law in the Case Law of the European Court of Justice: A Casebook Overview of Key Judgments since the Portuguese Judges Case* (Swedish

While a positive answer from EU institutions is understandable, the reaction of *national* institutions is of the utmost interest. As previously mentioned, for instance, national courts in some Member States have tried to compensate for the internally plummeting commitment to constitutionalism by referring to the Court of Justice and counting on its 'constitutional role' to safeguard judicial independency.[51] Moreover, even outside these pathological circumstances, a few constitutional courts have in the last decade started using the Charter of Fundamental Rights as an *internal* standard of constitutional review: the constitutional courts of Austria, Italy, and Germany have heightened the Charter to the level of a proper equivalent of their own catalogues of rights.[52] While there are internal reasons of judicial politics which partly explain this choice, especially the need of avoiding de facto decentralization of judicial review via independent application of the Charter by domestic judges *in lieu* of the national constitution,[53] the decision of directly using the EU standards is a recognition of the constitutional maturity of EU law that cannot be underestimated. In judgment 269/2017 by the Italian Constitutional Court (ICC), this recognition was plain:[54]

> Granted the principles of the primacy and direct effect of European Union law as consolidated in both European and constitutional case law, it bears considering that the aforementioned Charter of Rights is a part of Union law that is endowed with particular characteristics due to the typically constitutional stamp of its contents. The principles and rights laid out in the Charter largely intersect with the principles and rights guaranteed by the Italian Constitution (and by other Member States' constitutions).

Institute for European Policy Studies 2021) 33–93 www.sieps.se/en/publications/2021/respect-for-the-rule-of-law-in-the-case-law-of-the-european-court-of-justice/. Despite a significant reluctancy, though. See R Daniel Kelemen and Tommaso Pavone, 'Where Have the Guardians Gone? Law Enforcement and the Politics of Supranational Forbearance in the European Union' (Social Science Research Network 2021) SSRN Scholarly Paper 3994918 https://papers.ssrn.com/abstract=3994918.

51 Peter Van Elsuwege and Femke Gremmelprez, 'Protecting the Rule of Law in the EU Legal Order: A Constitutional Role for the Court of Justice' (2020) 16 European Constitutional Law Review 8.

52 See the comparative analysis of the three cases by Clara Rauchegger, 'National Constitutional Courts as Guardians of the Charter: A Comparative Appraisal of the German Federal Constitutional Court's *Right to Be Forgotten* Judgments' (2020) 22 Cambridge Yearbook of European Legal Studies 258. On the advantages for constitutional courts of such strategy, see Davide Paris, 'Constitutional Courts as European Union Courts: The Current and Potential Use of EU Law as a Yardstick for Constitutional Review' (2017) 24 Maastricht Journal of European and Comparative Law 792, 24–28.

53 Such risk had been assessed in the literature even before the Charter became binding. See Victor Ferrares Comella, 'The European Model of Constitutional Review of Legislation: Toward Decentralization?' (2004) 2 International Journal of Constitutional Law 461, 479–482. See also Jan Komárek, 'The Place of Constitutional Courts in the EU' (2013) 9 European Constitutional Law Review 420, 427–433.

54 Corte costituzionale, judgment 269/2017, para. 5.2.

Similarly, the German Constitutional Court recognized the constitutional status of the Charter a few years later.[55] Such statements regard the liberal more than the democratic element of modern constitutionalism, nevertheless they acknowledge explicitly the constitutional character of EU law.

Briefly, the claim that (part of) EU law has constitutional nature is accepted by a series of legal actors that belong to both the level of EU institutions and to national legal systems. Besides legitimate doubts, a certain degree of recognition of this nature must be registered as a social fact. The claim that EU law has a constitution of its own is de facto taken seriously.

It is this grounding of EU law on a 'constitutional charter', quoting again from *Les Verts*, that transforms the problem we started from, that of legal pluralism, into the riddle of *constitutional pluralism*: the plural and competing fundamental norms that lie at the basis of the involved systems (national and EU) coincide with constitutions.

This does not fundamentally change the riddle of pluralism but makes it more delicate and urgent. Indeed, structurally we still have a theory telling us that on top of the legal order we should find a single foundational norm, only to then encounter an uncomfortable bifurcation (the EU treaties or the national constitutions as *grundnorm*). However, whether the ultimate norm is a constitution or not is far from being irrelevant. Scholars like Carl Schmitt, Rudolf Smend, and Costantino Mortati, have emphasized long ago how the constitution has a particular way of performing the function of unification typical of ultimate norms: they identify the essential common values of a political community.[56] The fact that the competing basic norms are *constitutions* and not just any other norm does not structurally alter the riddle of pluralism, but the ethical-political sense of the constitution as a unifying instrument explains why the challenge of pluralism becomes more delicate after its transmutation into constitutional pluralism. Modern constitutionalism is not merely a description of how the highest norms of the system work, but most importantly a normative theory. Realizing whether the ultimate, foundational norm lies on one level or on the other becomes particularly pressing, for it strongly impacts on the legitimacy of law. The theoretical problem does not change, but the practical need to understand it gets stronger.

Here we can finally summarize the challenge of constitutional pluralism: most lawyers would describe their legal system as a series of hierarchically ordered norms with a constitution on top. Yet in the EU, a European constitution commands loyalty

55 BVerfG, 2 BvR 1845/18, para. 37. The judgment comes after the two *Right to be Forgotten* cases (BVerfG 1 BvR 16/13; BvR 267/17), which clarified that the German Constitutional Court would apply the Charter as a standard of review each time EU law fully harmonized an area of law (BvR 267/17, *Right to be Forgotten II*) and would in principle give priority to German constitutional rights in non-fully harmonized areas (BvR 16/13, *Right to be Forgotten I*).

56 See Carl Schmitt, *Constitutional Theory* (Duke University Press 2008) 75–89 and 125–135; Arthur Jacobson and Bernhard Schlink (eds), *Weimar: A Jurisprudence of Crisis* (2002) 213–247 for a partial translation and comment of Smend; Costantino Mortati, *L'ordinamento del governo nel nuovo diritto pubblico italiano* (Giuffrè 2000) 7–27.

to officials and citizens as much as the domestic constitution does. The pyramid seems to have two tops, which is nothing but a metaphor to refer to the disagreement on the question of ultimate authority, to the competing claims to ultimate authority that several institutions make. Was the traditional, one-top view mistaken in requiring agreement on the ultimate authority, then? Or is the EU perspective wrong? Or, perhaps, are the national constitutions obsolete? Finally, what happens when commands coming from the two levels collide?

1.3 Radical Pluralism, Positivism, Comparative Law

Naturally, attempts to answer these questions were made. Although there is no universal consensus regarding the constitutional nature of the EU and although there are scholars who still prefer to consider EU law as part of international rather than constitutional law,[57] others have tried to understand how the two constitutional layers relate one another. To name a few, multilevel constitutionalism was advanced to conceptualize the 'dual' structure of Europe: the constitution of Europe would be made of the constitutions of the States together with the complementary body of the Treaties.[58] Similarly, the idea of a 'composite' European constitution emphasizes the fact that the level of integration is so deep that the two levels cannot function on their own, but only in symbiosis.[59] The interpretation and meaning of EU rights, for instance, is allegedly influenced by the meaning they have in Member States (and *vice versa*).[60] The European constitution has also been described as a 'complex' entity, in which the changes that each level brings about are non-reversible and non-reducible to the action of a single layer, the future evolution unpredictable, the possibility of governing its evolution limited.[61]

All these works exemplify a wider scholarly movement that may be called 'constitutional pluralism', in the broad sense of a movement accepting the constitutional nature of EU law and trying to figure out how it relates to the constitutions of the Member States. A more detailed examination of the pluralist movement will be introduced in Chapter 2. It is necessary, however, to immediately introduce a major division among pluralists that is crucial to understand the position of this book.

57 E.g., Pavlos Eleftheriadis, *A Union of Peoples* (Oxford University Press 2020); Bruno de Witte, 'The European Union as an International Legal Experiment' in Grainne de Burca and JHH Weiler (eds), *The Worlds of European Constitutionalism* (Cambridge University Press 2011); Bruno de Witte, 'Direct Effect, Primacy, and the Nature of the Legal Order' in Paul Craig and Gráinne de Búrca (eds), *The Evolution of EU Law* (Oxford University Press 2021).

58 Ingolf Pernice, 'Multilevel Constitutionalism and the Treaty of Amsterdam: European Constitution-Making Revisited?' (1999) 36 Common Market Law Review 48.

59 Besselink (n 23).

60 E.g., consider the principle of proportionality: of German origin, it spread throughout Europe after being appropriated and diffused by the Court of Justice. See Alec Stone Sweet and Jud Mathews, 'Proportionality Balancing and Global Constitutionalism' (2008) 47 *Columbia Journal of Transnational Law* 73, 139–145.

61 Giuseppe Martinico, *The Tangled Complexity of the EU Constitutional Process: The Frustrating Knot of Europe* (Routledge 2013).

Most pluralists take a stance that may be labelled 'normative constitutional pluralism', but that is so diffused to have become a sort of constitutional pluralism *tout court*. This version of constitutional pluralism does not focus that much on how the interactions between the two constitutional layers work, but mostly on the desirability of such state of affairs. For normative pluralists, the dual constitutionalism of Europe is desirable and worth preserving as an adaptation of constitutionalism to the post-national scenario of the 20th century: the interaction between supranational and national powers will reinforce, not weaken, constitutionalism in Europe. The only concern is how to avoid that the involved layers collide. The focus of normative pluralists is on the interpretive methodologies that the main legal actors of the Union, the Court of Justice and national judges, shall use in order to preserve the suspension on the question of ultimate authority without colliding: saving pluralism while avoiding conflicts.

This normative version of constitutional pluralism is not the one I develop in this book. Instead, I endorse a version of pluralism usually defined *radical pluralism*. I understand radical constitutional pluralism as the theory according to which EU law has some minimum degree of constitutionalism, imperfect as it may be, so that it makes sense to talk about an EU as well as of a national constitutional layer. However, the focus of this approach is on realizing how two legal orders with an independent constitutional foundation can coexist, rather than judging its desirability. When it comes to the risk of conflicts, in radical pluralism there is no legal solution available: ultimately irreconcilable directives will at times be issued, and there is no interpretive method that can provide a legal solution to the contradiction. When juridical solutions run out, only political negotiation remains. Radical pluralism is, in other words, descriptive instead of normative, realist rather than idealist, and political as opposed to juridical. It is this framework that I develop in this book.

Radical pluralism is a quite underdeveloped theory, something that contributes to the more generalized relative thinness of studies on the law and constitution of the EU recently underlined by Neil Walker.[62] It is not easy to explain why, although it is possible that the denial of the possibility to provide legal solutions in conflictual cases makes radical pluralism less attractive than its normative twin to most lawyers. Yet, it has not always been so. Radical pluralism was the first perspective adopted by the intellectual father of constitutional pluralism, the Scottish jurist Neil MacCormick in a few articles published between 1993 and 1997,[63] a position which he abandoned in later years.

This book relies heavily on MacCormick's thoughts on pluralism, which are examined in detail in Chapter 3. This, in turn, also entails a commitment to legal positivism at the level of general jurisprudence. Positivism is perhaps not particularly

62 Neil Walker, 'Legal and Constitutional Theory of the European Union' in Paul Craig and Gráinne de Búrca (eds), *The Evolution of EU Law* (Oxford University Press 2021) 90.

63 Neil MacCormick, 'Beyond the Sovereign State' (1993) 56 The Modern Law Review 1; Neil MacCormick, 'The Maastricht-Urteil: Sovereignty Now' (1995) 1 European Law Journal 259; Neil MacCormick, 'Democracy, Subsidiarity, and Citizenship in the "European Commonwealth"' (1997) 16 Law and Philosophy 331.

popular among scholars working on European pluralism,[64] as the normative pull of the movement leads to the adoption of rival perspectives such as Dworkinism.[65] However, as the goal of the book is to figure out how a functioning legal order can be based on a twofold ultimate norm of constitutional nature, a positivist perspective is only natural. The kind of positivism endorsed here is a minimalist one based on two fundamental theses: that all law is the intentional or unintentional product of human activities while, conversely, there is no natural law (social thesis); and that it is possible to analyse the law without automatically expressing a moral judgment about it (separability thesis).[66] This version of positivism directly connects with H.L.A. Hart's self-evaluation of his theory as a form of 'descriptive sociology' of law, a theory that, as we will see, was used by MacCormick in elaborating radical pluralism.[67] Moreover, it is a version of positivism that reconciles it with legal realism. Law is conceived as a social phenomenon to be studied empirically by looking at the behaviour of institutions, especially judges.[68] The value of jurisprudence lies not so much in advising practitioners, but in explaining the legal culture and institutions of a society. Law is a social construct that can be studied looking at its crafters, officials and even citizens.[69]

Enter another tenet of this book, one that follows directly from the positivist-realist perspective, namely the use of *comparative (constitutional) law*. If theorizing

64 In the words of Kumm in Matej Avbelj and Jan Komárek, 'Four Visions of Constitutional Pluralism Symposium Transcript' (2008) 2 European Journal of Legal Studies 323, 354: 'But as the heartpiece of a theory of constitutional authority, the new post-statist, post-nationalist and post-positivist constitutionalism that many of us here embrace has the purpose to more generally reconceive the foundations of law as it's practiced in trans-nationally integrated liberal-democracies'.

65 E.g., see Mattias Kumm, 'The Jurisprudence of Constitutional Conflict: Constitutional Supremacy in Europe before and after the Constitutional Treaty' (2005) 11 European Law Journal 262; Eleftheriadis (n 57).

66 A series of other supposed commitments of positivism, including a special allegiance to *Rechtstaat* as the ideal form of government or the myth of the judge as the *bouche de la loi*, are enlisted by John Gardner, 'Legal Positivism: 5 1/2 Myths' (2001) 46 American Journal of Jurisprudence 199.

67 Herbert LA Hart, *The Concept of Law* (Oxford University Press 2012) vi. On the extent to which Hart was able to follow this aim, see Nicola Lacey, 'Analytical Jurisprudence Versus Descriptive Sociology Revisited' in Maksymilian Del Mar and Michael Giudice (eds), *Legal Theory and the Social Sciences*, vol II (Routledge 2010) 948–960.

68 Leslie Green, 'Positivism, Realism and Sources of Law' in Torben Spaak and Patricia Mindus (eds), *The Cambridge Companion to Legal Positivism* (Cambridge University Press 2021); Brian Leiter, 'Legal Positivism as a Realist Theory of Law' in Torben Spaak and Patricia Mindus (eds), *The Cambridge Companion to Legal Positivism* (Cambridge University Press 2021). As Green states (ivi 49–51), the most significant difference between Hart's jurisprudence and realism lies in the amount of indeterminacy that is typical of legal systems. For Hart, it is an exaggeration to state, as he attributes to realists, that ordinary legal controversies are indeterminate and depend for the most part on judicial discretion: 'hard' cases exist but do not epitomize the ordinary functioning of law. In Leiter's analysis (ivi 80–82), Hart is close to realism for four reasons: a) he recognizes that law mainly operates outside courts to guide people's behaviour; b) when legal disputes reach courts, judges exercise discretion; c) law is conceived law in naturalistic terms (as a series of social and psychological facts); d) law is not necessarily morally good.

69 Leslie Green, 'Introduction' in Herbert LA Hart, *The Concept of Law* (Oxford University Press 2012) xliv–lii.

about abstract legal concepts requires the analysis of their concrete application, then focusing on a single jurisdiction will hardly provide for the appropriate level of generality. A more fruitful approach consists in looking at how similar societal challenges have been dealt with in different jurisdictions and then theorize starting from the commonalities in responses. In the jargon of comparative law, this presupposes a certain degree of functionalism: the assumption is that, although elaborated in different contexts, legal doctrines and institutions provide answers to similar societal needs.[70] By studying answers to similar societal problems, key concepts denoting these problems become analytically sharper.[71] This way of proceeding has been applied to elaborate illuminating notions like 'unconstitutional constitutional amendments' or 'Commonwealth constitutionalism':[72] a series of pre-theoretical assumption guides the selection of cases (for instance, some prejudices about what jurisdictions belong to the 'Commonwealth constitutionalism'), but after these have been studied, a proper theory will be available and much likely at least part of the pre-theoretical assumptions will be different. Theory and practice go hand in hand in a sort of reflective equilibrium.

What I intend to do is similar but slightly different. I intend to look at whether in the experience of States there is indeed a single top of the pyramid or not. Since the problem we are attempting to analyse here is how a functioning legal order like the European one can have more than one foundational norm, we need to consider whether twofold and contested ultimate norms have functioned historically outside the EU order and compare them with our main case study. Cases considered in Chapters 4 and 5, such as that of the USA before the Civil War, perform this task. The result is not the formulation of a new abstract concept as 'Commonwealth constitutionalism' but rather some elucidation of the concept of 'constitution' itself, stressing its structurally plural and conflictual character and its meaning in the case of EU pluralism.

Here it is possible to anticipate that the conclusion I reach is that the idea of a single and uncontested foundational norm at the basis of legal systems is unrealistic. The riddle of constitutional pluralism is answered by noticing that a plurality of constitutions is often at stake when we look at how legal orders work. The view according to which there is only one foundational norm, one constitution per each legal system, was mistaken. Functioning legal orders show that it is indeed

70 James Gordley, 'Comparative Legal Research: Its Function in the Development of Harmonized Law' (1995) 43 American Journal of Comparative Law 555; Ralf Michaels, 'The Functional Method of Comparative Law' in Mathias Reimann and Reinhard Zimmermann (eds), *The Oxford Handbook of Comparative Law* (Oxford University Press 2019).

71 Hirschl called such method 'concept formation through multiple description'. See Ran Hirschl, 'Comparative Methodologies' in Roger Masterman and Robert Schütze (eds), *The Cambridge Companion to Comparative Constitutional Law* (Cambridge University Press 2019) 25. See also Vicki Jackson, 'Comparative Constitutional Law: Methodologies' in Michel Rosenfeld and András Sajó (eds), *The Oxford Handbook of Comparative Constitutional Law* (Oxford University Press 2012) 64–65.

72 Yaniv Roznai, *Unconstitutional Constitutional Amendments: The Limits of Amendment Powers* (Oxford University Press 2019); Stephen Gardbaum, *The New Commonwealth Model of Constitutionalism* (Cambridge University Press 2013).

perfectly normal to see disagreement and controversy regarding the ultimate legal authority, the interpretation of the constitution, or conflict-resolving rules. Officials and participants in the legal practice at large will frequently uphold different *rules* of recognition, largely coincident with their 'constitutions'. Occasionally, such divergences erupt into open conflict, but constitutional conflicts do not jeopardize the legal order, except in long-lasting and severe cases. Therefore, the European case is considered here as simply a more pronounced instantiation of what happens at the level of States too. Its conflictual character is harsher but not fundamentally different from the one that we experience at the State level. Briefly, I argue based on evidence from comparative law that the foundational norm of legal systems is structurally complex and conflictual.

Comparison also plays another role here, besides providing external experiences that help us understanding the riddle of EU pluralism, one that may be defined illustrative. Constitutional pluralism in Europe is the by-product of various legal formants,[73] two of which are dominant, case law and scholarship. For instance, and as we will see in Chapter 2, it was the 'constitutional' case law of the Court of Justice, backed by an active group of scholars and practitioners, which created the basis for the EU constitutional layer and, therefore, for the twofold European constitution. Other judges resisted this process of judicial integration, undermining the idea of a European constitution or limiting it. In doing so, courts both expressed their theoretical views on the problem of pluralism and influenced the grip of theories because of their authority. When the Court of Justice defined its order as autonomous on paper, for instance, it contributed to make it autonomous in practice. By comparing how different courts in Europe faced the problem of pluralism and upheld separate stances on the issue of the ultimate norm, we will illustrate the formation and practical meaning of the challenge of constitutional pluralism as well as its theoretical significance. In this second sense, comparative law is not that much aimed at forming new concepts or theories, but at illustrating the terms of the debate.

As a result, my answer to the riddle of constitutional pluralism is that a plurality of foundational criteria is possible and normal, rather than paradoxical. On the contrary, the foundations of law are often plural and controversial, and yet legal orders are overall capable of effective functioning despite this structural pluralism. The case of the EU is only a particularly extreme instantiation of such phenomenon.

1.4 Plan of the Book

In the last few paragraphs, I have introduced the research question to be answered and the theoretical as well as the methodological underpinnings of the book. Here I explain how the argument is developed in the book.

73 Rodolfo Sacco, 'Legal Formants: A Dynamic Approach to Comparative Law (Installment I of II)' (1991) 39 The American Journal of Comparative Law 1; Rodolfo Sacco, 'Legal Formants: A Dynamic Approach to Comparative Law (Installment II of II)' (1991) 39 The American Journal of Comparative Law 343.

The work consists of four substantive chapters (2 to 5), together with this Introduction (1) and the final Epilogue (6).

Chapter 2 examines the judicial and scholarly formants of European constitutional pluralism. As for the first, I compare three judgments that epitomize different stances on pluralism by peak courts. The *Maastricht Urteil* of the German Constitutional Court exemplifies the position of those who consider EU law as a merely delegated authority, while the *grundnorm* remains firmly at the level of domestic constitution. Opinion 2/13 of the Court of Justice illustrates the opposite position, in which EU law is depicted as autonomous, independent on external validation. Last, the *Granital* judgment of the ICC recognizes to both an independent origin and separate validation, this way being the closest to a properly pluralist position. I then consider the way in which scholars have conceived constitutional pluralism so far, especially focusing on the normative position according to which pluralism allows for a form of constitutionalism beyond the State. Normative pluralism must be distinguished from the radical kind I develop in the book.

In Chapter 3 I discuss Neil MacCormick's pluralism and his embryonic form of radical pluralism (from 1993 to 1997). I also consider his later turn towards 'pluralism under international law' (1998–1999) and criticize it. While radical pluralism rests on a Hartian theory of law and sovereignty, pluralism under international law introduces elements of Kelsen's theory on domestic-international law relations: the two perspectives are ultimately irreconcilable. Radical pluralism is on the other hand more promising, but MacCormick's version of it is underdeveloped.

Chapter 4 starts from MacCormick's radical pluralism to articulate the hypothesis that the problem of constitutional pluralism is founded on a myth, that of a single and straightforward ultimate norm, in the famous form 'what the Queen in Parliament enacts is law'. I compare the EU to a particular form of composite legal order called in the literature a 'union of States', lying in the middle between federal States and international organizations. The case of antebellum USA is considered to articulate such comparison and gives us evidence of a previous case in which simultaneous claims of ultimate constitutional authority were raised in a legal order, at times leading to declarations of *ultra vires*. I also consider evidence from contemporary States to show how even when there seems to be agreement on some kind of 'Queen in Parliament', the question of ultimate authority is anyway open to discussion because of interpretive disputes that occasionally arise. The basic norm is, in other words, complex and conflictual even when apparently reducibly to the concentration of ultimate legal power into a sovereign institution. It is more reasonable to conceive it as a complex series of norms, a sort of 'grammar' of legality, that can variate considerably.

Chapter 5 focuses on the cases of conflicts on the European constitution in the last years. I consider the *Taricco* saga, a confrontation between the ICC and the Court of Justice of the European Union, showing an example of disagreement on some fundamental elements of the foundational norm which did not eventually lead to open conflict. I also examine the cases of *ultra vires* judgments in Europe, which instead show what happens when conflict is not avoided. The Czech *Landtová* saga, the Danish *Ajos* case, the *PSPP* (Public Sector Asset Purchase Programme) judgment of the German Constitutional Court, are all instances of open constitutional conflict. Yet, I argue that these do not necessarily threaten the breakdown of the legal order, which remains broadly functioning. I finally compare them to the Polish K 3/21 judgment, decided in October 2021: the latter exemplifies a different case, in which the intensity of disagreement has gone beyond the physiology of constitutional conflicts and threatens a breakdown of EU law in Poland.

Lastly, in the Epilogue I recapitulate the main lines of the book and draw three conclusions. First, that it is possible to develop a radical theory of constitutional pluralism, and this leads us to see conflicts as both inevitable and less troubling than it might appear at first glance. Second, the theory shows the complexity of legal orders, both at domestic level and beyond the State, and the illusion of a single and straightforward foundational rule coinciding with the constitution. Finally, elaborating on radical pluralism means placing oneself on a third way between the optimistic idea that it is possible to govern conflicts through legal reasoning, and the sharp pessimism of anti-pluralists. Radical pluralism underlines at the same time the virtues and the limits of jurisprudence.

2

CONSTITUTIONAL PLURALISM IN THEORY AND PRACTICE

2.1 Premise: 1993, *Annus Mirabilis*

The year 1993 has a special role in the history of European law: it was a turning point in the juristic reflection regarding the relations between Member States and the European Union (EU). In that *annus mirabilis*, two crucial pieces of juristic knowledge were issued.

In January, the 'Modern Law Review' published an essay by Neil MacCormick entitled *Beyond the Sovereign State*, which was going to embody the spirit of the time. MacCormick, as anticipated in the Introduction, was a prominent figure both as a legal theorist and as an expert on European law. *Beyond the Sovereign State* and his later comment on the *Maastricht Urteil* lie at origin of the pluralist movement and specifically of radical pluralism, as they discussed the notions of sovereignty, modern State, *grundnorm*, and their place in the early '90s Europe.[1] In 1993, all these concepts entered with MacCormick into the standard vocabulary of constitutional pluralism.

On 12 October the second cornerstone of 1993 was published: the German Constitutional Court issued the famous *Maastricht Urteil*,[2] regarding Germany's access to the Maastricht Treaty. The judgment discussed the German participation to the Treaty in a theoretically unprecedented manner: the Court elaborated in detail on sovereignty, modern State, democracy, constitution, constitutionalism, and legal system as never before. In the *Maastricht Urteil* we find one of the possible descriptions of the relations between the EU and the Member States, one that denies the autonomy of supranational law, understands the Union as an association

1 Neil MacCormick, 'Beyond the Sovereign State' (1993) 56 The Modern Law Review 1; Neil MacCormick, 'The Maastricht-Urteil: Sovereignty Now' (1995) 1 European Law Journal 259.

2 BVerfG 2 BvR 2134/92, 2 BvR 2159/92.

DOI: 10.4324/9781003291572-2

of States, and reserves sovereignty to the Member States. It was the perfect anti-pluralist narrative and one that would have large influence, both in later judgments of the Federal Court, such as the *Lissabon Urteil* in 2009, and on other supreme and constitutional courts.

Briefly, 30 years ago constitutional pluralism was suddenly more debated than ever, in academia as well as in courts. *Beyond the Sovereign State* and *Maastricht* were sophisticated and very diverse investigations in the notions of sovereignty, modern State, democracy, constitution, constitutionalism, and legal system, which fostered a huge debate. The dual nature of pluralism epitomized by *Beyond the Sovereign State* and *Maastricht*, academic and judicial, requires a dual analysis. For this reason, this chapter is be divided in two parts as well.

Starting from the judicial formant, the riddle of constitutional pluralism, namely explaining a functioning legal order with two foundational norms on top, requires an illustration of how judges, and most importantly supreme or constitutional courts, dealt with the problem. Indeed, here we analyse three decisions which epitomize very different approaches to the riddle of pluralism.

The end of the chapter is devoted to the other formant of pluralism, namely legal scholarship, the progeny of *Beyond the Sovereign State*. I examine the normative (and dominating) side of constitutional pluralism, made of authors explicitly praising the undecidedness of the question of ultimate authority in Europe. I also consider the critiques moved to pluralism, looking at both those who endorse a scholarly version of the *Maastricht*-style state-centredness and, on the other hand, at scholars who blame pluralism for preventing the emergence of full primacy of EU law.

The upshot of the chapter is showing how constitutional pluralism was either accepted as a conceptualization of the uncertainty on the ultimate norm in Europe or strongly rejected by both courts and scholars, this way illustrating the theoretical presuppositions and practical implications of pluralism.

2.2 Constitutional Pluralism in Court: Three Judgments

The judgments examined in this paragraph epitomize three different approaches to constitutional pluralism by courts. In a logical rather than chronological order, we shall start by examining Opinion 2/13, which celebrated the uniqueness of the Union and its autonomy; second comes the *Maastricht Urteil* which, as anticipated, manifested the opposite and state-centred approach; finally, *Granital* attempted to find a middle way and develop a pluralist understanding of the relations between national and supranational law.

2.2.1 Opinion 2/13 and the Autonomy of EU Law

The accession of the Communities and later of the Union to the European Convention on Human Rights (ECHR) was an option considered for a long time.[3]

3 COM(79)210 final – Memorandum on the Accession of the European Communities to the Convention for the Protection of Human Rights and Fundamental Freedoms, 2 May 1979.

The process was halted a first time in the Nineties by the Court of Justice with Opinion 2/1994, based on the absence of adequate legal basis in the Treaties.[4] In June 2002 the Steering Committee for Human Rights (CDDH) of the Council of Europe adopted a study on legal and technical issues of the EU's possible adherence. Protocol 14 to the ECHR, allowing accession of the EU to the Convention (Art. 17), was drafted in 2004 and later ratified. In the meanwhile, with the drafting Article 6(2) and Protocol 8 to the Lisbon Treaty, the EU was explicitly allowed to join the Convention. Negotiations opened in 2012 and the draft Accession Agreement was finalized on 5 April 2013. Yet, the European Commission, pursuant to Article 218(11) of the Treaty on the Functioning of the European Union (TFEU), asked the Court of Justice to deliver an opinion on the compatibility of the draft agreement with EU law, paving the way for Opinion 2/13. Delivered on 18 December 2014, it famously rejected again the EU's accession to the Convention.[5]

Negotiations resumed in October 2020, so that EU's accession may eventually happen in the future, but it is not for us to follow these developments.[6] What we are interested in here is Opinion 2/13 *per se*, its legal reasoning and significance for EU law. Most importantly, its stance on the autonomy of EU law is crucial. Thus, I consider its discussion of the principle of autonomy of EU law and show the historical continuity with a series of cases starting with *Van Gend en Loos*. I argue that autonomy, rather than direct effect or primacy, is the principle of EU law that explains constitutional pluralism: once the Court of Justice declared its legal order autonomous (and kept asserting this), the first social fact that could eventually separate the reason of validity of EU law from that of Member States was posited. That also contrasting social facts exist, which deny the autonomy of EU law and assert its dependence on States (as the *Maastricht Urteil* to be examined later), makes for the riddle of pluralism.

To briefly recapitulate the content of Opinion 2/13, according to the Court the draft agreement was incompatible with EU law for several reasons.

First, the draft agreement did not coordinate Article 53 ECHR and Article 53 of the Charter, potentially allowing Member States to regulate differently the same right, when enshrined in both charters,[7] and therefore potentially harming the unity, uniformity, and effectiveness of EU law. Accession under the draft agreement could infringe the EU principle of mutual trust between Member States, forcing them to check on other States' protection of ECHR's standard. Moreover,

4 Opinion 2/94, ECLI:EU:C:1996:140.

5 Opinion 2/13 ECLI:EU:C:2014:2454.

6 European Council, EU accession to the ECHR ('46+1' Group), www.coe.int/en/web/human-rights-intergovernmental-cooperation/accession-of-the-european-union-to-the-european-convention-on-human-rights.

7 The relations between the two supranational courts, the Court of Justice of the EU and the European Court of Human Rights, are well summarized by Federico Fabbrini and Joris Larik, 'The Past, Present and Future of the Relation between the European Court of Justice and the European Court of Human Rights' (2016) 35 Yearbook of European Law 145, 147–159.

Protocol 16 to the ECHR, of which the EU did not become party according to the agreement, granted national judges the power to ask for advisory opinions to the European Court of Human Rights (ECtHR), the judicial body of the Convention, potentially circumventing the specular preliminary mechanism of reference to the Court of Justice (Article 267 TFEU). The agreement also risked circumventing Article 344 TFEU, which reserves to the Court of Justice exclusive jurisdiction over disputes regarding EU law, by letting Member States sue one another under Article 33 ECHR. Moreover, the power granted by the agreement to the ECtHR to decide whether to admit the EU or its Member States as co-respondents did entail a power to authoritatively interpret EU law which was reserved to the Court of Justice under the EU treaties. The mechanism of prior involvement of the Court of Justice was, as designed in the draft agreement, defective, as it did not ensure to the Court of Justice to intervene on all unsettled or undecided questions of EU law. Finally, the area of common foreign and security policy, excluded from review under the Treaties, was justiciable in front of the ECtHR according to the draft agreement.

This long series of reasons was pooled together by a sort of *fil rouge*, namely the defensive stance of the Court against external factors potentially affecting the autonomy of EU law (and the Court's role as ultimate interpreter): the possible involvement of an external arbiter in the interpretation of EU law was an unacceptable threat to the self-contained legal order of which the Court is the custodian. This attitude is especially visible in the Opinion which, rightly or not, defended the identity of EU law, but is hardly unique. To the contrary, the definition and defence of the EU's legal features against the ECtHR's influence was only the outward projection of an EU legal principle for long designed with that aim, the principle of autonomy.[8] As previously anticipated, the detailed characterization of the autonomy of EU law in Opinion 2/13 is what makes of it such important piece to understand constitutional pluralism from the perspective of the Court of Justice.

Autonomy has been one of the defining tenets of EU law since its inception. Strictly connected to the notion of sovereignty, it signals the self-referential character of a legal order, its capacity of self-validation: the norms created, applied, and interpreted in the system are valid based on higher provisions belonging to the same system, without the need of constant validation by an external order.[9] In the context of EU law, this translates into the question whether the Treaties, the 'constitutional charter of the Union', were and are autonomous from Member States' validation. Self-validation of the Treaties can be interpreted in two senses which, following Schilling's classic classification, are called 'original' and 'derivative' autonomy.[10] The former refers to a legal order created by its own constituent

8 Daniel Halberstam, '"It's the Autonomy, Stupid!" A Modest Defense of Opinion 2/13 on EU Accession to the ECHR, and the Way Forward' (2015) 16 German Law Journal 105, 144–146.

9 René Barents, *The Autonomy of Community Law* (Kluwer 2004) 171–173.

10 Theodor Schilling, 'The Autonomy of the Community Legal Order: An Analysis of Possible Foundations' (1996) 37 Harvard International Law Journal 389, 389–390.

power, working in legal *vacuo*, and validating the first historical constitution, in Hans Kelsen's vocabulary.[11] This validation cuts the ties with the previous legality and marks the beginning of a new and independent legal order: '[i]f one prefers a cosmological metaphor, this constitution is the big bang out of which the new legal order develops. It is a revolution replacing the previous historically first constitution with a new one'.[12] Thus, original autonomy entails the sudden rupture of the previous chain of validity and the equally sudden relocation of the *grundnorm* from one *locus* to another (in our case, from the Member States' constitutions to the EU constitution).[13] Derivative autonomy, instead, refers to a legal order that, although not being born autonomous, becomes independent with time: it later emancipates from the legal order which validated it and at some point, establishes a basic norm of its own. Despite the lack of a clear, symbolic moment of transition, from the moment of the *grundnorm*'s relocation on, we expect to see officials, especially judges, pledging allegiance to a new fundamental norm-constitution.[14]

Original autonomy likely does not fit the historical evolution of EU law. As argued by Schilling himself, there is no reason to believe that the Treaties originally meant anything different from the institution of an international organization for the Member States.[15] It remains to be seen if derivative autonomy, acquired through time, fits the evolution of the Union. To answer this question, it is necessary to briefly go back to the foundational cases of Community law, when autonomy was first conceived. Indeed, Opinion 2/13 explains in a richer, more detailed, and with a more 'constitutional' tone something that *in nuce* was already in *Van Gend en Loos* and *Costa*.[16]

The idea of self-validation of EU law, of its autonomy, developed slowly throughout the decades starting with the 1960s. In fact, historical research shows how since 1958 growing pressure had mounted on the Court of Justice for a 'constitutional' interpretation of the Treaties from both civil servants, especially the Commission's legal service, and scholars reunited in the new pan-European lawyers' association, the *Fédération internationale pour le droit européen* (FIDE).[17] These diverse formants pushed for the establishment of direct effect and primacy as legal principles to counter the reluctancy of both States' governments in

11 Hans Kelsen, *General Theory of Law and State* (Transaction Publishers 2005) 115–116.
12 Schilling (n 10) 391.
13 ibid 390–395.
14 ibid 395–397.
15 ibid 394–395.
16 C-26/62 Van Gend en Loos v Nederlandse Administratie der Belastingen ECLI:EU:C:1963:1; C-6/64 Flaminio Costa v E.N.E.L. ECLI:EU:C:1964:66.
17 See Eric Stein, 'Lawyers, Judges, and the Making of a Transnational Constitution' (1981) 75 American Journal of International Law 1, 3–10. More recently, see Morten Rasmussen, 'Revolutionizing European Law: A History of the Van Gend En Loos Judgment' (2014) 12 International Journal of Constitutional Law 136, 146–153; Morten Rasmussen, 'Law Meets History: Interpreting the Van Gend En Loos Judgment' in Fernanda Nicola and Bill Davies (eds), *EU Law Stories* (Cambridge University Press 2017) 111–117; Antoine Vauchez, *Brokering Europe: Euro-Lawyers and the Making of a Transnational Polity* (Cambridge University Press 2015) 116–124.

the Council in implementing the (at that time) European Economic Community Treaty (EEC) and that of national judges in using the preliminary reference mechanism. Only a radical reinterpretation of the legal nature of the EEC Treaty, from a mere international organization to a partly constitutional one based on direct effect and primacy (and a centralized interpretation in Luxembourg), would ensure the uniformity and effectiveness necessary for a common market to be developed. Direct effect was meant to confer to citizens rights directly enforceable in national courts, while primacy would avoid that adoption of later and conflicting domestic norms by States.

It was far from obvious that the Court would eventually accept this constitutionally oriented logic, but eventually it did.[18] By a narrow majority, direct effect was accepted in *Van Gend en Loos*, in which the Court mostly followed the Commission's *memorandum*.[19] Relying on the 'scheme and spirit' of the Treaties,[20] the Court established the direct effect of clear and unconditional Treaty provisions. Direct effect was born, although limited to 'negative' obligations for Member States (obligations not to act).[21] Two years later, in *Costa*, the Court of Justice also addressed the problem of primacy. As the Italian Constitutional Court (ICC) in its own *Costa* judgment had affirmed that later national provisions of the same legal rank of the law implementing the EEC would prevail over treaty provisions, it posited an existential threat to Community law.[22] Again backed by officials and scholars,[23] the Court of Justice immediately unharmed it by specifying that one of the characteristics of Community law was primacy, again a specific characteristic of the newly established legal order. Primacy, as well as direct effect, followed from the autonomy.[24]

Briefly, recent historical reconstructions of the foundational cases tend to emphasize that what happened was in fact a sort of legal revolution, radically changing the nature of the Communities. A new and 'revolutionized' legal order

18 Also because of a change in the Court's composition between 1958 and 1962. See Rasmussen, 'Revolutionizing European Law' (n 17) 148.

19 Despite the opposition of various Member States, see ibid 154; Rasmussen, 'Law Meets History' (n 17) 115–116; Vauchez (n 17) 122.

20 Since the foundational era, teleological reasoning has remained the most frequently used argument in the case law of the Court of Justice. See Giulio Itzcovich, 'The European Court of Justice' in András Jakab, Arthur Dyevre and Giulio Itzcovich (eds), *Comparative Constitutional Reasoning* (Cambridge University Press 2017) 298–300. In foundational cases, the Court has looked not only at the *telos* of the examined provisions, but also at the general spirit of the Treaties, the meta-*telos* of EU law. See Miguel Poiares Maduro, 'Interpreting European Law: Judicial Adjudication in a Context of Constitutional Pluralism' (2008) 1 European Journal of Legal Studies 137, 140.

21 Vauchez (n 17) 122–123.

22 Corte costituzionale, judgment 6/1964. See Amedeo Arena, 'From an Unpaid Electricity Bill to the Primacy of EU Law: Gian Galeazzo Stendardi and the Making of Costa v. ENEL' (2019) 30 European Journal of International Law 1017, 1023–1026.

23 Vauchez (n 17) 135–140; Morten Rasmussen, 'From Costa v ENEL to the Treaties of Rome: A Brief History of a Legal Revolution' in Miguel Poiares Maduro and Loïc Azoulai (eds), *The Past and Future of EU Law: The Classics of EU Law Revisited on the 50th Anniversary of the Rome Treaty* (Hart Publishing 2010).

24 Gráinne de Búrca, 'Sovereignty and the Supremacy Doctrine of the European Court of Justice' in Neil Walker (ed), *Sovereignty in Transition* (Hart Publishing 2003) 450–455.

was established, constitutional rather than international and based on direct effect and primacy. Severing the connection to the will of the States and asserting the autonomy of the new legal order helped justifying its specificities: specifically, again, it helped legitimizing the direct effect and primacy of Community law. Concepts as 'supranational' and '*sui generis*' stably entered the jargon of lawyers to denote such unusual object, suspended in between a State and an international organization.[25] Such change was grounded in the reinterpretation of Treaty provisions by the Court of Justice, severing the connections with national constitutional law and with the will of the drafters. Both cases insisted on the special character of the EEC. Many of the interpreters and commentators were eager to stress this specialty in their observations.[26] As a result, in the eyes of several scholars and practitioners, the constitutionalization translated into severance of the validation of Community law by national constitutional law and into the shift of the foundational norm to the Treaties.[27] Using again Schilling's vocabulary, it was the beginning of European derivative autonomy.

However powerful, the Member States did not significantly oppose the judicial constitutionalization of Community law by the Court of Justice, nor the advent of derivative autonomy. Why such silent legal revolution or, to use Stone Sweet's powerful wording, this 'juridical *coup d'état*',[28] was allowed is very much debated and various explanations have been proposed.[29] To begin with, despite scepticism, national governments did not consider the areas at that time under Community law salient enough to justify treaty revision,[30] and in any case, they did not agree on how to change them.[31] Second, while the foundations of an autonomous legal order were posited, States were reassured by the introduction of the informal right of the national veto, which secured a certain equilibrium.[32] Third, first instance judges at the national level were often interested in the direct connection with the Court of Justice as a tool to win internal controversies with peak courts.[33] Moreover, the

25 Robert Schütze, *European Constitutional Law* (Cambridge University Press 2012) 12–18, 67–68.

26 Vauchez (n 17) 127–128.

27 Giulio Itzcovich, 'Legal Order, Legal Pluralism, Fundamental Principles. Europe and its Law in Three Concepts' (2012) 18 European Law Journal 358, 363; Giulio Itzcovich, *Teorie e ideologie del diritto comunitario* (Giappichelli 2006) 115–133.

28 Alec Stone Sweet, 'The Juridical Coup d'État and the Problem of Authority' (2007) 8 German Law Journal 915: 'By the phrase juridical coup d'état, I mean a fundamental transformation in the normative foundations of a legal system through the constitutional lawmaking of a court.'

29 Some of the most common explanations are enlisted in Monica Claes, *The National Courts' Mandate in the European Constitution* (Hart Publishing 2006) 246–265.

30 Rasmussen, 'Revolutionizing European Law' (n 17) 161–162.

31 E.g., see Vera Fritz, 'The First Member State Rebellion? The European Court of Justice and the Negotiations of the "Luxembourg Protocol" of 1971: The ECJ and the Luxembourg Protocol of 1971' (2015) 21 European Law Journal 680, 685–697. She studies the failed French-lead attempt to limit the scope of the preliminary ruling procedure in 1971.

32 Joseph HH Weiler, 'The Transformation of Europe' (1991) 100 The Yale Law Journal 2403, 2410–2431.

33 Karen J Alter, 'Explaining National Court Acceptance of European Court Jurisprudence: A Critical Evaluation of Theories of Legal Integration' in Anne Marie Slaughter, Alec Stone Sweet and Joseph

overall success of the Communities in establishing a more and more integrated single market provided for a functionalist reason to leave the constitutionalization of Community law be.[34] By the time the Community expanded with the Single European Act (1986) and the European Union was established with the Maastricht Treaty (1992), it was too late to come back: the advantages of supranationalism seemed to have overall overcome its disadvantages. At that point, the constitutional doctrines had solidified into the *acquis Communautaire* and the autonomy of EC/EU law with it. If it really was a juridical *coup d'état*, fifth columns were operating in the Member States.

Briefly, the revolutionized European legal order consolidated. Later, the autonomous foundations of its law were confirmed again, explicitly stating primacy over constitutional law of Member States.[35] Together with this internal side, the Court parallelly affirmed the autonomy of its legal order against external legal regimes as well.[36] In *Kadi* it affirmed and developed the autonomy of EU law against international law, following the line begun with *Van Gend en Loos*.[37] *Kadi* bridged autonomy and constitutionalism, explicitly clarifying that the content of the EU autonomous constitution matched that of liberal constitutionalism by securing individual rights.[38] This substantive commitment was justified by looking at the rights which the Court had progressively integrated into its own case law since the 1970s.[39]

Opinion 2/13 comes as the end of this process and as the ultimate accomplishment (so far) of the project of autonomization and constitutionalization of EU law. The Court rejected the compatibility of the draft agreement with the Treaties and prevented the potential access to the ECHR for the time being. In doing so, it grounded its objections to the accession in the need to preserve the

HH Weiler (eds), *The European Court and National Courts: Doctrine and Jurisprudence: Legal Change in Its Social Context* (Hart Publishing 1998); Karen J Alter, *Establishing the Supremacy of European Law: The Making of an International Rule of Law in Europe* (Oxford University Press 2003).

34 Turkuler Isiksel, *Europe's Functional Constitution: A Theory of Constitutionalism Beyond the State* (Oxford University Press 2016) 86–94.

35 E.g., C-11/70 Internationale Handelsgesellschaft mbH v Einfuhr- und Vorratsstelle für Getreide und Futtermittel ECLI:EU:C:1970:114.

36 E.g., Opinion 1-91 ECLI:EU:C:1991:490, paras. 17–21. On the external side of autonomy, see Marja-Liisa Öberg, *The Boundaries of the EU Internal Market: Participation without Membership* (Cambridge University Press 2020) 188–194.

37 Joined Cases C-402/05 P and C-415/05 P, Yassin Abdullah Kadi and Al Barakaat International Foundation v Council and Commission ECLI:EU:C:2008:461; Joined Cases C-584/10 P, C-593/10 P, and C-595/10 P, Commission, Council, United Kingdom v Yassin Abdullah Kadi ECLI:EU:C:2013:518. On the continuity between *Van Gend en Loos* and *Kadi*, see Andrea Gattini, 'Joined Cases C–402/05 P & 415/05 P, Yassin Abdullah Kadi, Al Barakaat International Foundation v Council and Commission, Judgment of the Grand Chamber of 3 September 2008' (2009) 46 Common Market Law Review 213.

38 Giuseppe Martinico, 'The Autonomy of EU Law – A Joint Celebration of Kadi II and Van Gend En Loos' in Matej Avbelj, Filippo Fontanelli and Giuseppe Martinico (eds), *Kadi on Trial: A Multifaceted Analysis of the Kadi Judgment* (Routledge 2014) 166–171.

39 C-29/69, Erich Stauder v City of Ulm - Sozialamt, ECLI:EU:C:1969:52; C-11/70 Internationale Handelsgesellschaft; C-4/73 J. Nold, Kohlen- und Baustoffgroßhandlung v Commission of the European Communities EU:C:1974:5.

autonomy of EU law and its specific characteristics. There were later reaffirmations of EU's autonomy on behalf of the Court of Justice, and others will most likely follow.[40] Yet, Opinion 2/13 is perhaps the most paradigmatic case so far: although it does not affirm EU law's autonomy in relation to the Member States but rather towards international law, it iterates a narrative on autonomy ongoing since *Van Gend en Loos* and developed in relation to States. Moreover, and most importantly, Opinion 2/13 elaborates on how the autonomy of EU law relates to the principles of modern constitutionalism as never before, even more than in *Kadi*. This makes of it the best case to consider in order to analyse the view on autonomy from the side of EU law.

Specifically, in Opinion 2/13 the Court states that not only EU law is an autonomous legal order (it has a *grundnorm* of its own as in the *Van Gend en Loos-Costa* doctrine), but this system is endowed with 'its own constitutional framework and founding principles', as well as a 'structured network of principles, rules and mutually interdependent legal relations linking the EU and its Member States, and its Member States with each other' which made the European constitution.[41] Marking one step forward on the path opened by *Kadi*, the Court kept filling in the substantive content of EU's autonomy by aligning it to the tenets of liberal constitutionalism: separation of powers and guarantee of rights. The first prong, concerning the separation of powers, encompassed both the norms governing the institutions of the Union (Articles 13 to 19 Treaty on the European Union, TEU), so to ensure the horizontal separation, and those governing the vertical separation between the Union and the States, as the principles of conferral (Article 5 TEU) and that of loyal cooperation (Article 4(3) TEU).[42] A special role was reserved to the preliminary ruling procedure, the keystone of the EU's judiciary connecting national judges to the Court of Justice.[43] As for the second prong, concerning rights, the structured network of EU constitutional principles comprised a series of shared values (Article 2 TEU), of fundamental rights (Article 6 TEU and the Charter), and of common objectives (Article 3 TEU), such as the common market, the citizenship of the Union, and the area of freedom, security and justice. Rights lied 'at the heart of that legal structure' and worked as requirements for the lawfulness of any EU measure and of any national provision of implementation.[44]

40 See C-621/18 Andy Wightman and Others v Secretary of State for Exiting the European Union ECLI:EU:C:2018:999 paras. 44–45; Opinion 1/17 ECLI:EU:C:2019:341 paras. 109–111.

41 Opinion 2/13 paras. 158 and 167.

42 ibid paras. 165 and 173.

43 ibid paras. 174–176. Originally modelled on the Italian system of constitutional review, especially after *van Gend en Loos* the preliminary ruling mechanism became more and more a characteristic feature of EU law, as it directly connected the Court to national judges. See Leonardo Pierdominici, *The Mimetic Evolution of the Court of Justice of the EU: A Comparative Law Perspective* (Palgrave Macmillan 2020) 66–75.

44 ibid paras. 169–171. The Court here endorses a functional notion of fundamental right as a ground of validity for other provisions in the hierarchy of norms: the 'fundamental' character of a right consists in its function of standard of review. On such conception, Gianluigi Palombella, 'Arguments

Here it is not particularly relevant to speculate how much of this commitment is truly reflected in the practical functioning of the Union. What counts is that the Court explicitly filled the content of the fundamental norm of the EU with principles that belong to this pattern. The objections to the EU's accession to the ECHR were then presented by the Court as specific aspects of the EU's autonomy that would be in danger in case the agreement was ratified. On such specificities of EU law, the Court would not negotiate or derogate.[45]

The Court's reasoning in Opinion 2/13 has been criticized by pointing out that it asserted EU law's supremacy and self-sufficiency over international law to the detriment of fundamental rights' protection and that it could have taken a more 'discursive' and less exclusive approach to autonomy.[46] Paradoxically, the Court has exposed itself to such critique right in its most overtly constitutionalist decision. Indeed, Opinion 2/13 is the transposition in supranational law of the standard theory examined in the Introduction: EU law is structured hierarchically, with a basic norm of constitutional content making it autonomous from other legal systems. Yet, constitutionalism can mean cultural idiosyncrasy, closure, and expressivism.[47] As it was correctly pointed out, the Court mimicked the typical attributes of national legal systems.[48]

To the aim of this chapter, Opinion 2/13 is the epitome of the first side of the bifurcation in the riddle of constitutional pluralism. The other side, as we will see in a moment, was aptly expressed by national courts, in the reasoning of the German Constitutional Court more clearly than anywhere else.

2.2.2 *The* Maastricht Urteil*: The Masters of the Treaties' Oracle*

As previously stated, 1993 was a notable year in the history of constitutional pluralism for two reasons, one being the publication of MacCormick's seminal essay *Beyond the Sovereign State*, the other lying in the decision of the German Constitutional Court regarding Germany's access to the Treaty of Maastricht, the *Maastricht Urteil.*

in Favour of a Functional Theory of Fundamental Rights' (2001) 14 International Journal for the Semiotics of Law 299.

45 This is the 'existential extremism' of EU autonomy emphasized by Niamh Nic Shuibhne, 'What Is the Autonomy of EU Law, and Why Does That Matter?' (2019) 88 Nordic Journal of International Law 9, 22–30.

46 Louise Halleskov Storgaard, 'EU Law Autonomy versus European Fundamental Rights Protection – On *Opinion 2/13* on EU Accession to the ECHR' (2015) 15 Human Rights Law Review 485; Benedikt H Pirker and Stefan Reitemeyer, 'Between Discursive and Exclusive Autonomy – Opinion 2/13, the Protection of Fundamental Rights and the Autonomy of EU Law' (2015) 17 Cambridge Yearbook of European Legal Studies 168.

47 Mark Tushnet, 'The Possibilities of Comparative Constitutional Law' (1999) 108 The Yale Law Journal 1225, 1269–1274.

48 Justin Lindeboom, 'Why EU Law Claims Supremacy' (2018) 38 Oxford Journal of Legal Studies 328, 335–355.

The new Treaty, signed in 1992 and entered into force in 1993, was a huge step forth in the process of European integration. After the fall of the Berlin Wall and the German reunification, it posited the basis for much deeper cooperation: it instituted the European Union, created the three pillars structure, and most importantly formalized and constitutionalized an unprecedented level of fiscal and monetary integration, including the future introduction of the single currency.[49] Briefly, the Maastricht Treaty set a system of macroeconomic governance that remained mostly unchanged until the reforms of the 2010s[50] and the post-pandemic recovery plan.[51] The Treaty, it is worth mentioning, had the twofold effect of on the one hand vastly transferring sovereign powers from States to the new-born Union[52] and on the other provoking the first signs of popular indifference towards European integration and even of Euroscepticism. The close majority of the French referendum on the Treaty and the Danish rejection in the first referendum are cases in point of the latter effect.[53]

It was from Germany, however, that the most theoretically thick and legal rather than political contestation of the integration process eventually came. On 12 October, the German Constitutional Court issued its judgment on the Treaty, granting German participation. However, in doing so, the Court also introduced a new way of adjudicating about European integration: the Federal Court exposed a complex and thick constitutional theory, discussing in detail the notions of State, sovereignty, constitution, and association of States.[54] This thickness was the main novelty of the judgment and inaugurated a typically German way of adjudicating that extended to later decisions like *Lissabon*, *Gauweiler*, and *PSPP*.[55] Truly, the Court had already reacted to the autonomization and constitutionalization of European law in the *Solange I* judgment (1974),[56] stating that as long as European integration did not endow the Community with a charter of rights, established by a democratically elected parliament and comparable in terms of level of protection to the Basic Law, the Federal Constitutional Court would have possibly admitted complaints regarding the constitutionality of German measures implementing Community norms, if necessary disapplying them. Later, in the softer *Solange II*

49 Kaarlo Tuori, *European Constitutionalism* (Cambridge University Press 2015) 174–187.

50 See a summary in Robert Schütze, *European Union Law* (Oxford University Press 2021) 781–799.

51 Bruno de Witte, 'The European Union's Covid-19 Recovery Plan: The Legal Engineering of an Economic Policy Shift' (2021) 58 Common Market Law Review 635.

52 Tuori (n 49) 178.

53 Julio Baquero Cruz, 'The Legacy of the Maastricht-Urteil and the Pluralist Movement' (2008) 14 European Law Journal 389, 390.

54 Matej Avbelj and Jan Komárek, 'Four Visions of Constitutional Pluralism Symposium Transcript' (2008) 2 European Journal of Legal Studies 323, 333–336; Leonardo Pierdominici, 'The Theory of EU Constitutional Pluralism: A Crisis in a Crisis?' (2017) 9 Perspectives on Federalism 119, 123.

55 BVerfG, 2 BvR 2/08; 2 BvR 2728/13; 2 BvR 859/15.

56 BVerfGE 37, 271 2 BvL 52/71. On the historical context of *Solange I*, see Bill Davies, *Resisting the European Court of Justice: West Germany's Confrontation with European Law, 1949–1979* (Cambridge University Press 2012) 21–29.

decision (1986),[57] given the growing protection of fundamental rights in the case law of the Court of Justice, it ensured that, as long as the level of protection ensured by the Court of Luxembourg to fundamental rights was sufficiently high, the Federal Court would not exercise its jurisdiction over German measures implementing Community law.[58] However, *Solange I* and *II* never elaborated in the almost academic tone of *Maastricht*.

The *Maastricht Urteil* epitomized a theory that is opposite and specular to the Opinion 2/13: if the Opinion is the paradigm of the state-mimicking reasoning that places the European constitution as the foundational norm of the new European legal order, *Maastricht* announced the opposite perspective. According to the Federal Court, the Maastricht Treaty was not a 'constitution' for a new State based on a European people,[59] but only the legal basis for *a sui generis* international organization, 'a compound of States'.[60] Indeed, for the Treaty to establish a constitution, a *pouvoir constituant* would be required. In a democratic legal order, a constituent power would be legitimate only if directly or indirectly expressed by the *people*, and there was no such thing as a European people. Only European *peoples* existed.[61] Modern democracy works by means of free elections of representatives and only under the existence of some privileged conditions. Free interaction of social forces must be possible, decision-making shall be transparent and comprehensible, political parties, trade unions, and media, shall work as medium between citizens and institutions. Given this definition of democracy, it was possible for Germany to join the Treaty, but only if this association of States remained a *sui generis* international organization, with limited and sufficiently specified competences, obligations, aims, and rights. If too many powers were transferred or if they were not sufficiently determined, Germany (and Member States in general) would cease to be democratic organizations. Only States whose authority is based on democratic participation of the people can, and to a certain extent must, retain some ultimate competences and possibly delegate them to international organizations.

57 BVerfGE 73, 339 2 BvR 197/83.

58 This presumptive reasoning (the *Solange* method) has spread significantly. See Nikolaos Lavranos, 'The Solange-Method as a Tool for Regulating Competing Jurisdictions among International Courts and Tribunals' (2008) 30 Loyola of Los Angeles International and Comparative Law Review 275.

59 Matthias Herdegen, 'Maastricht and the German Constitutional Court: Constitutional Restraints for an "Ever Closer Union" and Document "Extracts from: Brunner v. The European Union (*Bundesverfassungsgericht*)"' (1994) 31 Common Market Law Review 235, 241–242.

60 The precise wording is *Staatenverbund*, a neologism. It expresses the idea of a legal institution connecting various States, although not representing either a Federation or a Confederation. It will be developed and explained in more detail in the *Lissabon Urteil* (para. 229): it denotes an association of States, a system that remains derivative and subject to disposal of the States. See Christian Wohlfahrt, 'The Lisbon Case: A Critical Summary' (2009) 10 German Law Journal 1277, 1281.

61 This is the so-called no-*demos* thesis. According to Nicolaïdis, it was the true 'force' of the Maastricht *Urteil*, for it asked in a radical fashion the question of how to connect the polity (citizens) and the governance structure (the EC). See Kalypso Nicolaidis, 'The Idea of European Demoicracy' in Julie Dickson and Pavlos Eleftheriadis (eds), *Philosophical Foundations of European Union Law* (Oxford University Press 2012) 250.

The Court interpreted restrictively the amendments to the German Constitution aimed at ensuring participation to the EU (e.g., art 23 of the *Grundgesetz*)[62] and only allowed participation insofar as the Treaty stated the EU powers in a sufficiently clear manner.

In terms of practical consequences, the *Maastricht Urteil* was especially influential in the years to come for two reasons. First, it allowed German citizens to bring individual complaints to the Constitutional Court to check the compatibility of European integration with the Constitution.[63] Second, it created the much influential *ultra vires* review, the most significant legal export of the German Constitutional Court in the field of European integration: provisions would possibly be revised by German institutions,[64] if 'European institutions or governmental entities were to implement or to develop the Maastricht Treaty in a manner no longer covered by the Treaty in the form of it upon which the German Act of Consent is based' so that 'any legal instrument arising from such activity would not be binding within German territory'.[65] This doctrine would later be adopted by other constitutional or supreme courts, as we will see in Chapter 5.

However, from the theoretical point of view, it is the exposed theory of sovereignty that turned out to be especially influential, for it entailed no recognition of genuine normativity outside the boundaries of the State.[66] States remained the 'masters of the Treaties' and the Treaties' validity depended on their will. The *kompetenz-kompetenz* did not belong to the Union and unilateral withdrawal from the Treaties was always possible: one can hardly imagine a stronger denial of the idea of autonomy of EU law in the sense of derivative autonomy described while commenting on Opinion 2/13.

Summing up, a strong commitment to democratic constitutionalism and the disqualification of other forms constitutionalism, the no-*demos* thesis, firm limits to cession of State sovereignty, the possibility of *ultra vires* review against EU acts overstepping the conferred powers, and most importantly, the conceptualization of the Union as an association of States, mere agent of the masters of the Treaties, all occurred in *Maastricht*. The strong similarity and at the same time the resounding difference between the *Urteil* and Opinion 2/13 could not be more evident. Both were judicial attempts to solve the riddle of constitutional pluralism,

62 In *Maastricht* the Court clearly dismissed the importance of amendments to the German Constitution aimed at fostering further European cooperation, to the point that '[t]he power of constitutional revision is seen as a subordinate power. The original *pouvoir constituant* has become a myth and the German Constitutional Court is the maker and the guardian of that myth'. Baquero Cruz (n 53) 407.

63 Peter Hilpold, 'So Long Solange? The PSPP Judgment of the German Constitutional Court and the Conflict between the German and the European "Popular Spirit"' (2021) 23 Cambridge Yearbook of European Legal Studies 159, 166–168.

64 It was not clear in the *Maastricht Urteil* which institution was then endowed with the power to declare the inapplicability of European norms in Germany, whether the Constitutional Court itself or every court (and maybe every administrative body). Baquero Cruz (n 53) 393–394.

65 BVerfG, 89 155, 1993, I, C, 3.

66 Itzcovich, 'Legal Order, Legal Pluralism, Fundamental Principles' (n 27) 364.

and both ultimately relied on the same, pyramidal view of the legal system. Yet, *Maastricht* showed the nationalist perspective: the ultimate norm had to be placed at the state level, as only states had the democratic credentials to carry the burden of a modern constitution. A rigid interpretation of democratic constitutionalism radically disqualified the idea of a European constitution and hence of a European *grundnorm*. States remained sovereign and almighty; EU law was derivative and not autonomous.

The *Maastricht Urteil*'s importance is hard to underestimate also because of the broader cultural impact it had on other judges and on scholars.

As just mentioned, several national courts followed the main lines of the *Bundesverfassungsgericht*'s reasoning: judgments by supreme or constitutional courts in Denmark, Poland, Cyprus, and the Czech Republic mimicked *Maastricht* and imported the *ultra vires* review. Softer revisions of the relations between national law and EU law inspired by *Maastricht* were at the centre of judicial decisions in France, Spain, and Belgium.[67] The most important contributor to the persistency of the *Maastricht* line, however, was the German Constitutional Court itself. Some evidence of this continuity was already at stake in the 2005 judgment on the European arrest warrant,[68] when the German Constitutional Court refused to address a preliminary reference to the Court of Justice, but a full-fledged reassertion of the *Maastricht* narrative only came with the *Lissabon Urteil*.[69] Issued on 30 June 2009 and concerning the German participation to the Lisbon Treaty, it did not fundamentally change the theory expressed two decades before.[70] Two elements were added to the Federal Court's previous picture: first, the possible review of EU provisions infringing German constitutional identity, introducing a third reason of scrutiny together with fundamental rights (*Solange I*) and *ultra vires* (*Maastricht*);[71] second, the explicit enlisting of a series of areas that could be handed over to the Union without creating a proper federal State, areas including criminal law, defence and internal affairs, education, social security, and budgetary decisions. Yet, conceptually, the judgment reiterates *Maastricht*'s brainchildren: States as the sovereign 'masters of the Treaties' and the Union as a delegated 'association of States',[72] the no-*demos* thesis, the strict conditions for the development of a European democracy.[73] The list of not transferable powers, if anything, strengthened *Maastricht*'s legacy by making the limits

67 On all these cases, see Baquero Cruz (n 53) 397–403.

68 BVerfG, 2 BvR 2236/04.

69 BVerfG, 2 BvR 2/08.

70 Daniel Halberstam and Christoph Möllers, 'Special Section: The Federal Constitutional Court's Lisbon Case' 10 German Law Journal 18, 1241; Christoph Schönberger, 'Lisbon in Karlsruhe: Maastricht's Epigones at Sea' (2009) 10 German Law Journal 1201, 1207.

71 Constitutional identity is an idea with an old tradition in Germany, rooted in Weimar. It was used by the Constitutional Court in relation to EC/EU law even before *Lissabon* and later codified in Article 79 III GG. See Monika Polzin, 'Constitutional Identity, Unconstitutional Amendments and the Idea of Constituent Power: The Development of the Doctrine of Constitutional Identity in German Constitutional Law' (2016) 14 International Journal of Constitutional Law 411, 426–432.

72 See paras. 231, 233, 278, 279, 298 of the decision.

73 See paras. 248–252 and 286.

to European integration more explicit and endorsing an almost Schmittian theory which ultimately presupposes a pre-existent, homogeneous, and largely mythical people as the sole democratically legitimate constituent power.[74]

As for *Maastricht*'s impact on legal scholarship, it was equally momentous. In a sense, *Maastricht* was the engine of the entire scholarly movement of pluralists. Reflection among both judges and scholars on the plurality of constitutional claims made in Europe existed at least since the foundational cases examined in the last paragraph. Yet, *Maastricht* worked as a catalyst and boosted the discussion considerably. Apart from the role it had for courts outside Germany, within academic circles, many scholars got involved in the discussion trying to understand, explain, criticize, or endorse the *Maastricht* judgment.[75]

The collection of essays published in 1995 in the third number of the 'European Law Journal' is particularly instructive, as it exposed *in nuce* the full spectrum of later academic stances of pluralism.

To begin with, Dieter Grimm's article *Does Europe Need a Constitution?* was a clear endorsement of the *Urteil*, a refinement of its theoretical apparatus, and the scholarly version of the state-based pyramidal view.[76] He stressed the democratic element of modern constitutions: the lack of a European *demos* as source of legitimacy and the absence of a structure of parties, associations, trade unions, media, public debate, and common language necessary to build it a the European level.[77] Grimm's endorsed *Maastricht* and radically questioned the possibility of a European constitution.

Similar to Grimm's but more moderate was the opinion expressed by Jürgen Habermas.[78] According to Habermas, Grimm was right in underlining the lack of a European demos and of a European public sphere. Yet, he did not share Grimm's pessimism on the possibility of little by little building a European *demos*. A *demos* is not a *volk*, ethnically homogeneous and endowed with an original identity, but a communicative community, and a communicative community can be developed. There was no *a priori* reason to exclude this possibility, while on the other hand there were many reasons to aim at the incremental development of a European entity, democratically legitimized and well equipped to face issues that States were not able to tackle anymore at the national level.

A different interpretation came from MacCormick himself. In his *The Maastricht Urteil: Sovereignty Now*,[79] he claimed that the decision by the German Constitutional Court proved instead of falsifying his claims regarding constitutional pluralism. Based on his developing theory of pluralism, examined in detail in the next chapter,

74 Lars Vinx, 'The Incoherence of Strong Popular Sovereignty' (2013) 11 International Journal of Constitutional Law 101, 114–124.

75 Avbelj and Komárek (n 54) 333.

76 Dieter Grimm, 'Does Europe Need a Constitution?' (1995) 1 European Law Journal 282.

77 Grimm wrote extensively about the shift from the ancient to the modern sense of 'constitution'. See Dieter Grimm, *Constitutionalism: Past, Present, and Future* (Oxford University Press 2016) 89–124.

78 Jürgen Habermas, 'Remarks on Dieter Grimm's "Does Europe Need a Constitution?"' (1995) 1 European Law Journal 303.

79 MacCormick, 'The Maastricht-Urteil' (n 1). MacCormick commented further the *Maastricht Urteil* in a subsequent article in which he addressed the conception of 'people' and 'democracy' endorsed

he stated that the correct analysis of the relation between Member States and the EU was pluralistic rather than monistic: each system recognized the others as sources of valid law and accepted that its own judicial institutions would be the final arbiter within their material sphere of validity. Each claimed primacy in its own sphere; none claimed absolute, all-purpose supremacy. If so, then the *Maastricht Urteil* proved that pluralism was correct: the German Court had indeed recognized the validity of EU law in its separate sphere and endorsed cooperation; on the other side, it preserved its own field of jurisdictional competence. The systems were separate and yet interacting. This twofold reading of the *Urteil* was possible to the Scottish scholar because in his view the reasoning of the Federal Court itself was ambiguous and contradictory.

Finally, Joseph Weiler criticized harshly the decision.[80] In his view, the key error of *Maastricht* lied in the misleading notion of 'people'. A late 20th century version of the concept of *volk* echoed in the judgment, as an ethically and culturally homogeneous unity. This Schmittian, organic notion, in which *demos* and *ethnos* collapse, inevitably led the Court to the no-*demos* thesis and to the impossibility of a European democracy. Yet, there was no evidence of constant presence of a homogeneous polity behind democratic States. Indeed, the opposite has historically happened more than once: States artificially created peoples. The other way around, we have experience of States in which the *demos* was made of a series of *ethnoi*. As a result, in Weiler's view *Maastricht* radically blundered in understanding European supranationalism, which was not about building a European *ethnos*-state, but about creating a community where one could be at the same time member of an *ethnos* and citizen of a broader polity.

To sum up, the *Maastricht Urteil* was perhaps the most important judgment in the history of European constitutional pluralism: it exposed the first theoretically thick judicial elaboration on the topic; placed firmly the *grundnorm* in the hands of the masters of the Treaties, in a manner specular and opposite to pieces like Opinion 2/13; influenced immensely the subsequent case law of other courts, as well as later German developments; fostered a scholarly debate on constitutional pluralism that grew quickly and rages on still today.

2.2.3 Granital*: Pluralism and Institutionalism*

Of the Inner Six that established the Communities in the first place, four had a monist conception of the relations between domestic and international law

by the German Constitutional Court. He argued in favour of a 'civic' conception of *demos* in opposition to the 'ethnic' understanding of the Court: what unites the latter are ethnic or ethnic-cultural boundaries, while what unites the former would be loyalty to the values of a common constitutional order. Neil MacCormick, 'Democracy, Subsidiarity, and Citizenship in the "European Commonwealth"' (1997) 16 Law and Philosophy 331, 340–342.

80 Joseph HH Weiler, 'Does Europe Need a Constitution? Demos, Telos and the German Maastricht Decision' (1995) 1 European Law Journal 219.

(Belgium, France, Luxembourg, and the Netherlands) and two a dualist perspective (Germany and Italy).[81] Dualism entails that external law is internally valid once incorporated, with a rank determined by the norm of incorporation.[82] This doctrinal perspective made the reception of the foundational principles of direct effect and especially primacy predictably difficult in Germany and Italy.[83] Moreover, both were paradigmatic cases of European post-World War II constitutionalism, endowed with long, rigid, ethically thick constitutions, with a centralized system of constitutional review.[84] As in Germany, the newly instituted *Corte costituzionale* (1956) had to gain the authoritativeness necessary to perform its role in a delicate context. Indeed, in Italy both the political branches and the judiciary initially had little patience for the *Consulta*.[85] Moreover, the absence of a direct action available to individuals, substituted by the indirect review that was later transposed in the preliminary reference mechanism, marked a crucial difference with the *Bundesverfassungsgericht* and forced the ICC to actively look for a cooperative relation with ordinary judges.[86]

Thus, the acceptance of direct effect, primacy, and autonomy of Community law was problematic in Italy: the dualist tradition, combined with the need for the Constitutional Court to build its own authority rather than that of the Court of Justice, made quite difficult the recognition of an external legal order claiming autonomy, direct effect, and primacy. Indeed, the Court of Justice's affirmation of primacy in *Costa* was, after all, triggered by the ICC: by ranking the Treaty at the same level of the internal provision ratifying it, the Italian Court took a strictly dualist approach and exposed Community law to the will of the domestic legislator.[87] The reasoning exposed by the *Corte costituzionale* was in fact an answer to the challenge of constitutional pluralism, and one perfectly consistent with the standard model. The single and ultimate norm justifying the validity of law was the national Constitution which allowed for international cooperation and for the limitations of sovereignty necessary to it (Article 11). The nature of the EEC, supranational, quasi-federal, international, or anything else, was irrelevant. Thus, the rank of the

81 Claes (n 29) 45–57.

82 Bruno de Witte, 'Direct Effect, Primacy, and the Nature of the Legal Order' in Paul Craig and Gráinne de Búrca (eds), *The Evolution of EU Law* (Oxford University Press 2021) 189. Generally on monism and dualism see James Crawford, *Brownlie's Principles of Public International Law* (Oxford University Press 2012) 48–50.

83 Rasmussen, 'From Costa v ENEL to the Treaties of Rome: A Brief History of a Legal Revolution' (n 23) 71.

84 Andrea Buratti, *Western Constitutionalism: History, Institutions, Comparative Law* (Springer 2019) 148–163.

85 Vittoria Barsotti and others, *Italian Constitutional Justice in Global Context* (Oxford University Press 2015) 11–37; Andrea Simoncini, 'The Success of a Constitutional Experiment: When History Matters. The Italian Constitutional Court in Global Context' (2016) 8 The Italian Journal of Public Law 79, 81–89.

86 Armin von Bogdandy and Davide Paris, 'Power Is Perfected in Weakness: On the Authority of the Italian Constitutional Court' in Vittoria Barsotti and others (eds), *Dialogues on Italian constitutional justice: a comparative perspective* (Routledge-Giappichelli 2021) 267–269.

87 Arena (n 22) 1023–1026.

EEC Treaty corresponded to that assigned internally to the act of incorporation. This neat and clear reasoning failed to be eventually accepted in Luxembourg in the face of the ongoing process of autonomization and constitutionalization of the Communities. However, it well exemplified one of the possible paths to deal with the problem of pluralism.

Later developments are quite known.[88] A decade after *Costa*, in the *ICIC* case, the Court stated that internal norms in conflict with previous supranational norms had to be quashed by the Constitutional Court as inconsistent with Article 11 of the Constitution.[89] The Court of Justice did not accept a mechanism that would involve time-consuming national declarations of invalidity and in *Simmenthal* asserted that national judges had to disapply immediately every conflicting national norm in order to ensure direct effect and primacy.[90] Finally, after another decade,[91] in *Granital* the Italian Court reached an arrangement that satisfied the Court of Justice: Community norms with direct effect enjoyed primacy over domestic law and disapplication of conflicting Italian norms was possible for ordinary judges without any previous declaration of invalidity by the Constitutional Court.[92] The only reservation was made for those basic constitutional principles and inalienable human rights which are usually referred to as the *counter-limits* to the European integration:[93] such hendiadys, once again recalling the enduring pair of modern constitutionalism (public powers and rights), referred to a core of the Italian Constitution that could not be disapplied.[94] Although the Italian Court never distinguished between fundamental rights, *ultra vires*, and identity control, as the *Bundesverfassungsgericht* did, *Granital* effectively established the Italian side of the Italo-German model of conditional primacy which later spread in other countries as well.[95] *Granital* has been since the keystone of the legal relations between Italy and

88 Antonio La Pergola and Patrick Del Duca, 'Community Law, International Law and the Italian Constitution' (1985) 79 American Journal of International Law 598, 609–616; Marta Cartabia, 'The Italian Constitutional Court and the Relationship Between the Italian Legal System and the European Community' (1990) 12 Michigan Journal of International Law 173; Giulio Itzcovich, 'Sovereignty, Legal Pluralism and Fundamental Rights: Italian Jurisprudence and European Integration (1964-73)' (2004) 10 European Public Law 28.

89 Corte costituzionale, judgment 232/1975.

90 C- 106/77 Amministrazione delle Finanze dello Stato v Simmenthal SpA ECLI:EU:C:1978:49.

91 In the meanwhile, the Court had commanded to Italian judges to interpret Italian norms consistently with EC law (Corte costituzionale, judgments 176–177/1981).

92 Corte costituzionale, judgment 170/1984. See the unofficial translation in Giorgio Gaja, 'Constitutional Court (Italy), Decision No. 170 of 8 June 1984, S.p.a. Granital v. Amministrazione Delle Finanze Dello Stato' (1984) 21 Common Market Law Review 756, 758–764.

93 Paolo Barile, 'Il cammino comunitario della Corte' *Giurisprudenza costituzionale* (1973) 2406.

94 This doctrine was elaborated throughout decades, starting already in the 1960s (see Corte costituzionale, judgment 98/1965, *Acciaierie San Michele* and 183/1973 *Frontini*). It is also worth mentioning that a few years later, in the *FRAGD* case, the Italian Court specified that it would possibly review and disapply individual EC norms, abandoning any threat of a general check on the entire Treaty system (which was previously asserted, e.g., in *Frontini*). This made the use of the counter-limits more likely, but also less disruptive. See Corte costituzionale, judgment 239/1989.

95 de Witte (n 82) 217–223.

the EC/EU.[96] The latest significant development, judgment 269/2017 mentioned in the Introduction, allowed Italian judges to refer first to the Constitutional Court and then to the Court of Justice in case of provisions possibly violating both constitutional and EU rights, but did not change the conceptual reconstruction of the relations between Italian and EU law.[97]

While this is known, what is less reported is the way in which *Granital* dealt with the challenge of pluralism. This is the reason why *Granital* is discussed here: compared to both Opinion 2/13 and *Maastricht*, it is characterized by a different and interesting perspective. In *Granital*, we find an attempt to escape the view according to which supranational law is valid and binding only *qua* delegated regulation on behalf of the Member States.

In *Granital*, the *Corte costituzionale* stated something that can be defined as a form of pluralism *in nuce*: it claimed that Italian and Community law existed side by side, each one independent and autonomous, although coordinated. Community law had its own, separate validity and its norms did not operate within the Italian system because of an act of delegation, but in the light of their own binding force. The Court explicitly stated that the domestic order was 'opening itself' to Community provisions, whose rank in a hierarchy of norms was determined by its system of origin only, not by Italian law. Article 11 of the Italian Constitution merely allowed such recognition, it did not internalize Community law. Crucially, the national recognition of its norms within internal sources was limited to granting efficacy and application to supranational norms, not their validity. Therefore, Community law enjoyed direct effect and primacy on its own grounds and within its own competences.

The immediate and practical effect of such conceptualization was allowing judges to disapply conflicting Italian legislation without any previous reference to the Constitutional Court. Indeed, there was no invalidity to be declared by the *Corte costituzionale*, for the involved norms belonged to different systems. Moreover, *Granital* made cases like *Costa*, based on a diametrically opposite conceptualization of the relations between national and supranational law, just impossible. Symmetrically, it meant that Italian legislation would be merely disapplied, not voided by domestic judges. The autonomy of Community law, in other words, was not only accepted in theory, but also considered in its pragmatic meaning and 'carried to its logical conclusion'.[98]

These practical results of *Granital* cannot be forgotten and likely were strong motivating factors in adopting it. Yet, this point must not be overemphasized. Indeed, the picture of the two systems as autonomous yet coordinated had first appeared

96 *Granital*'s reasoning regarded Regulations. Later cases decided by the Italian Constitutional Court extended its rationale and ordinary judges' power of disapplication to other EC norms, including decisions of the Court of Justice (judgment 113/1985), Treaty provisions (judgment 389/1989), and self-executing Directives (judgment 168/1991).

97 Giuseppe Martinico and Giorgio Repetto, 'Fundamental Rights and Constitutional Duels in Europe: An Italian Perspective on Case 269/2017 of the Italian Constitutional Court and Its Aftermath' (2019) 15 European Constitutional Law Review 731, 748–751.

98 Pergola and Duca (n 88) 614.

in the case law of the Court already in the *Acciaierie San Michele* judgment (1965), right after *Costa* and well before the Court accepted that ordinary judges could disapply domestic provisions autonomously.[99] The Court iterated such idea again in *Frontini* (1973). Thus, the practical results of the 'autonomous yet coordinated' view follow, do not precede the theory. What is visible in *Granital* is, in other words, more the blossoming of a cultural change, from the typically dualist approach of *Costa* to a pluralist theory, rather than a reasoning strategically aimed at solving the specific problem the Court was concerned about.

Dualism is, as a matter of fact, perfectly consistent with judgments like *Maastricht*. Any norm that is external to the system must be validated through direct or indirect mechanisms of reference before counting as law.[100] Whatever its role externally, it is a sheer fact from the perspective of a dualist system. Validation must happen according to internal mechanisms which, in turn, must directly or indirectly be validated by the ultimate norm, the constitution. *Granital* escaped this perspective by accepting that supranational law had a validity of its own. The judgment did not affirm that the Community was developed enough to have a constitution of its own, thus it did not clearly reveal a form of constitutional pluralism, but it is safe to say that it was a pluralist, rather than a dualist decision.[101] Not by chance, it was suggested that *Granital*'s pluralism may have been influenced by the pluralist and institutionalist theory of law developed by the public lawyer and former President of the Council of State Santi Romano.[102] Romano, as his contemporary Maurice Hauriou in France, was concerned with the development of organized societal structures, like mass political parties or trade unions, that between the end of the 19th century and the beginning of the 20th, were flourishing in Europe beyond any control or recognition of the State. Romano called such organized structures 'institutions' and depicted them as proper and independent legal orders. As a matter of fact, their normative grip did not depend on State recognition but on their independent capacity to obtain the allegiance of people. Only a dogmatic faith in the idea that all law derives from State recognition could deny this social fact. What followed, in his view, was a deeply pluralist theory of law, in which institutions of various kinds, from States and international organizations to parties and religious groups, developed autonomously.[103] This theory was and still is perfectly know in

99 Corte costituzionale, judgment 98/1965.

100 Pavlos Eleftheriadis, 'Pluralism and Integrity: Pluralism and Integrity' (2010) 23 Ratio Juris 365, 368–370; Gianluigi Palombella, 'Theory, Realities, and Promises of Inter-Legality: A Manifesto' in Gianluigi Palombella and Jan Klabbers (eds), *The Challenge of Inter-Legality* (Cambridge University Press 2019) 366–369.

101 Itzcovich, 'Sovereignty, Legal Pluralism and Fundamental Rights' (n 88) 115–120.

102 ibid; Itzcovich, *Teorie e ideologie del diritto comunitario* (n 27) 236–242; Diletta Tega, 'The Italian Constitutional Court in Its Context: A Narrative' (2021) 17 European Constitutional Law Review 369, 382–383.

103 Romano's main work can now be read in English, see Santi Romano, *The Legal Order* (Routledge 2017). See also the commentaries by Massimo La Torre, *Law as Institution* (Springer 2010) 98–109; Massimo La Torre, 'Institutionalism as Alternative Constitutional Theory: On Santi Romano's

Italy and may well have influenced the line of cases that, from *Acciaierie San Michele* to *Granital*, recognized the autonomous value of Community law.

The distance from *Maastricht*, with its emphasis on the ultimate, foundational national constitution as the only justification for the validity of supranational law, could not be greater.

Granital is different from *Maastricht* in another sense too. While the latter is known for its thickness and complexity, its magisterial and almost academic tone, *Granital* was much thinner. Although compared to the previous Italian cases it seemed at that time an 'unusually theoretical decision',[104] to the eyes of those who assisted to the much thicker reasoning of later cases, this sensation is reversed. The Court sketches its pluralist perspective in a few pages and in brief formulas. Autonomy within coordination, openness to Community law, basic principles and inalienable rights: all is vague and blurred. *Granital* is a pluralist decision without a full-fledged theory of pluralism. What is especially puzzling is the coexistence of pluralism and of the counter-limits doctrine. For, if supranational law is autonomous and its validity is not assessed at the national level, how can then the ICC still assert its jurisdiction on possible although unlikely violations of the core of the Constitution? *Granital* seems really the last page of a twofold, paradoxical stream of cases, on the one hand accepting the foundational principles of the new supranational legal order, on the other positing limits on them.[105] Perhaps the most likely explanation for such contradiction lies in the new meaning given to Article 11 of the Constitution: not anymore a rule establishing the rank of internalized treaty law in Italy, but a principle allowing participation to international cooperation.[106] Principles, more likely than rules, are the object of balancing and defeasible application.[107] When, in the eyes of the Constitutional Court, the damage to equally basic constitutional norms outweighed the advantage of participation into the process of European integration, the recognition of the binding force of the autonomous European order would be withdrawn.

2.2.4 Comparative Assessment

It is now possible to pause and compare the three decisions. Opinion 2/13, the *Maastricht Urteil*, and *Granital* show how real the riddle of constitutional pluralism is for

Concept of Law and His Epigones' (2020) 11 Jurisprudence 92; Martin Loughlin, *Political Jurisprudence* (Oxford University Press 2017) 114–118.

104 Gaja (n 92) 764.

105 Cartabia (n 88) 176–186.

106 Itzcovich, 'Sovereignty, Legal Pluralism and Fundamental Rights' (n 88) 124–126.

107 Whether rules apply in an all-or-nothing manner while principles are balanced (qualitative distinction) or whether also rules are at times object of balancing (quantitative distinction) is controversial. For the former view, see e.g., Ronald Dworkin, *Taking Rights Seriously* (Harvard University Press 1978) 22–28; for the latter, see e.g., Neil MacCormick, *Institutions of Law: An Essay in Legal Theory* (Oxford University Press 2007) 24–31. I am inclined to accept the latter option. This does not prevent from recognizing that the defeasible application of principles is much more likely and frequent.

judges: far from being a mere academic and theoretical concern, it had and still has an impact on the way specific controversies are solved. The EU's accession to the ECHR, Germany's participation to the Treaty of Maastricht, and even the more mundane tax import controversy which was at the basis of *Granital*, were all occasions for the three courts to think about the nature of the EU, the effects of its provisions, and ultimately the justification of its primacy.

After the difficult process of acceptance of the EU's foundational principles which the German and Italian experiences witness, the most accepted solution from the perspective of national supreme and constitutional courts has been conditional primacy, which recognizes the primacy of EU law while making some reservations for the core of the national constitution. The Court of Justice, on the other hand, does not make such exception. Even when it has granted exceptions to the application of EU law,[108] it did so based on EU principles or clauses such as the principle of proportionality or Article 4.2 TEU on respect for national identity.[109] This divergence in the scope of EU primacy of course entails the possibility of conflicts whenever cases within the area of constitutional courts' reservations emerge. Chapter 5 will be devoted to an analysis of recent judicial conflicts. It will demonstrate again that the riddle of constitutional pluralism is far from being theoretical.

Apart from showing the persistent relevance of constitutional pluralism for the practice of law, Opinion 2/13, *Maastricht*, and Granital expose the diversity of judicial solutions to the riddle of pluralism, that is, ultimately to the question of EU law's autonomy, rather than primacy. Exceptions to the primacy of EU law may be justified from both a national and a supranational perspective, but what counts is whether EU law is autonomous and can determine them alone or whether it is a second order legality derived from States, which in turn hold the power of fixing the limits of EU's attributions. In the vocabulary of *Maastricht*, it is a problem of *kompetenz-kompetenz*. Posited in front of the same problem, namely, how to understand the autonomization and constitutionalization of EU law since *Van Gend en Loos*, the approaches developed by the three courts diverge.

The Court of Justice, in a series of decisions epitomized by Opinion 2/13, insisted that EU law is autonomous, that the Treaties have independent legal value, and that the specific characteristics of EU law make for a network of principles that in fact compose the EU constitution. By grounding the value of EU law in an autonomous source of constitutional nature, the Court of Justice mimicked the standard pyramidal picture typical of States.

108 E.g., C-112/00 Eugen Schmidberger, Internationale Transporte und Planzüge v Austria ECLI:EU:C:2003:333; C-36/02 Omega Spielhallen- und Automatenaufstellungs GmbH v. Oberbürgermeisterin der Bundesstadt Bonn ECLI:EU:C:2004:614; C-208/09 Ilonka Sayn-Wittgenstein v. Landeshauptmann von Wien ECLI:EU:C:2010:806.

109 On proportionality in EU law, see Tor-Inge Harbo, 'The Function of the Proportionality Principle in EU Law' (2010) 16 European Law Journal 158. As for Article 4.2 TEU, its origin, interpretation, and application, see Leonard FM Besselink, 'National and Constitutional Identity before and after Lisbon' (2010) 6 Utrecht Law Review 36.

The *Maastricht Urteil* is symmetrical and opposite to Opinion 2/13. It followed the same logic which identifies a single foundational norm from which legality emerged but situated it at the level of State constitutions. In a theoretical, thick, almost academic judgment, the Federal Court rejected the idea of a European constitution based on a connection between the people (the only true *pouvoir constituant* in democratic societies), the constitution (the only acceptable basic norm), and the validity of any other legal provision (necessarily to be authorized by the constitution). EU law was de-autonomized and de-constitutionalized in such reasoning, transformed into an association of States whose legal order was valid only insofar it was delegated by the States.

Lastly, *Granital* took a different path. It tried to avoid the reductionist perspective which reconnects all legal norms to a single foundational norm and accepted that supranational law had a validity of its own, although not taking an explicit position on the constitutional nature of the Treaties. By accepting the autonomy of Community law, it was able to recognize its independent legal effects without recurring to the picture of the domestic legal system which, like Midas, recognized external norms and transformed sheer facts into law.[110] *Granital* is an example of how to come to terms with the riddle of constitutional pluralism from a pluralist perspective. However, it also was a quite thin judgment, in which a proper theory of pluralism is not defined, but only hinted at. Most importantly, it never explained how the autonomy and separateness of Community and Italian law, coexisting side by side, could be reconciled with the persistence of the counter-limits doctrine, which kept the ICC's reservations to the principle of primacy well alive.

2.3 The Debate on Pluralism: New Incarnation of Constitutionalism or Oxymoron?

While, as we have just seen, the riddle of constitutional pluralism was well visible for courts and these struggled to find an adequate approach to European integration, scholarship too was at work to provide one. In this specific sense, constitutional pluralism primarily was and is the collective academic endeavour to develop an understanding at the same time alternative to *Maastricht*, thicker than *Granital*, and inspired by MacCormick's hints in *Beyond the Sovereign State*. Indeed, although attempts to describe the process of autonomization and constitutionalization of supranational law were made even before,[111] it was only after the influential writings

110 See Kelsen (n 11) 161: 'Just as everything King Midas touched turned into gold, everything to which law refers becomes law.'

111 E.g., Stein (n 17); Weiler, 'The Transformation of Europe' (n 32); G Federico Mancini, 'The Making of a Constitution for Europe' (1989) 26 Common Market Law Review 595; Koen Lenaerts, 'Constitutionalism and the Many Faces of Federalism' (1990) 38 American Journal of Comparative Law 205. On these scholars, see Daniel Halberstam, 'Joseph Weiler, Eric Stein, and the Transformation of Constitutional Law' in Marlene Wind and Miguel Poiares Maduro (eds), *The Transformation of Europe: Twenty-Five Years On* (Cambridge University Press 2017) 221–223.

by MacCormick in the early Nineties and after the *Maastricht* judgment that constitutional pluralism became a large, widely discussed academic topic.[112]

In the wake and immediately after the *Maastricht Urteil*, the first intellectual reaction was understanding the puzzling phenomenon of competing claims to ultimate constitutional authority. This perspective, which inspires this book as well, has usually been known as *radical constitutional pluralism*. As anticipated in the Introduction, it was a mainly descriptive one. It aimed at understanding more than correcting, at explaining rather than advising. It also came to the somewhat sceptical conclusion that, at some point, legal principles would prove to be insufficient and that only political negotiation would effectively mediate between competing claims of authority. In a sense, radical pluralism assigned a limited role to law and to lawyers and a much bigger one to politics and politicians. This might explain radical pluralism's overall academic unpopularity: giving up any hope to reconcile competing claims under a legal framework was later perceived as a yielding concession to instability and an invitation to open conflict.[113] Moreover, radical pluralism was criticized for allegedly being too thin and poor to explain the relative stability of European constitutional pluralism despite the possibility of conflicts.[114] As a result, besides MacCormick's articles between 1993 and 1995, on which we will return in the next chapter, few and limited attempts have been made to revitalize such perspective.[115]

It is my opinion, of course, that this condemnation is overall wrong. Radical pluralism was a realistic attempt to comprehend a complex phenomenon. There is no reason to accuse an attempt to explain constitutional pluralism of anything that is failing to explain, and certainly none to blame it for constitutional conflicts (which have happened anyhow, despite radical pluralism being a fairly minoritarian view). It is true though that the theory has never been developed enough and has remained a thin account of European pluralism, but this is an invitation to further development, not to prematurely abandon the theory. This book is aimed at filling this gap with arguments coming from both constitutional

112 Avbelj and Komárek (n 54) 333; Baquero Cruz (n 53) 412–418.

113 E.g., Pavlos Eleftheriadis, *A Union of Peoples* (Oxford University Press 2020) 69–72.

114 Cormac S Mac Amhlaigh, 'The Anatomy of Constitutional Pluralism in the European Union' in Gareth Davies and Matej Avbelj (eds), *Research Handbook on Legal Pluralism and EU Law* (Edward Elgar 2018) 68–70.

115 Nico Krisch, *Beyond Constitutionalism: The Pluralist Structure of Postnational Law* (Oxford University Press 2010); Nico Krisch, 'Who Is Afraid of Radical Pluralism? Legal Order and Political Stability in the Postnational Space' (2011) 24 Ratio Juris 386; Nicholas Barber, *The Constitutional State* (Oxford University Press 2010). None, however, openly claims to adopt a form of radical pluralism. It is only admitted that multiple claims to ultimate authority, grounded on different foundational norms, can coexist, while no overarching legal framework to accommodate conflicts is vindicated. Moreover, the focus is not solely or even mainly the European context: there is no detailed analysis of how the various basic norms of Europe interact and collide. Instead, this is what I attempt to do here: filling the gap by deepening radical pluralism as a theory of European constitutional pluralism. Finally, these works predate the cases of constitutional conflict that I examine in Chapter 5.

theory and from comparative law. As we will see in Chapter 5, once this is done, the relative stability of the composite European constitution is explainable from a radical perspective.

That said, however, it is worth recalling how most scholars have not accepted such perspective and have instead taken a different and *normative* turn, one so diffused that constitutional pluralism in its academic sense has for the most part become a synonym for this normative position. The core tenet of normative pluralism is that the undecidedness of the question of ultimate authority which derives from the rival constitutional claims is not only an empirical fact but also a desirable one. In the words of Kalypso Nicolaidis:[116]

> Constitutional pluralists ... push this idea further and start from the empirical observation that the question of final constitutional authority in the EU remains open in law, in order, ultimately to ground their normative claim that the question of final authority (between European and national courts) ought to be left open.

It is not necessary explain in detail how this view has been articulated in the past years.[117] Just to recall some of the most iconic views on normative pluralism, Neil Walker has pointed out that conceptualizing the EU either as an international organization whose masters are the States or as a purely autonomous entity necessarily means that we will lose something of significance, while to redeem constitutionalism in the post-state 21st century, it is necessary to accept a minimum degree of mutual recognition for rival and incommensurable constitutional conceptions. The question of inter-systemic superiority must remain open and undecided.[118] Joseph Weiler developed a substantive version of constitutional pluralism, based on the principle of constitutional tolerance: the two levels of constitutional authority, the European and the national one, should understand each other as equal, so that no monism, prone to abuse, can ever prevail.[119] Matthias Kumm argued that national constitutional courts should accept the primacy of EU law as an instantiation of the value of the rule of law in Europe, except when this is outweighed by concerns connected to State democracy or guarantee of constitutional values. In his Dworkinian account of pluralism, the rival constitutional claims must be

116 Kalypso Nicolaidis (n 61) 265.

117 For a comprehensive overview see Klemen Jaklic, *Constitutional Pluralism in the EU* (Oxford University Press 2014).

118 Neil Walker, 'The Idea of Constitutional Pluralism' (2002) 65 Modern Law Review 317. See also N Walker, 'Legal Theory and the European Union: A 25th Anniversary Essay' (2005) 25 Oxford Journal of Legal Studies 581; Neil Walker, 'Constitutional Pluralism Revisited' (2016) 22 European Law Journal 24.

119 Weiler, 'Does Europe Need a Constitution?' (n 80); Joseph HH Weiler, *The Constitution of Europe* (Cambridge University Press 1999); Joseph HH Weiler, 'In Defence of the Status Quo: Europe's Constitutional Sonderweg' in Joseph HH Weiler and Marlene Wind (eds), *European Constitutionalism beyond the State* (Cambridge University Press 2003).

treated as competing principles in need of balancing.[120] The scholar who expressed the main tenets of normative pluralism in the clearest possible fashion probably is the former Advocate General of the Court of Justice Miguel Poiares Maduro. In his view, not only we experience a plurality of competing constitutional authorities (descriptive claim) and not only this heterarchical equilibrium among them is normatively preferable to a hierarchical setting (normative claim), but today this scenario expresses a superior fidelity to the ideal of constitutionalism than every possible monistic constitutionalism, be it national or European (thickly normative claim).[121] In Poiares Maduro's view, at the core of modern constitutionalism lies a never-ending tension between a 'unitary conception of law and political authority' and 'the pluralist conception of society and the political space'. Pluralism on ultimate constitutional authority is therefore a constitutive part of the concept of constitutionalism and equilibrium between different legal orders is necessary to a well-ordered constitutionalism. This project requires a balance between different systems to ensure mutual respect and minimize the risk of conflict. Poiares Maduro calls for a balance based on the 'harmonic principles of contrapunctual law'. If legal actors in the European order share some common principles of legal reasoning, namely pluralism, consistency, universalizability, and institutional choice, then coherence and integrity of the European legal order will be granted.[122] As a result, normative constitutional pluralism was developed as an ambitious theory that started from an empirical point (the fact of pluralism), praised it (as the modern incarnation of constitutionalism), and tried to elaborate complex interpretive methods allowing for an equilibrium between the involved legal orders.

It goes without saying that the narrative of pluralists like Kumm or Poiares Maduro has not gone unchallenged: an impressive barrage of critiques of various kinds has targeted it. Some argued that the question of ultimate authority indeed is not or shall not be left undecided: ultimate authority lies at the level of State constitutions.[123] Martin Loughlin went even further and stated that 'constitutional

120 Mattias Kumm, 'Who Is the Final Arbiter of Constitutionality in Europe?: Three Conceptions of the Relationship Between the German Federal Constitutional Court and the European Court of Justice' (1999) 36 Common Market Law Review 351; Mattias Kumm, 'The Jurisprudence of Constitutional Conflict: Constitutional Supremacy in Europe before and after the Constitutional Treaty' (2005) 11 European Law Journal 262; Mattias Kumm, 'The Moral Point of Constitutional Pluralism: Defining the Domain of Legitimate Institutional Civil Disobedience and Conscientious Objection' in Julie Dickson and Pavlos Eleftheriadis (eds), *Philosophical Foundations of European Union Law* (Oxford University Press 2012).

121 Miguel Poiares Maduro, 'Three Claims of Constitutional Pluralism' in Matej Avbelj and Jan Komárek (eds), *Constitutional Pluralism in the European Union and Beyond* (Hart Publishing 2012).

122 Miguel Poiares Maduro, 'Contrapunctual Law: Europe's Constitutional Pluralism in Action' in Neil Walker (ed), *Sovereignty in Transition* (Hart Publishing 2003); Miguel Poiares Maduro, 'Interpreting European Law: Judicial Adjudication in a Context of Constitutional Pluralism' (n 20); Miguel Poiares Maduro, 'Three Claims of Constitutional Pluralism' (n 121).

123 Grimm (n 76). See also Grimm (n 77) 271–294; Gareth Davies, 'Constitutional Disagreement in Europe and the Search for Pluralism' in Matej Avbelj and Jan Komárek (eds), *Constitutional Pluralism in the European Union and Beyond* (Hart Publishing 2012); Alexander Somek, 'Monism: A Tale of the Undead' in Matej Avbelj and Jan Komárek (eds), *Constitutional Pluralism in the European*

pluralism' is a contradiction in terms, an oxymoron.[124] On the other side of the spectrum, Daniel Kelemen stated that by applauding undecidedness, pluralism favoured conflicts and prevented the development of full-fledged primacy of EU law.[125] It was also pointed out that the celebration of undecidedness, a form of constitutional postmodernism, favoured undue uncertainty and conflict.[126] Finally, in the wake of the rule of law crisis in Hungary and Poland, normative pluralism was criticized for being a powerful tool in the hands of autocrats: easily used to justify disapplication of EU law and implement illiberal political programmes under a patina of alleged legality.[127]

The debate rages on though: a new generation of scholars has by now emerged and has focused on discussing the critiques to constitutional pluralism. Most importantly, given the conflicts which have erupted in the last years and on which we will return in Chapter 5, how to distinguish destructive from acceptable disagreements is now at the centre of pluralists' concerns.[128]

2.4 Conclusion: Back to 1993

To sum up, the autonomization and constitutionalization of supranational law in Europe was fostered by a combination of judicial, academic, and bureaucratic support on the one hand and by a certain degree of tolerance on behalf of national governments and parliaments on the other. This created a bifurcation when it comes with the ultimate reason of validity of EC/EU norms or national provisions implementing them. That is the riddle of constitutional pluralism in the EU. This apparently theoretical problem turns into a real one when one realizes that the result of where the fundamental norm is situated is either full or conditional primacy of EC/EU law.

Union and Beyond (Hart Publishing 2012); Michel Troper, 'Sovereignty' in Michel Rosenfeld and András Sajó (eds), *The Oxford Handbook of Comparative Constitutional Law* (Oxford University Press 2012).

124 Martin Loughlin, 'Constitutional Pluralism: An Oxymoron?' (2014) 3 Global Constitutionalism 9.

125 R Daniel Kelemen, 'On the Unsustainability of Constitutional Pluralism: European Supremacy and the Survival of the Eurozone' (2016) 23 Maastricht Journal of European and Comparative Law 136.

126 Baquero Cruz (n 53); Julio Baquero Cruz, 'Another Look at Constitutional Pluralism in the European Union' (2016) 22 European Law Journal 356.

127 R Daniel Kelemen and Laurent Pech, 'The Uses and Abuses of Constitutional Pluralism: Undermining the Rule of Law in the Name of Constitutional Identity in Hungary and Poland' (2019) 21 Cambridge Yearbook of European Legal Studies 59.

128 E.g., Ana Bobić, 'Constitutional Pluralism Is Not Dead: An Analysis of Interactions Between Constitutional Courts of Member States and the European Court of Justice' (2017) 18 German Law Journal 1395; Ana Bobić, 'Constructive Versus Destructive Conflict: Taking Stock of the Recent Constitutional Jurisprudence in the EU' (2020) 22 Cambridge Yearbook of European Legal Studies 60; Jessica C Lawrence, 'Constitutional Pluralism's Unspoken Normative Core' (2019) 21 Cambridge Yearbook of European Legal Studies 24; Matej Avbelj, 'Constitutional Pluralism and Authoritarianism' (2020) 21 German Law Journal 1023; Tom Flynn, 'Constitutional Pluralism and Loyal Opposition' (2021) 19 International Journal of Constitutional Law 241.

Courts have faced this problem differently, conceptualizing the relations between EU and national law in ways that range from full assertion of the autonomy and constitutionality of EU law (as in Opinion 2/13) to rejection of such claims, describing the EU as a mere association of States with no constitutional nature (as in the *Maastricht Urteil*). In the middle, cases like *Granital* attempted to find a middle way which at the same time recognizes the autonomy of EU law and preserves the supremacy of at least the core of national constitutional law.

Legal scholarship has reacted to such conceptualizations, and specifically to the *Maastricht Urteil*, by developing academic theories of constitutional pluralism. Although heavily criticized, especially in the last few years, constitutional pluralists are committed to a tolerant, cosmopolitan, liberal, and integrationist view in which hierarchy between legal systems is substituted by heterarchy. Both EU law and national constitutional law have independent legal value and constitutional nature. They interact but none enjoys full supremacy over the other. If we relate to the decisions previously examined, pluralists side with *Granital* against both Opinion 2/13 and *Maastricht*. Most importantly, they praise heterarchy as a desirable state of things, a manifestation of constitutionalism beyond the State. To preserve this state of peaceful heterarchy, some of them have developed methods of interpretation based on principles of legal reasoning that shall guide courts and allow peaceful and mutually respectful interactions. In other words, normative pluralists embrace heterarchy and look for legal (as opposed to merely political) principles which can avoid conflicts and inconsistencies. They recognize the riddle of constitutional pluralism but attempt to neutralize it through legal reasoning. Briefly, constitutional pluralism combines a descriptive claim (the recognition of pluralism), a normative one (the value of heterarchy and its role in preserving constitutionalism even beyond the State), and the elaboration of methods of legal reasoning that avoid conflicts.

While this is the picture drawn by pluralists, this book aims at taking a different path. It is my view that by shifting most of the attention from the descriptive to the normative point the debate is missing something relevant, namely the 'anatomy' of constitutional pluralism.[129] How does the coexistence of several foundational norms work and what can we learn from it? What happens when conflicts cannot be avoided? Too much time has perhaps been spent in praising pluralism and avoiding conflicts, instead of understanding the former and scrutinizing the latter.

One of the internal strands of pluralism, the radical one, was indeed aimed at exposing the anatomy of pluralism in the first place. However, this line of research was mostly abandoned in the last few decades. The promise of explaining the coexistence of EU law and domestic law was overshadowed by the justification of pluralism on normative grounds and by the development of methods of interpretation. The normative tenet of pluralism obscured the descriptive one.

It is worth noting, anyway, that pluralism was originally and primarily radical. Its roots lied in the works of MacCormick published in the Nineties, starting with

129 Mac Amhlaigh (n 114).

Beyond the Sovereign State in 1993. An effort in understanding before influencing pluralism lies at the roots of the movement. As the aim of the book is developing radical pluralism, it is to these roots that we must return. Specifically, MacCormick's works since 1993 must be carefully examined: realizing how MacCormick understood European legal orders to be interlocked, how he came to such views, what hints and what shortcomings they expose, and finally how MacCormick progressively abandoned them, is the first step to then move forth and elaborate a full-fledged theory (Chapters 4 and 5). To redeem radical pluralism and show why it is the best theory we currently have, we must go back to its origins.

3

REVISITING RADICAL PLURALISM

The Jurisprudence of Neil MacCormick and Beyond

3.1 Introduction

This chapter is devoted to discussing radical pluralism in the writings of Neil MacCormick, the intellectual father of the pluralist movement.[1] Trained as a pupil of Herbert Hart,[2] he never was an orthodox positivist and often sought for a synthesis between positivism and the most intriguing ideas of its critics. He worked on a variety of topics, including legal reasoning and argumentation,[3] and the institutional theory of law, developed together with Ota Weinberger.[4] Although it is possible to discuss the essays on constitutional pluralism separately from the rest of his work, it is anyway important to realize that part of the conceptual apparatus he used to decipher constitutional pluralism owes something to his views on legal reasoning, institutionalism, and positivism.

MacCormick was politically committed too: a Scottish nationalist, close to the progressive Scottish National Party (SNP), he was also a Europhile. He was a member of the European Parliament for the SNP between 1999 and 2004 and

1 For an analysis of MacCormick's place in the pluralist movement, see chapter 1 in Klemen Jaklic, *Constitutional Pluralism in the EU* (Oxford University Press 2014).

2 It has been claimed that, among the three great pupils of Hart, namely Dworkin, Raz, and MacCormick, the last was perhaps the closest to Hart's legacy. See Massimo La Torre, 'Reform and Tradition: Changes and Continuities in Neil MacCormick's Concept of Law' in Agustín José Menéndez and John Erik Fossum (eds), *Law and Democracy in Neil MacCormick's Legal and Political Theory* (Springer 2011) 58.

3 Neil MacCormick, *Legal Reasoning and Legal Theory* (Oxford University Press 1994).

4 Neil MacCormick and Ota Weinberger, *An Institutional Theory of Law* (Springer 1986); Neil MacCormick, 'The Legal Framework: Institutional Normative Order', *Questioning Sovereignty* (Oxford University Press 1999); Neil MacCormick, *Institutions of Law: An Essay in Legal Theory* (Oxford University Press 2007).

DOI: 10.4324/9781003291572-3

joined the Convention on the Future of Europe in the effort to draft the later failed Constitutional Treaty.[5]

Thus, he reunited a deep theoretical knowledge of law with the practical experience of a scholar directly involved in high-level law-making. This particularly wide understanding of law, both practical and theoretical, helps explaining why he was well suited to provide a challenging perspective on fundamental legal concepts such as legal system, constitution, State, or sovereignty.

MacCormick's ideas on the construction of a new European legal order coalesced into a series of essays published between 1993 and 1999. These papers lie at the origin of the pluralist movement, and it is hard to underestimate their intellectual influence: it is also hard to find a single scholar working on constitutional pluralism not engaged in citing, building on, or criticizing MacCormick's works.

Besides being extremely influential, MacCormick's reflection on constitutional pluralism is also internally composite. While a few core ideas remained the same throughout the entire time span, a fundamental shift in MacCormick's perspective on pluralism, from strictly descriptive to normative, can be identified as well. These two different phases are usually known by the etiquettes that the author himself used, 'radical pluralism', ideally referring to the 1993–1997 time frame, and 'pluralism under international law', mostly situated into the 1998–1999 period. This chapter aims at assessing MacCormick's pluralism, starting from his first essay in 1993 (the already mentioned *Beyond the Sovereign State*) and then moving towards the writings of the late 1990s.

The perspective of this book, as I have repeatedly stated, is that of radical pluralism. Therefore, it is the first part of MacCormick's writings that is of particular interest here: from there a basis for conceptualizing constitutional pluralism in Europe can be extrapolated. His later essays, on the other hand, will be object of substantive criticism here. I argue that MacCormick's later stance on pluralism conflates two irreconcilable perspectives, one inspired by his former mentor Hart and aimed at a descriptive and sociological explanation of pluralism (a perspective well-established also in the radical phase), and one reconnecting to Hans Kelsen's writings on international law, which, on the other hand, is eminently normative, aimed at directing pluralism rather than merely describing it. A dual inspiration of this kind is motivated by MacCormick's late aspiration to both keep the sociological angle of the first essays and at the same time to tame the risk of constitutional conflicts in Europe. However, this dualism eventually generates contradictions.

Nevertheless, MacCormick's late works on pluralism have had a crucial historical function that must be acknowledged. They have prompted one of the first attempts to elaborate legal principles to tame constitutional pluralism, a pioneering project

5 Neil Walker, 'Reconciling MacCormick: Constitutional Pluralism and the Unity of Practical Reason' (2011) 24 Ratio Juris 369, 369–371; Hugo Canihac, 'Is Constitutional Pluralism (Il)Liberal? On the Political Theory of European Legal Integration in Times of Crisis' (2021) 22 German Law Journal 491, 493–494.

that is today systematically pursued by the vast crowd of contemporary pluralists mentioned in Chapter 2. Moreover, by also recapitulating the main findings of the radical phase, they contributed to their diffusion in a non-negligible manner. Thus, the criticism that follows must not be considered as an attempt to deny the value of such essays, but rather as the effort to distinguish within MacCormick's intuitions what is historically relevant for constitutional pluralism at large and what is theoretically useful from the perspective of this book.

The chapter is structured as follows.

First, MacCormick's essays on pluralism are summarized, exposing their main tenets and giving an overview of his ideas from 1993 to 1999. To illustrate the shift between the radical phase and the so-called pluralism under international law, this first section is split into two paragraphs, examining the two phases separately.

Reverting the timeline, I then focus on the later pluralism under international law, assessing its content and pointing the finger toward the contradictions that make this phase ultimately flawed. However, as the shortcomings of these later essays likely depend on the impossible attempt to simultaneously rely on both Hart and Kelsen, I first briefly introduce the Hart-Kelsen debate on international law to underline the incompatibility between the two and show why pluralism under international law was inevitably doomed to collapse when committing to both at the same time.

Finally, I end the chapter by focusing on the radical phase and underline its takeaways, namely the methodological commitment to 'sociological realism', a certain scepticism towards the notion of 'sovereignty', and the view that the foundational norms-constitutions are complex and possibly even conflictual, far from the irenic simplicity of purely theoretical models like the famous 'what the Queen in Parliament enacts is law'.

3.2 MacCormick's Pluralism: From *Beyond the Sovereign State* to *The Risk of Constitutional Conflict*

As just mentioned, here I summarize the main tenets of MacCormick's pluralism, splitting his work in two. First, we find the radical phase, mostly exposed in the first essay *Beyond the Sovereign State* (1993).[6] As stated in Chapter 2, this essay had a large influence on the later development of constitutional pluralism and, together with the *Maastricht Urteil*, marks in a sense the very beginning of the academic movement. Radical pluralism as conceived by MacCormick is further elaborated in his commentary of *Maastricht* too (1995).[7] The later stage of MacCormick's thinking, pluralism under international law, can instead be summarized by looking at the essay, very telling already in its title, *Risking Constitutional Collision in Europe?* (1998)[8] and at the

6 Neil MacCormick, 'Beyond the Sovereign State' (1993) 56 The Modern Law Review 1.
7 Neil MacCormick, 'The Maastricht-Urteil: Sovereignty Now' (1995) 1 European Law Journal 259.
8 Neil MacCormick, 'Risking Constitutional Collision in Europe?' (1998) 18 Oxford Journal of Legal Studies 517.

later chapter *Juridical Pluralism and the Risk of Constitutional Conflict* (1999).[9] In the middle, we find *Democracy, Subsidiarity, and Citizenship in the European Commonwealth* (1997), a moment of transition in which the argument starts shifting.[10]

The first paragraph of this section considers the two essays of the radical phase, while the last two and the intermediate *Democracy, Subsidiarity, and Citizenship* are analysed in the second paragraph.

3.2.1 Shaping Radical Pluralism (1993–1997)

As previously pointed out, *Beyond the Sovereign State* lies at origin of the entire pluralist movement. Published in the renowned 'Modern Law Review', it is for sure the clearest and most detailed exposition of MacCormick's radical pluralism and, consequently, requires adequate scrutiny.

The first thing to notice is the year of publishing: 1993, the year of the Maastricht Treaty's ratification in several States all around Western Europe. The Treaty would eventually enter into force on 1 November 1993, but its drafting and ratification fostered extensive debate. As mentioned in the last chapter, the Treaty established the European Union, created the three pillars structure, and transferred an unprecedented number of powers from States to the European Union (EU), most notably monetary policy for States adhering to the forthcoming single currency. In a sense, it was really the birth of the European 'Union', something much closer to a federation than the previous and relatively narrow Communities, focused on the creation of a single market only. It is only natural that such step forward on the path to political, legal, and economic integration raised a series of questions. Indeed, the ratification met serious opposition in Denmark, France, and the United Kingdom.[11]

For constitutional lawyers, the most pressing issue was of course the problem of sovereignty. As we have seen in the last chapter, when assessing the compatibility of the Treaty with the *Grundgesetz*, the German Constitutional Court provided its own, and rather traditionalist, answer to the issue of States' sovereignty after the Treaty. *Beyond the Sovereign State*, whose title is already quite revealing, must be placed within this background. Even more so as it came from a Scottish scholar, someone trained and operating in a legal system in which the dogma of parliamentary sovereignty is very pronounced.[12]

Beyond the Sovereign State is, therefore, dominated by the problem of the sovereign State: what is it and how to make sense of it in the light of the process of European integration? MacCormick challenges the foundations of the concept of

9 Neil MacCormick, 'Juridical Pluralism and the Risk of Constitutional Conflict', *Questioning Sovereignty* (Oxford University Press 1999).

10 Neil MacCormick, 'Democracy, Subsidiarity, and Citizenship in the "European Commonwealth"' (1997) 16 Law and Philosophy 331.

11 Desmond Dinan, *Europe Recast: A History of the European Union* (Lynne Rienner Publishers 2014) 244–247.

12 Peter Leyland, *The Constitution of the United Kingdom* (Hart Publishing 2016) 47–65.

sovereignty, perhaps with the view of disconnecting UK constitutional theory from an uncompromising doctrine of parliamentary sovereignty and facilitate the Treaty's ratification.[13]

To do so, he splits sovereignty into two, a political and a legal sense.[14] In the political sense, MacCormick argues, sovereignty, in a line of thinking that relies on Austin, is the supreme power of decision-making in a social organization: it is the ultimate factual authority, obeyed by subjects but not obedient to any authority. Sovereign is who is habitually obeyed by its subjects. On the other hand, in a legal sense that MacCormick traces back to Dicey, sovereignty is a position of normative power defined by the law: the near absolute law-making power conferred by legal (constitutional) norms.[15] Sovereign is who is empowered by the law. The legal conception of sovereignty allows conceivable procedural or substantive constraints in the conferring constitution.[16] Moreover, sovereignty in a legal sense can be divided among different institutions, so that none will be the only 'sovereign': federations and other cases of division of the supreme legislative power are cases in point.[17] Yet, the looser these limitations and the more concentrated the power conferred, the more the empowered institution will be sovereign and its legal authority 'near-absolute'.[18]

After sovereignty, MacCormick moves to the concept of 'State'. Here too he distinguishes between a political concept of the State, namely a political body subject to a de facto sovereign, and a legal one, which defines the State as the legal system, following a tradition exemplified, in MacCormick's view, by Kelsen. He discards the latter as too connected to German constitutional theory and to the 'potentially dangerous idea' that 'a State could not itself be the subject of genuine legal constraints, or of a critique in terms of legal values, because the State is itself constituted by the law'.[19] Thus, he accepts a mainly political notion according to which the State is a 'territorially organized political community', where power is exercised effectively.

13 Probably also to facilitate the process of internal devolution towards the constitutive nations: a Scottish nationalist like MacCormick could appreciate not only the supranational, but also the subnational political potential of a looser notion of sovereignty. See Nico Krisch, 'Who Is Afraid of Radical Pluralism? Legal Order and Political Stability in the Postnational Space' (2011) 24 Ratio Juris 386, 390–392.

14 The distinction between 'internal' and 'external' sovereignty is one of the classic analytical divides in the theory of sovereignty. See recently Nicholas Barber, *The Principles of Constitutionalism* (Oxford University Press 2018) 25–29.

15 Similarly, Noel Malcolm, whose views on sovereignty are otherwise much different from MacCormick's, claimed in the same period that a usual mistake in discussions about sovereignty lies in the missing distinction between power (de facto authority) and proper authority (de iure): sovereignty is a matter of authority, not of sheer power. See Noel Malcolm, 'Sense on Sovereignty' in Martin Holmes (ed), *The Eurosceptical Reader* (Palgrave Macmillan 1996) 10–14.

16 MacCormick, 'Beyond the Sovereign State' (n 6) 11–13.

17 ibid 12–13.

18 See also Neil MacCormick, 'On Sovereignty and Post-Sovereignty', *Questioning Sovereignty* (Oxford University Press 1999) 127.

19 MacCormick, 'Beyond the Sovereign State' (n 6) 13.

Combining the two definitions, a legal notion of sovereignty and a political notion of State, we reach that idea of 'sovereign State' as 'a territorial political order coupled with a legally defined position of near absolute legislative power'.[20] In MacCormick's view, this is an extremely concise account of the traditionally accepted notion of sovereignty developed by modern legal and political thinkers.

The State's monopoly on legal and political legitimate power entails, internally, the identification of the supreme governing institution; externally, it means absence of superior powers or legal constraints. This omnipotent creature of modernity, governing any human activity alone, is the brainchild of a line of thinking that MacCormick traces back to the work of early modern scholars as Bodin and Hobbes. These, in the light of the disastrous religious wars, looked for certainty and stability above all: being ultimate, unitary, unquestionable, and indivisible, sovereignty is the source of certainty they looked for. Alternative normative orders such as international or canon law were inevitably marginalized by the rise of the sovereign State to the paradigm of law. This 'foundationalist' perspective was the equivalent in law and politics of Descartes' search for indubitable truths in epistemology.[21]

Briefly, in MacCormick's view, sovereignty is partly a political concept, defining a certain obedience of citizens to political authority and therefore a certain degree of efficacy of social rules in organized societies. Yet, it is also a legal one, denoting ultimate normative authority on the community, meant as a near absolute power of law-making, conferred by constitutive (and constitutional) norms: as such, it can be restrained by the latter and possibly divided among several authorities. This twofold concept is usually coupled with the State, a social organization that claims ultimate, near absolute normative authority over a certain territory and population and exercises it effectively. A sovereign State claims monopoly of legitimate authority over its own jurisdiction. This understanding comes from the troubled time in which the modern State developed, an era of painful searching for stability and certainty of social rules.

After reconstructing the traditional idea of the sovereign State in modern legal thinking, MacCormick attempts to show how inadequate it is to describe the process of European integration.[22] Given this demanding definition of sovereign State and how important the European Community is in the law-making process of its Member States, there seems to be no sovereign State in contemporary Europe.[23] The extent of powers conferred and effectively exercised at the European level is already wide enough to invalidate the demanding traditional requirement of full authority and independency. Of course, on the other hand, the EC does not enjoy the authority of a State either. Yet, this is a merely apparent paradox: the notion that legal orders must necessarily resemble a sovereign State is, in MacCormick's

20 ibid 14.
21 ibid 14–16.
22 On MacCormick' theory of sovereignty, see extensively Peter C Oliver, 'Sovereignty in the Twenty-First Century' (2003) 14 King's Law Journal 137, 157–173.
23 MacCormick, 'Beyond the Sovereign State' (n 6) 16.

view, simply mistaken. The sovereign State is just contingent, it is one of the possible forms of social organization, one which prevailed in early modernity by concentrating power into a single body, be it the king, the parliament, or the *volonté générale*. MacCormick states that it is wrong to conceptualize the situation of European law as if there necessarily were a sovereign, be it at the level of Member States or in the EU itself.[24] We must substitute to this 'monocular view' a 'broader, more diffuse' one, that understands normative power as not necessarily reduced to unity, but potentially widespread. It is possible that 'different systems can overlap and interact, without necessarily requiring that one be subordinate or hierarchically inferior to the other or to some third system'.[25]

Critiques of sovereignty are not new in constitutional theory.[26] Yet, MacCormick's characterization of this 'broader view' is perhaps one of the reasons why his remarks gained so much attention. In his view, each system recognizes the others as sources of valid law, yet none claims absolute supremacy: the question of ultimate authority remains open. This already is *in nuce* the central claim of constitutional pluralism.

MacCormick elaborates on the coexistence of several claims to ultimate authority.

First, we find a critique of 'monocular' explanations, starting from Austin's theory of the European legal order as based on a general habit of obedience backed by the threat of sanction to a single sovereign, be it in Brussels or in the national capitals.[27] For this to be true we should conceptualize European authorities as agents of national ones by means of the Treaties or, the other way around, national authorities as delegates of the European bureaucrats. Both perspectives seem to him implausible. The latter is particularly lame and awkward: it is clearly unrealistic to depict national branches as dependent on European validation. The right of States to withdraw at any time or judgments like *Maastricht* are evidence of that. Yet also the opposite seems problematic to MacCormick. First, because the European officials and bureaucrats do not regard themselves as delegates, but as officials of an autonomous order, and probably so does a wide number of scholars and practitioners.[28] Second, in the European context, the Austinian sovereign would consist of a *bunch* of States altogether. Yet, it is unlikely that many different sovereigns can make up for a single and coherent one. Thus, the sovereign which commands European officials to act as delegates would be a heterogeneous one, exposed to a high risk of contradiction. The Austinian picture seems therefore inadequate to MacCormick.

24 See also Neil MacCormick, 'Sovereignty: Myth and Reality' (1995) 11 (First Series) Scottish Affairs 1; MacCormick, 'On Sovereignty and Post-Sovereignty' (n 18).

25 MacCormick, 'Beyond the Sovereign State' (n 6) 8.

26 Some of these critiques are recalled in Barber (n 14) 46.

27 MacCormick, 'Beyond the Sovereign State' (n 6) 2–5.

28 ibid 4. Here MacCormick refers to the *Costa v Enel* judgment, but last chapter's analysis of Opinion 2/13 should illustrate even better how cases affirming EU law's autonomy look like.

An alternative is proposed: we can try with a different picture, namely 'a Hartian model, with its conception of legal systems as unions of primary and secondary rules'.[29] Notoriously, in Hart's view at the apex of every legal system there is a 'rule of recognition'.[30] MacCormick defines the rule of recognition as the procedural and substantive criteria for the validity of law, plus their hierarchical order, and the binding character of valid law. The rule of recognition is the result of the complex activity of legal officials, of their beliefs and self-understanding. As such, it can change along with the practice. This allows MacCormick to make two points. First, the deepest beliefs regarding how to judge of a rule's validity change throughout the time when officials change their minds. Second, an observer is not committed to endorse them. This notion will be later expressed through the wording 'sociological realism'.[31]

In analysing the rule of recognition of the interlaced legal order of the early Nineties, MacCormick therefore looks at the perspective of officials, both national and supranational. If we consider the practice of national officials, exemplified by the British example, we can see a sharp fracture before and after the *European Communities Act* (1972). Before the entry in force of the *Act*, we envisaged three criteria of validity: rules deriving from unrepealed parliamentary acts, delegated and unrepealed parliamentary delegation, and precedents of superior UK courts.[32] We can maybe add customs and unwritten general principles of the law, but this roughly exhausts the rule of recognition of pre-1972 United Kingdom. After the accession to the EC, we add a new criterion of validity: EC law under the *European Community Act* approved by the Parliament is valid law and prevails over every other norm, 'unless Parliament explicitly derogates form this priority ranking of Community Law'.[33] MacCormick wrote before the Brexit process and, if *Beyond the Sovereign State* was drafted today, this sketch of the rule of recognition in the UK would be quite different,[34] but his point seems clear: among the criteria used by officials to assess a norm's validity, we also find reference to Community (now EU) law. If we now move to the criteria employed by European officials, we find a different scenario. Primary law, as contained in the Treaties and in sources of equal rank, enjoys primacy as valid law. At the same level, we find standards deriving from 'other treaties', such as the European Convention on Human Rights (ECHR). Then we find secondary law. Last, we have criteria 'subject to some debate', such as the case law of the Court of Justice or the common constitutional traditions of Member States.[35]

29 ibid 5.

30 Herbert LA Hart, *The Concept of Law* (Oxford University Press 2012) 94–95 and 105–117.

31 MacCormick introduces this wording only in his work on the *Maastricht Urteil*. See MacCormick, 'The Maastricht-Urteil' (n 7) 264. However, his commitment to this idea seems established already in *Beyond the Sovereign State*.

32 This listing of criteria of recognition is quite close to the previous characterization of the rule of recognition in MacCormick, *Legal Reasoning and Legal Theory* (n 3) 242–244.

33 MacCormick, 'Beyond the Sovereign State' (n 6) 6–7.

34 The European Communities Act 1972 (UK) was repealed by the European Union (Withdrawal) Act 2018.

35 MacCormick, 'Beyond the Sovereign State' (n 6) 7.

MacCormick notices that these criteria partly overlap. By adding EU norms to the domestic criteria of recognition, British officials adopted a rule of recognition partly coinciding with that adopted by EU officials. If we then asked to both groups of officials why these are the criteria of recognition, the former would likely say that it is the will of the Parliament or of the Queen in Parliament that gives them the status of validity criteria, while the latter would say the same about the Treaties as autonomous sources. Here is where they may diverge as none recognizes the other's rule of recognition as hierarchically superior, as a validating norm. The self-referential validation of EU law's autonomy in cases like *Costa* 'suggests the conclusion that, as an external fact of social reality, there already exist two self-standing constitutional orders'.[36]

This analysis in Hartian terms entails two conclusions, in MacCormick's view.

The first is that, as a matter of fact, the partial convergence de facto allows the functioning of the system. The potential and inevitable instability of constitutional pluralism is clearly a phenomenon that he considers possible. Some tools to avoid conflicts are consequently recalled: the preliminary ruling mechanism, the principles shared among different European systems, the interpretation of human rights embodied by the Court of Strasbourg's case law, the principle of proportionality as developed by the Court of Justice. Yet, these remedies remain theoretical in his view, mere hypothesis on which practices could bring stability within pluralistic uncertainty.[37] Although conflict is possible, it is not necessary: empirically we see that in most cases the two orders coexist and are largely merged: national officials apply supranational law every day. In MacCormick's view, it is the 'high degree of relatively willing cooperation and a relatively low degree of coercion' that more than anything else ensures stability within constitutional pluralism.[38]

Second, and most importantly, methodologically we must not presuppose the existence of a sovereign issuing commands or wonder whether the complex European legal order conforms to some abstract model necessarily looking for a Kelsenian *grundnorm*. Instead, we should look at the beliefs of officials, at their statements and views concerning what grounds the norms they apply, at how they change and overlap throughout the time.

> [Escaping] the idea that all law must originate in a single power source, like a sovereign, is thus to discover the possibility of taking a broader, more diffuse, view of law. ... different systems can overlap and interact, without necessarily requiring that one be subordinate or hierarchically inferior to the other or to some third system.[39]

36 Jaklic (n 1) 19. MacCormick analyses the British participation to the EC again in similar terms later, see Neil MacCormick, *Questioning Sovereignty* (Oxford University Press 1999) 87–91. See also the commentary by Oliver (n 22) 171–173.

37 MacCormick, 'Beyond the Sovereign State' (n 6) 8, 18.

38 ibid 17.

39 ibid 8.

Briefly, the bulk of radical pluralism is fully contained in *Beyond the Sovereign State*: the conclusion that no EU State is 'sovereign' anymore; the rejection of any monistic abstract model necessarily looking for a *grundnorm* at the level of States or of the Union; an allegedly realistic analysis of the officials' beliefs, pointing at their concrete convergence and divergence in criteria of recognition; a description of the riddle of constitutional pluralism precisely starting with this realistic analysis; finally, acceptance of the possibility of conflicts, coupled with the empirical consideration that de facto convergence and cooperation make them remote.

While most of MacCormick's radical pluralism is contained in *Beyond the Sovereign State*, a few other notes are added two years later, in the already mentioned comment of the *Maastricht Urteil* for the 'European Law Journal'.[40]

Apart from commenting on the *Urteil*, as we have seen in the last chapter, the essay broadly confirms many of the points previously made: the idea that neither States, nor the EC can convincingly claim to validate each other, a rejection of a Kelsenian picture of hierarchical relations, and the Hartian approach to the rule of recognition and to sovereignty.[41] Yet, there is also room for some refinement. Now MacCormick explicitly claims the commitment of his theory to 'a degree of sociological realism' and elaborates a little further on his notion of interaction, claiming that in the 'interactive' European context States and the EC enjoy not an 'all-purpose' superiority, but only one limited to their sphere of competence. In the Hartian vocabulary, this means that the rule of recognition of national and European officials incorporates a criterion that ranks national law under EC law only where the EC is assigned law-making competence and that reverses supremacy in all other cases. Consequently, on that area the 'interpretive competence-competence' will belong respectively to the European Court of Justice or to national ones.[42]

Moreover, and crucially, we find an explicit statement of a truly 'radical' pluralism: the possibility of conflict is always at stake, for in same cases institutions could disagree irremediably. When this happens, there is no legal answer and the solution (or prevention) of conflict is a matter of political sensibility: 'acceptance of a pluralistic conception of legal systems entails acknowledging that not all legal problems can be solved legally'. Conflict is not 'logically embarrassing', but theory can provide no guidance.[43] In the previous essay, MacCormick had only claimed that it would take a 'high degree of willing cooperation' to ensure stability within constitutional pluralism, while here he explicitly talks about 'political sensitivity' as the instrument of conflict management. This is perhaps the most radical statement of his analysis: here we find the moment in which MacCormick is probably furthest from the normative version of constitutional pluralism which dominated the movement in later years: officials in Europe hold partly overlapping, partly

40 MacCormick, 'The Maastricht-Urteil' (n 7).
41 ibid 263–264.
42 ibid 264.
43 ibid 265.

diverging rules of recognition, and conflicts are solved not through legal reasoning, but rather through political bargain.

3.2.2 Pluralism under International Law: 1998–1999

Two years later, we find a new contribution on European pluralism. In *Democracy, Subsidiarity, and Citizenship in the European Commonwealth* MacCormick takes again a 'radical' position, but the very first hints of future development start being visible. He draws the lines of a possible Kelsenian explanation of European pluralism in which instead of claiming that EC law grounds national law or *vice versa*, both EC and national law are conceived as based on international law.[44] This view is known today as 'pluralism under international law' and instantiates the last phase of MacCormick's reflection on pluralism. In *Democracy, Subsidiarity, and Citizenship*, the simultaneous validation of both national and EU law by international law is still theoretical speculation: MacCormick is faithful to the 'sociological realism' of his theory and, in the light of the practice of national and European institution, dismisses this perspective as implausible. Yet, this perspective will be much more appreciated soon: the stage for the normative turn is set.

In 1998 he publishes, as a review of Phenal's *Revolt or Revolution: On Constitutional Boundaries of the European Community*, an essay whose title is revealing of the new focus: *Risking Constitutional Collision in Europe?*[45] Several previously developed views are recalled again: the emphasis on 'governmental roles', that is, on officials and their practices, the change in national rules of recognition 'to include validity-in-EC-law as a criterion of validity domestically', the already described understanding of sovereignty and State.[46] Moreover, some further thought is added to this picture. For instance, MacCormick claims that at the basis of a legal order's obedience lie reasons of several kind, from fear backed by threat of force to genuine adherence. In modern democratic States, constitutionalism plays a key role in generating legitimacy by dividing powers and safeguarding rights.[47]

The crucial point, anyway, lies in the new assessment of what grounds the intertwined orders in Europe. Once again, MacCormick rejects the view that EC law validates national law or *vice versa*.Yet, when it comes to providing an alternative view, the chosen path diverges significantly from his previous essays. Here we find a clear distinction between 'radical pluralism' and 'pluralism under international law'. Both are forms of 'pluralism', since they affirm the autonomy of EC law and national law, rejecting a hierarchical structure and endorsing a heterarchical view. Yet, they diverge as for what validates both EC and national law.

From the perspective of radical pluralism, each order is simply autonomous, there is no point in looking for further legal grounding and we can only ascertain

44 MacCormick, 'Democracy, Subsidiarity, and Citizenship in the "European Commonwealth"' (n 10) 336.

45 MacCormick, 'Risking Constitutional Collision in Europe?' (n 8).

46 ibid 524–528.

47 ibid 525.

that this is the ultimate level of justification. We have reached the point where, to quote out of context a famous philosophical motto, 'if I have exhausted the justifications, I have reached bedrock and my spade is turned. Then I am inclined to say: "This is simply what I do"'.[48]

On the other hand, according to pluralism under international law, there is a common ground for both: MacCormick builds on the Kelsenian idea that a global *grundnorm* commands to observe international customary law as valid law. As we will see in more detail later in this chapter, Kelsen claimed that the law must be understood as a unity based on a single validating norm, a *grundnorm* that may be placed either at the national or at the international level.[49] EC and national law can therefore be traced back to an independent validation directly in international law. This is quite different from claiming, as MacCormick did in shaping a mere theoretical possibility in *Sovereignty Now*, that domestic law is a sub-system of EC law which, in turn, is validated by international law:[50] both EC and domestic law find their grounding directly in international law. The argument is close to the one deployed the previous year in *Democracy, Subsidiarity, and Citizenship in the European Commonwealth*, but the fundamental contribution to the debate lies in the explicit *endorsement* of pluralism under international law. Recommending one account or another has considerable practical consequences: under radical pluralism in case of conflict there are no legal solutions, for some problems are only political; pluralism under international law, on the other hand, allows for remedies in the form of international obligations. Conflicts, thus, do not occur in a legal vacuum, but can find legal solutions, for instance in international arbitration.[51]

One year later, in *Juridical Pluralism and the Risk of Constitutional Conflict*, MacCormick publishes is legacy on pluralism. A large part of the essay is a *summa* of the basic concepts of constitutional pluralism: constitution and constitutionalism, legal system and legal order, the concept of 'sovereign State' and the reasons for its success, the rule of recognition and legal validity. However, what really characterizes the work is again the resolute attempt to tame the risk of conflict. In the context of pluralism, now specifically defined as 'the idea that there can coexist distinct but genuinely normative legal orders', we know that 'two such distinct legal orders can generate different answers to the same question'.[52] Again, there is recognition of the fact that conflict cannot be avoided by merging different legal orders into one: social facts, to whom MacCormick's sociological realism is sensible, prevent the possibility to conceive the European and the national level as united. Again, MacCormick holds that there only are two 'reasonably arguable analyses' of the European intertwined context, namely radical pluralism and pluralism under international law. Definition and understanding of both perspectives are the same as in

48 Ludwig Wittgenstein, *Philosophical Investigations* (Blackwell 1988), para. 217.

49 Hans Kelsen, *General Theory of Law and State* (Transaction Publishers 2005) 214–217 and 369–370; Hans Kelsen, *Pure Theory of Law* (The Lawbook Exchange 2003) 323–324.

50 MacCormick, 'The Maastricht-Urteil' (n 7) 6.

51 MacCormick, 'Juridical Pluralism and the Risk of Constitutional Conflict' (n 9) 527–531.

52 ibid 102.

Risking Constitutional Collision in Europe?. Yet, we can slightly deepen the picture by relying on MacCormick's definition of 'legal validity' as the result of 'valid exercise of legislative power'.[53] Pluralism under international law claims that both EC and national law are 'validated' by international law in the sense that their norms are enacted according to norms on law-making that belong to international law. Thus, the latter prescribes the rules for correct exercise of normative powers within EC law or national law. The consequences, as we know, of choosing one account over another lie in the different account of conflicts that they provide. Pluralism under international law is now MacCormick's favourite option because it is not a normatively inert position: it provides guidance.

How exactly does it handle potential conflicts? According to MacCormick, there are two possible paths to consider. First, both the Community and the States are subject to international obligations, to respect in good faith, and this prevents unilateral actions in breach of legal obligations. Second, if it is not possible to avoid conflicts appealing to respect for international obligations, adjudication or arbitration to which both States and the EC must abide by under international law can be resorted to in order to solve controversies.[54]

As a result, there is quite a significant shift in MacCormick's argument from the merely descriptive approach held between 1993 and 1995 to the normative one adopted in 1998 and 1999. The position expressed in *Democracy, Subsidiarity, and Citizenship in the European Commonwealth* lies in between, as the moment in which the normative turn was conceived, but not endorsed yet.

The reasons for this turn may lie in the different political scenario of the later 1990s. By that time, not only the Treaty of Maastricht was ratified and consolidated, but also the British process of devolution was progressing.[55] For a Europhile and Scottish nationalist, the need of attacking the classic picture of undivided sovereignty was at this point less pressing, while worries about possible constitutional conflicts grew.[56] Radical pluralism derived directly from MacCormick's adherence to Hart's understanding of legality as determined by the practice of officials.[57] Yet, this normatively inert registration of the factual unfolding of the practice left the possibility that the practice of officials could diverge too open. Such perspective becomes unacceptable to MacCormick in the late 1990s.

Besides political considerations, from the strictly intellectual point of view, radical pluralism seems problematic to MacCormick in his late writings on pluralism for two reasons.

53 ibid 115.

54 ibid 121.

55 Leyland (n 12) 246–273.

56 See Krisch (n 13) 390–397. See also Agustín José Menéndez, 'From Constitutional Pluralism to a Pluralistic Constitution? Constitutional Synthesis as a MacCormickian Constitutional Theory of European Integration' in Agustín José Menéndez and John Erik Fossum (eds), *Law and Democracy in Neil MacCormick's Legal and Political Theory* (Springer 2011) 227–228, and Matej Avbelj, 'Questioning EU Constitutionalisms' (2008) 9 German Law Journal 1, 14 footnote 61.

57 Krisch (n 13) 391.

First, the possibility of conflict engendered what has been called the 'rule of law critique': lack of agreement among institutions, especially courts, on legal norms, generates uncertainty regarding rights and duties on citizens.[58] Yet, this problem seems to be a minor one. Indeed, we know that full predictability and certainty are not fully ensured within States too, so that this defect does not seem to depend particularly on the pluralist nature of the European law.[59]

The second problem is far more important in the overall balance of MacCormick's ideas: the risk of radical disagreement and possibly explicit conflict between competing orders (inter-systematic fragmentation). Let aside consequences on individuals, the point here is that there may be cases in which disagreement emerges on the very fundamental norms of the system, the 'constitution' in MacCormick's sense.[60] There is a general unease with the idea that on the fundamental norms sharp disagreement might emerge without any *legal* device as a possible solution to conflict. Here MacCormick inaugurates a tendency to distrust politics and always look for a legal solution to inter-systematic conflicts that was never abandoned by constitutional pluralists.[61]

This ends our analysis of MacCormick's constitutional pluralism, developed over a period of six years, rich of intuitions, and significantly diverse from one phase to the other. The rest of this chapter is devoted to assessing the two phases separately. I will reverse the chronological order and start form the latter, pluralism under international law, to then consider radical pluralism. Critically examining MacCormick's version of radical pluralism, collecting the takeaways and discarding the imperfections, is an inevitable step in a book devoted to renewing radical pluralism. Yet also an examination of the pluralism under international law is a worthy enterprise as it shows the kind of problems a theory may run into when the purported aims, descriptive or normative, are not clearly identified and distinguished. Such is a problem to which scholars working on constitutional pluralism are particularly exposed and may therefore benefit from reading a critique of.

3.3 Pluralism under International Law: A Critique

This section scrutinizes pluralism under international law, MacCormick's latest take on pluralism, and shows why it offers a problematic perspective. However, to do so, a digression is needed. Indeed, I argue that the reason why pluralism under

58 ibid 394–395.

59 As Krisch himself points out, contemporary theories on the rule of law tend to recognize that the value of predictability within the rule of law is not absolute and must sometimes be balanced against other substantive values. See ibid 394. Also Gianluigi Palombella, 'The Rule of Law beyond the State: Failures, Promises, and Theory' (2009) 7 International Journal of Constitutional Law 442, 449–458; Jeremy Waldron, 'The Rule of Law and the Importance of Procedure' in James Fleming (ed), *Getting to the Rule of Law* (New York University Press 2011) 18–23.

60 MacCormick, 'Juridical Pluralism and the Risk of Constitutional Conflict' (n 9) 102–103. See also MacCormick, *Institutions of Law* (n 4) 45–49.

61 Krisch (n 13) 406–407.

international law is ultimately flawed lies in its attempt to simultaneously maintain the Hartian theory of law that MacCormick used to make the case for radical pluralism and at the same time endorse a Kelsenian view on the relations between the legal orders. These perspectives are irreconcilable and failing to choose one inevitably generates contradictions. However, to properly unfold this critique of pluralism under international law, it is first necessary to expose the mainlines of the Hart-Kelsen debate on international law (3.3.1). After exposing this debate, I return to MacCormick's writings on pluralism between 1998 and 1999 and show the inconsistencies ignited by this tentatively twofold perspective (3.3.2).

3.3.1 The Hart–Kelsen Debate on International Law

The debate between Kelsen and Hart concerning international law, its status, and its links to domestic law, is mainly instantiated by Kelsen's extensive discourse on the matter in several works[62] and by Hart's objections in *The Concept of Law*[63] and in the essay *Kelsen's Doctrine of the Unity of Law*.[64] This confrontation between two of the most important positivists of the 20th century is a unique opportunity to compare their understandings of law. In fact, the debate is a complex one, touching fascinating areas such as the concept of legal system and its evolution, the stage of development of international law, and the logic of norms. However, here it is not necessary or possible to reconstruct the debate entirely. It will suffice to recall how it concerns the relations between State and international law so to understand how they affected MacCormick's pluralism.[65]

Let us start considering Kelsen's claims on international law, focusing on three points: the possibility to conceive international law and national law as a unity, his conception of conflicts between the two levels, and the effects of the alleged unity on positive law.

According to Kelsen, international and domestic law must be considered as belonging to a single system of norms. Here a crucial role is played by Kelsen's epistemological postulate of unity: the science of law, as every other science, tries to describe its object as unitary, as a comprehensive system of propositions describing every legal norm through statements (descriptive ought-statements) that must be consistent with one another. All the described norms will belong to the common epistemic category, an internally coherent discourse which pictures 'the law'. This

62 See at least Kelsen, *General Theory of Law and State* (n 49) 328–388; Kelsen, *Pure Theory of Law* (n 49) 320–348. See also, Hans Kelsen, 'Sovereignty' in Stanley Paulson (ed), *Normativity and Norms: Critical Perspectives on Kelsenian Themes* (Oxford University Press 1999).

63 Hart, *The Concept of Law* (n 30) 232–237.

64 Now reprinted in Herbert LA Hart, *Essays in Jurisprudence and Philosophy* (Oxford University Press 1983) 309–342.

65 On the debate see Michael Giudice, 'Hart and Kelsen on International Law' in Leslie Green and Brian Leiter (eds), *Oxford Studies in Philosophy of Law: Volume 2* (Oxford University Press 2013); Nicola Lacey, *A Life of H.L.A. Hart: The Nightmare and the Noble Dream* (Oxford University Press 2006) 249–253.

requirement of internal consistency, the principle of non-contradiction, is defined by Kelsen the 'negative criterion' of unity.[66]

Given this understanding, we can only conceive international and national law as a single system of valid norms. Yet, Kelsen is not claiming that there already is a single global State or any other kind of centralized global organization. He is perfectly aware that there is no such thing. Nor is he saying that international and domestic law are identical: in his view, there certainly is a difference between State law and international law. In particular, the degree of centralization of coercion as a response to violation of legal norms allows us to identify the structural differences of the two. It is centralized within States, as only public authorities on behalf of citizens exercise it; it is decentralized in international law, where States, subjects of international obligations, exercise it directly, through war and reprisal.

Thus, Kelsen is not claiming that a global State governs our lives nor that the two kinds of law are identical. He is simply pointing out that a theoretical unity of all law is possible: we can take the entire legal materials and interpret them as belonging to a single system. More, we *must* interpret them this way for the sake of the epistemological postulate of unity.[67] If we could claim that a norm is legal from the point of view of the State or from the point of view of international law, then there would be several points of view on the law. Thus, the epistemological postulate of unity would be violated, and no science of law would be possible.

As a result, international and domestic law must belong to a single and internally consistent system of norms. Let us consider these two points, the unity of law and its internal consistency, separately.

How can we describe international law and national law as a single system of norms? According to Kelsen, there are two equally possible constructions, both 'monist' but different as they recognize primacy to either international or national law. For Kelsen, two systems of norms are united in one if the reason of their validity ultimately lies in the same basic norm.[68] An ordinance enacted by a local authority and a statute passed by the parliament both belong to the same system if they are both ultimately validated by the same *grundnorm*. They share the same reason of validity. Similarly, international law and State law can be part of the same system if they share the same basic norm.

If we start by assuming the primacy of international law, the *grundnorm* will necessarily validate international customary law as valid law. Thus, it will validate the principle of effectivity, namely the idea that as long as a State is effective on a certain population and territory, it will be a validly delegated sub-system of

66 See Kelsen, *Pure Theory of Law* (n 49) 328–329. It is worth remembering that in his late works Kelsen rejected the idea of absence of contradictions as a necessary feature of legal systems. On the other hand, he accepted the possibility of antinomies. See Hans Kelsen, *General Theory of Norms* (Oxford University Press 1991) 123–127 and 211–225.

67 See Kelsen, 'Sovereignty' (n 62) 526–527, for the idea that the unity of law is the implication of an epistemic necessity.

68 Kelsen, *General Theory of Law and State* (n 49) 110–115.

international law. Once validated, States are free to specify international law by organizing within the very wide (one could maybe claim, almost unlimited) discretion left by the overarching international level through delegation. State law, in other words, completes and specifies international law.

If, on the other hand, we start from the primacy of State law, then international law will be valid only as recognized and delegated by State law through explicit or implicit acts. It will be a sub-system of State law and, ultimately, the reason of validity of its norms will lie in the norm that commands to obey the first historical constitution of the State. Since it delegates the international level as a sub-system of its legal construction, the grounding domestic system will also be the ultimate reason of validity of every other State. This happens because international law, a sub-system of the grounding domestic system, through the principle of effectivity validates the law of other States, so that then they are sub-systems of the former system too.

As for the second issue, that of the internal consistency of the overarching system of legal norms, Kelsen faces the most intuitive objection to his theory, namely that we experience several times conflicts between norms of international law and norms enacted by States. How can we claim that there is no conflict, but internal consistency? Here the idea is that we can construct the norms so that conflicts are only apparent. Kelsen builds on an analogous situation quite common in domestic law: a norm conflicting with the constitution, in absence of mechanisms of review, would still be considered as valid law. If no constitutional review and consequent voiding is available, it is still possible to regard the non-compliance with the provisions of the constitutional norm as a reason for the lower norm to be abolished in the future (while not being 'expelled' immediately) or for the responsible organ to be sanctioned.[69] Kelsen transposes this reasoning to the international level. The case of (apparent) conflict between a domestic norm and international law would only entail that an international norm was violated and that, consequently, a sanction could be applied to the responsible State. The object of the domestic norm is the behaviour of national citizens or officials, guaranteed by internal sanction. If a norm of this kind is applied, the State may be considered as violating its international obligation. On the other hand, international norms regulate the sanction to be inflicted on the State or on domestic officials, for instance by means of reprisal, in case the State does not abide by its obligations. In other words, the two norms have different objects, therefore logically they cannot conflict, but the fact that State's organs did not abide by their international obligations because of domestic norms justifies the application of

69 ibid 153–162. Of course, we know of perfectly functioning legal systems which indeed work with limited mechanisms of constitutional review of legislation. For instance, consider the case of the Commonwealth model of constitutionalism. Stephen Gardbaum, 'The New Commonwealth Model of Constitutionalism' (2001) 49 The American Journal of Comparative Law 707; Stephen Gardbaum, *The New Commonwealth Model of Constitutionalism* (Cambridge University Press 2013).

international sanctions. As a result, as in the case of domestic voidable norms, their conflict is only apparent.[70]

How can we choose between the two possible constructions? Ultimately, this turns out to be simply a matter of choice. The two constructions build upon the same legal materials; the dispute cannot be settled by considering one of the two as more accurate. By giving primacy to international law as the foundational level, we express our adherence to a 'pacifist' view of the world, committed to a growing centralization of law beyond States. Similarly, by looking at State law as the foundational level, we articulate a preference for an 'imperialist' view of the world, in which the State we accord our predilection to enjoys absolute freedom in preserving its own interests. However, this adherence to one construction or to another according to ideological preferences has no impact on positive law: choosing one construction over the other has no influence on the content of international or of national law.[71] International law *qua* part of the national legal order has the same content as international law *qua* superior to the national legal orders and vice versa. For instance, primacy of domestic law does not entail that a State can never be subject to the jurisdiction of an international court. Similarly, from the primacy of international law does not follow that domestic legislation is automatically void, but only that sanction against the non-compliant State is possible.[72] The task of the pure theory of law is to unveil these apparently cogent arguments and show their ideological nature.[73]

Briefly, Kelsen points out that for epistemological reasons we need to conceive the whole law as a single legal system including both domestic and international law, that this system cannot be affected by inconsistencies, and that it can be alternatively constructed starting from State law or from international law. This merely turns out to be a matter of ethical-political choice. Finally, opting for one construction or another has no direct impact whatsoever on the State of positive law.

Having considered the main lines of Kelsen's argument, let us now move to Hart's critique, which is quite radical. It is possible to distinguish three main critiques in Hart's dense pages.[74]

First, Hart rejects Kelsen's view that there are methodological and epistemological reasons requiring the unity of law. The descriptive ought-statements that Kelsen takes as representation of norms have truth-values and, if the system they constitute must be consistent, they cannot conflict with each other, precisely as every other system of statements that is the discourse of a scientific enterprise. Yet, according to Hart we can simply point out that ought-statements' truth-value are system-dependent. From an external point of view, one could account for inconsistent descriptive ought-statements without committing fallacies by simply

70 Kelsen, *General Theory of Law and State* (n 49) 371–372.
71 Kelsen, *Pure Theory of Law* (n 49) 342.
72 ibid 339–344.
73 Kelsen, *General Theory of Law and State* (n 49) 387–388.
74 Here I mostly follow Giudice (n 65) 156–164.

claiming that if they derive from different systems, the descriptive ought-statements can have different truth-values.[75] For instance, the death penalty may be banned under Austrian law and permitted under Texan law: these are system-dependent statements describing an ought, the norm on death penalty accepted under Austrian and Texan criminal law. Austrian or Texan law are actual legal orders and not abstract epistemic categories. There is no *a priori* reason to exclude the possibility that, in describing the law under the two systems, we find conflicts and provide a 'scientific' account of them. The fact that we understand the norms under the same epistemic category of 'legal norm' does not entail the impossibility of conflict.[76]

Second, in chapter XI of the *Concept of Law* Hart points out that the international legal order is a form of primitive law and, consequently, it does not have secondary norms, such as a validating *grundnorm*.[77] Thus, in his view there is no reason to suppose, as Kelsen does, that there *must* be a basic norm in international law. Kelsen's view that we may foresee a *grundnorm* of the kind 'States should behave as they have customarily behaved' is mistaken for this formulation is empty, it cannot be employed to assess another norm's validity. For Hart, the statement 'States should behave as they have customarily behaved' is nothing but a restatement of the *fact* that States accept some customs as rules. It does not establish criteria that work as a test for recognition or, in Kelsen's language, as a reason of validity for international law. This artificial construction only derives from our difficulty in accepting that the international order is a primitive one and has no ultimate rule unifying it. In other words, the mere sense of normativity of customary behaviour cannot work as a rule of recognition, for it is empty in content and provides no guidance at all in distinguishing legal from illegal behaviour.[78]

Finally, Hart claims that Kelsen misrepresents the state of affairs of law when asserting that between international law and domestic law, we have relations of validation. According to Hart, simply stating that international law purports to validate domestic law through the principle of effectivity or any other criterion does not mean that de facto this criterion is accepted as the reason of validity of domestic law. To prove the validation link, mere correspondence between the content of international validating rules and domestic behaviour would be a necessary, but

75 Here the typically Hartian distinction between the internal point of view of participants in the legal practice and the external perspective of the observer who understands the attitudes of insiders is crucial. See Hart, *The Concept of Law* (n 30) 102–105. See also Dennis Patterson, 'Explicating the Internal Point of View' (1999) 52 Southern Methodist University Law Review 67; Scott Shapiro, 'What Is the Internal Point of View?' (2006) 75 Fordham Law Review 1157.

76 Hart, *Essays in Jurisprudence and Philosophy* (n 64) 331–332.

77 Hart, *The Concept of Law* (n 30) 232–237.

78 Here I disagree with Giudice (n 65) 159–160. He claims that one can reformulate the criterion 'states should behave as they have customarily behaved' as a Hartian conventional rule of recognition. Hart would perhaps claim that we should accurately describe what test of recognition a community ultimately chooses, but that not everything can work as a test of recognition. Purely referring to the content of the rules perceived as binding does not provide a test to *recognize* them as legal or not. Similarly, we can claim that rules of etiquette bind us, but the mere fact that we observe them does not constitute a viable test to separate them from other social rules.

not a sufficient condition. Of course, the same would be true for the validation of international law by domestic law. To reinforce this claim, Hart points out as an example that if the British Parliament issues an act validating the precise content of Soviet law, *this* will not necessarily be the reason of validity for Soviet law used by Soviet officials: they will recognize the very same norms by relying on other criteria, the Soviet Constitution most likely. The English act would validate Soviet law only if Soviet officials used it as a criterion of validity. Briefly, a relation of validating purport is a necessary, not a sufficient condition for actual validation: norms of international law must not only purport to validate State law but must be used by officials to validate the legal materials they operate. Consequently, that international law purports to validate domestic law by means of the principle of effectiveness is not enough to prove that this validation is in fact at stake.[79]

Having briefly recapitulated the main points, how to appraise the debate? Although it is my opinion that each of Hart's criticisms makes an important point, it is hard to deny, as benevolent as one can be towards Kelsen's views, that at least the last objection is fundamentally correct.[80] Even authors as Lars Vinx, inclined to take a Kelsenian stance, recognize this point.[81] Hart had a point when he underlined the descriptive inaccuracy of Kelsen's view on the relations between domestic and international law. We had and still have reasons to believe that de facto officials see themselves as belonging to separate and distinct legal orders, no matter what external norms purport to validate.

On the other hand, there is something we can learn from Kelsen's position too. As Giudice underlines,[82] Kelsen was trying to provide a hypothetical construction able to connect international and domestic law in a harmonious unity. This position can be interesting even though quite likely it is not an accurate description of current relations between international and domestic law. Kelsen's position is useful if we take the perspective of the participant, eager to figure out how to reconcile separate legal orders for reasons that are, at least in part, ethical. This disagreement on what perspective we shall take (that of the external observer or of the participant) is what motivates contemporary defenders of Kelsen's approach[83] and maybe

79 Hart, *Essays in Jurisprudence and Philosophy* (n 64) 312–313 and 317–321.

80 See again Giudice (n 65) 163–164.

81 Lars Vinx, 'The Kelsen-Hart Debate: Hart's Critique of Kelsen's Legal Monism Reconsidered' in Jeremy Telman (ed), *Hans Kelsen in America – Selective Affinities and the Mysteries of Academic Influence* (Springer International Publishing 2016) 73–74. Vinx claims that a form of weak monism remains plausible insofar as it is not empirically proven that judges do not look at international law for validation of national law. However, at least in the context of European pluralism, cases like *Maastricht* or Opinion 2/13 examined in the last chapter and stating the autonomy of EU law, seem to me abundant proof that they do not.

82 Giudice (n 65) 161.

83 See, tellingly, David Dyzenhaus, 'The Janus-Faced Constitution' in David Dyzenhaus, Jacco Bomhoff and Thomas Poole (eds), *The Double-Facing Constitution* (Cambridge University Press 2020) 45–46 footnote 83: 'In general, Hart seems to assume that because we can, say, assert without contradiction that the law of country X requires A and the law of country Y requires -A, we can thereby identify a contradiction between two valid systems of norms. But, as I have argued, we need to ask that

also explains why an author like Dworkin has tried to defend Kelsen's views against Hart's critique.[84]

Be it as it may, what is important for us here is to realize the differences between the two perspectives. Kelsen's understanding influences MacCormick's later essays on pluralism, while Hart's perspective is fundamental to MacCormick's early writings. Yet, they are irreconcilable. Hart did not accept Kelsen's argument for the unity of law and remained faithful to an ultimately 'sociological' approach to the relations between domestic and international law. Kelsen, on the other hand, struggled to show the possibility of the theoretical unity of law and provided reasons that are both epistemological and ethical. Once this difference is clarified, we can assess how the shift from the former to the latter theory affects MacCormick's later account of pluralism.

3.3.2 The Paradox of Pluralism under International law

There are two fundamental objections against MacCormick's turn in his 1998–1999 essays on constitutional pluralism. The first one regards the internal consistency of MacCormick's argument, while the latter concerns the efficacy of his strategy in reaching his fundamental goal, namely avoiding constitutional conflicts.

As for the first, even in pluralism under international law, MacCormick kept his commitment to the observation of social facts, when he advocated for a 'degree of sociological realism' as his key methodological tenet. This argument is at work even in his last essay, where the normative turn is complete.[85] MacCormick claims that international law works as a common ground of validity for both EC/EU law and Member States' law:[86]

> If system X enjoys supremacy over system Y, why trouble to have a theory about separate systems, rather than a theory which acknowledges the fact that Y belongs to X as a sub-system of it? … For contemporary Europe, this could hold good only with the added complexity that the Community legal order alone is a subsystem of international law, validated by the international law norm pacta sunt servanda, while the state systems, validated by Community law, would constitute sub-sub-systems. Other readings could suggest, for example, that international law continues to be the ground of validity of Member State law, while these systems jointly validate community law, which is then the sub-sub-system. *Perhaps most credibly of all*, it might be held that

question not from the perspective of an external observer, but from the perspective of a judge faced with a dispute in private international law, who must decide which system's norms are valid for the purpose of determining the result'.

84 Ronald Dworkin, 'Comments on the Unity of Law Doctrine (a Response)' in Howard Evans Kiefer and Milton Karl Munitz (eds), *Ethics and Social Justice* (State University of New York Press 1968) 201–205. See also Dyzenhaus (n 83) 40–42.

85 MacCormick, 'Juridical Pluralism and the Risk of Constitutional Conflict' (n 9) 117–119.

86 ibid 116–117.

> in a coordinate way, international law functions as a common ground of validity both of member-State systems and of Community law, neither being therefore a sub-system of the other, but both cohering within a common legal universe governed by the norms of international law. Since this position involves pluralistic relationships between the law of the Community and the member-states (and among the States inter se), albeit within a 'monistic' framework of international law, I shall in subsequent discussion refer to this position as that of 'pluralism under international law'. (Italics added)

Thus, in pluralism under international law, the overarching international order validates both EC and domestic law.[87] This is not surprising, for MacCormick claims that pluralism under international law is 'an instance of monism in Kelsen's sense'[88] and a Kelsenian theory can only conceive of validity relations between international and domestic law.[89]

What is interesting, however, is the wording 'most credibly of all', somehow suggesting that pluralism under international law is the most likely explanation of the current relations between EC and domestic law.[90] Yet, if he is still committed to 'sociological realism', as he seems to be, even more when he dismisses once again the claim that national law can be considered as a subset of EC law, then he must remain committed to it also when it comes to the relations between international law and its alleged sub-systems, EC and domestic law. In other words, if he dismisses the claim that there is a single European system based on the actual beliefs and practice of officials, then he must use the same method to argue that EC and domestic law are both validated by international law or provide a reason for not doing so.

However, he does not: there are no empirical observations to ground this claim. Quite the opposite, the idea that international law validates EC and domestic raises a few eyebrows: cases as *Van Gend en Loos*, *Costa*, or Opinion 1/91, which assert EC law's autonomy, were perfectly known at that time, but are not discussed. Today, in the light of further developments, there is little doubt that at least European officials see their legal order as independent from both domestic and international law.[91] However, even an advocate of pluralism under international law in the 1990s

87 See also the following paragraphs again in ibid 118: 'According to pluralism under international law, the obligations of international law set conditions upon the validity of state and of Community constitutions and interpretations thereof, and hence impose a framework on the interactive but not hierarchical relations between systems'. Later ibid 119: 'Hence the validity and partial mutual independence of EC law and member-state law is authorized by (public) international law'.

88 MacCormick, 'Juridical Pluralism and the Risk of Constitutional Conflict' (n 9) 119 and 121.

89 Kelsen, *Pure Theory of Law* (n 47) 332–333. Two dynamic normative systems can be either coordinated, as both validated by a superior normative system, or subordinated, so that one validates the other.

90 Moreover, he used the same wording ('most credibly of all') in an identical paragraph in his previous essay on pluralism under international law, see MacCormick, 'Risking Constitutional Collision in Europe?' (n 8) 527. It is quite hard, therefore, to imagine an occasionally misfortunate phrasing.

91 Besides cases like Opinion 2/13, see more recently C-156/21 Hungary v Parliament and Council ECLI:EU:C:2022:97 para. 125: 'That premise is based on the specific and essential characteristics of

should at least try to dismiss this objection, perhaps by claiming that *Van Gend en Loos*, *Costa*, and Opinion 1/91 only establish autonomy against State law, not against international law. Yet there is no argument of this kind in *Juridical Pluralism*.[92] We only find the claim that the fact that EC law and domestic law do not validate each other does not mean that they have no international obligations.[93] However, having international obligations clearly does not mean being validated by international law.

The view that there actually is some amount of officials' practice to ground pluralism under international law is even less likely when we read in *Juridical Pluralism* that if officials assumed that international law grounded both EC and State law, then 'the same thesis as to the coordination without subordination of legal orders would be available within pluralism under international law as under radical pluralism'.[94] This line seems to imply that a 'sociologically realist' account (radical pluralism) would observe a common validation of EC and State law by international law in the practice of officials, but that this is *not* the view that officials at both the European and the domestic level hold for the time being. Otherwise, why should we distinguish at all between radical pluralism and pluralism under international law? They would collapse into one position.

One could advance a last defence by claiming that MacCormick here implicitly accepts *ex hypothesi* the Kelsenian idea that the principle of efficacy, as a custom of international law, validates State law, while the custom *pact sunt servanda* validates EC law. Both would then be reducible to the common *grundnorm* 'States shall behave as they have customarily behaved'. Yet, this line of argument is not advanced, it must be imagined, and if it were advanced it would still be at odds with some puzzling empirical evidence, as *Van Gend en Loos*, *Costa*, or Opinion 1/91, evidence that sociological realism cannot ignore.

The only thing that, at this point, seems to ground pluralism under international law is a normative need, that of finding a legal solution to possible constitutional conflicts. Inevitably this entails falling into a is-ought problem, since we derive a descriptive conclusion (that EC and domestic law are part of a single international order) from a merely normative premise (the risk of inter-systematic conflict). Pluralism under international law seems in trouble when trying to simultaneously be descriptively accurate and normatively useful to avoid conflicts. An alternative may be to phrase it as a fully normative proposal: when there is risk of collision, officials of the two jurisdictions should rely on international obligations, especially

EU law, which stem from the very nature of EU law and the autonomy it enjoys in relation to the laws of the Member States and to international law'.

92 Furthermore, during his 'radical' phase, he expressed the opposite view. See MacCormick, 'Sovereignty' (n 24) 8: 'Since at least 1964 (Costa v ENEL, case 6/64), it has been the doctrine of the European Court of Justice that the Communities, now "Community", constitute a new legal order, neither a subordinate part of the laws of the Member States, nor simply a sub-system of International Law'. In other words, MacCormick was previously happy to provide empirical observations to ground his claims about the relations between EC and international law.

93 MacCormick, 'Juridical Pluralism and the Risk of Constitutional Conflict' (n 9) 119.

94 ibid 119.

the duty to interpret and implement subscribed Treaties in good faith, to try to avoid conflict at the interpretive level. If this solution is not available, international adjudication should be accepted to settle the controversy. This understanding of pluralism under international law seems more faithful to MacCormick's later essays. Yet, it also necessarily entails that, at some point, commitment to sociological realism which is instead typical of radical pluralism is dropped: he who decides to embrace pluralism under international law accepts not to be providing anymore the best 'theory' that is, the most credible explanation of constitutional pluralism. That pluralism under international law is 'contextually more persuasive and appropriate'[95] will necessarily mean that it provides a good framework to conflict management, not that it is more accurate.

Having clarified the first problem with pluralism under international law, namely its running into an is-ought fallacy, we can now consider a second (and shorter) objection. As we have seen, the point of the entire turn to pluralism under international law is the problem of conflicts in the face of possible constitutional collision in Europe. Suppose now that pluralism under international law is descriptively accurate, so that both EC and domestic law are validated by international law. Yet, if this is true and if it is simultaneously correct that pluralism under international law is a Kelsenian theory, there are serious doubts that it can have any utility in solving conflicts. As we have seen in the last paragraph, Kelsen's view is that no matter whether you interpret the legal materials according to international or national monism, the state of positive law will not change.[96] If a certain behaviour is commanded under domestic law and forbidden under EU law, both norms remain valid from a Kelsenian point of view. Recalling their international obligations has no practical effect, apart from clarifying that States are infringing international law and maybe authorizing sanctions on responsible organs. As for international adjudication, it is not justified legally, for a Kelsenian theory cannot ground new institutional arrangements without repudiating its purity. Surely, if recourse to international obligations or arbitration de facto happens, it may be a legal solution to conflicts. Yet, the point is that this happens independently from pluralism under international law. The justification of a solution to conflicts via international obligations or arbitration can only be political, it is not commanded by the theory. Thus, pluralism under international law, if it really is a Kelsenian theory, fails to deliver and must accept political solutions, precisely as radical pluralism.

Briefly, MacCormick's turn to pluralism under international law raises serious concerns. If it must be taken as a correct picture of the entanglement of European law, then it is not clear how it can account for some of the beliefs expressed by officials and how it would even differ from radical pluralism. If it must be interpreted as a normative account, then one must drop sociological realism at some point.

95 ibid 121.
96 Kelsen, *Pure Theory of Law* (n 49) 342–347.

Finally, if it is a Kelsenian theory of inter-systematic relations, then it is not clear whether it can ever provide guidance to solve conflicts.

Despite these critiques, it is likely that MacCormick's last works still had a crucial role in the history of constitutional pluralism: they were founding works of normative pluralism. For sure, theories of contemporary pluralists as Poiares Maduro or Kumm recalled in Chapter 2 are much more sophisticated and thicker in their attempts to solve conflicts. Nevertheless, we probably should see MacCormick not only as the father of descriptive pluralism, but also as one of the founders of its normative version. Even if the importance of these essays were a purely historical one, that would still be a role to remember.

3.4 Revisiting Radical Pluralism

It is now time to return to MacCormick's radical pluralism. While pluralism under international law is, as I have just explained, overall untenable, radical pluralism is much more promising. The rest of the book is devoted to developing a theory of radical pluralism in Europe. Therefore, here it is worth recalling the takeaways from radical pluralism as developed by MacCormick, four of which are of particular importance. They will guide the rest of the inquiry in the book. I also state how these are all deeply influenced by Hart's theory of law. In the Introduction it was anticipated that the radical pluralism here developed is a positivist theory, positivism being defined in a minimalist sense as the conjunction of the social thesis and of the separability thesis. Stressing how the takeaways from MacCormick's essays are influenced by Hart's positivism only confirms that radical pluralism must be a positivist theory at the jurisprudential level.

The first takeaway is methodological. Differently from the standard normative approach of constitutional pluralists recalled at the end of the last chapter and differently from the mixed perspective adopted by MacCormick himself between 1998 and 1999, radical pluralism is consistently *descriptive*. It is an attempt to explain the riddle of constitutional pluralism from a perspective that MacCormick defined as sociologically realist.

Second, MacCormick points his finger towards the *complexity* or *plurality* of the foundational norms, which he defines through the Hartian concept of the rule of recognition. By comparing the criteria of recognition used by British and European officials after 1972, MacCormick is showing that these are indeed several: complex legal orders do not work based on straightforward rules of recognition commanding respect for the authority of a commanding authority. On the contrary, they use various criteria that to a certain extent overlap: after accession to the Union, a domestic official internalizes the vast series of EU sources of law as criteria of validity, placing them within an already plural national rule of recognition. MacCormick stresses that, in the European context, officials share criteria of validity coming from various legal orders and the system broadly works effectively 'without any necessary assumption of sub- or superordination of one to the other'.[97] Perfectly functioning legal orders can exist in which the question of ultimate authority has no single answer.[98]

What immediately follows is a third takeaway concerning the notion of *sovereignty*. The idea of a single sovereign body, Austin's uncommanded commander (political sovereignty), or of a unitary constitution empowering a governing institution (legal sovereignty), is the equivalent in constitutional theory of the single basic norm in legal theory. MacCormick is sceptical towards this view: the existence of a sovereign institution or of a sovereign constitution is a merely contingent feature of modern States, not an essential characteristic of legal orders. Moreover, while it is the scenario of European integration that he has in mind, MacCormick also points out that limitations to sovereignty are typical of States as well, especially of federal States.[99] This suggests a continuity between States and non-state organizations like the EU which is particularly interesting: it would be a matter of degree, the degree of sovereignty-sharing. The neat State/non-state dichotomy seems rejected in MacCormick's radical pluralism, and so is the idea that sovereignty must necessarily move swiftly from one ultimate body or norm to another.

The last takeaway concerns another feature of the foundational norm, apart from complexity, namely its *conflictual* character. Although legal orders with complex foundational norms often work effectively and peacefully, cases of conflict cannot be ruled out. When this happens, legal mechanisms of various kinds may initially be used and at times they will be enough to solve the conflict. However, in other cases we may just run out of legal remedies and what would be left is political negotiation. This is the moment in which radical pluralism becomes a thesis about the limits of jurisprudence, this time meant not as legal theory, but as the series of interpretive methods and legal principles which contemporary pluralism devotedly attempts to develop. At some point, we run out of legality and must leave room to politics.[100]

It is my opinion that all these four theses are fundamentally correct and represent the pillars of a theory of radical pluralism. MacCormick's thoughts on them are intellectual contributions of the utmost importance.

It is also worth noting that, as previously anticipated, they all share a common inspiration in Hart's theory of law, quite influential on MacCormick's mature writings. To briefly recapitulate how influential Hart's theory was on MacCormick's radical pluralism (and therefore also on this book), it is worth recalling that, as indicated in the Introduction, Hart's commitment to a legal theory that explains the law as a socially constructed cultural and institutional object is plain. MacCormick's 'sociological realism' derives from it. Also, and again as already mentioned, this

97 MacCormick, 'Beyond the Sovereign State' (n 6) 8.

98 ibid 9: 'Where systems overlap, neither is necessarily a part of the ultimate reason for the validity of the other, nor do we have to presuppose some common reason for, or ground of, validity external to them both'.

99 ibid 12–13; MacCormick, 'Sovereignty' (n 24) 6–7; MacCormick, 'On Sovereignty and Post-Sovereignty' (n 18) 130.

100 MacCormick, 'The Maastricht-Urteil' (n 7) 265.

entails that any approach prosecuting the Hart-MacCormick line is close to a form of legal realism. This is compatible with a minimalist understanding of positivism, meant as the conjunction of the social thesis (all law is product of human activities) and of the separability thesis (it is possible to analyse the law without endorsing it).[101] The first takeaway from MacCormick's radical pluralism is, therefore, quite close to Hart.

Second, Hart's theory of sovereignty is quite similar to MacCormick's as well.[102] Hart did not provide a full-fledged theory of sovereignty, but he offered several interesting remarks both when criticizing Austin's[103] picture of a legally unconstrained sovereign body[104] and when assessing sovereignty under international law.[105] He criticized this understanding by claiming that the way in which we identify the sovereign is by referring to secondary rules conferring normative powers. Even an absolute monarch would be identified as an institution (the king or queen) by means of power-conferring norms which 'may well be called constitutional'[106] and which necessarily limit the sovereign.[107] In chapter X of *The Concept of Law*, we find a similar line of reasoning, stating that even external sovereignty of State is subject to legal norms: to limit themselves by means of agreements, 'sovereign States' must be subject to rules that identify what counts as a valid agreement.[108] Finally, in his later *Essays on Bentham*, Hart even admitted the possibility of a plurality of sovereign under the same constitution, as in the case of federal States:[109]

101 See Introduction, 3.

102 MacCormick, 'Beyond the Sovereign State' (n 6) 12.

103 It is not fully clear whether authors of the Anglophone positivist tradition as Hobbes, Bentham, and especially Austin by 'unlimited' sovereign meant an authority completely unbound by law, even by power-conferring constitutional rules, or simply one able to change any law, including power-conferring constitutional rules. See David Dyzenhaus, 'Hobbes on the Authority of Law' in David Dyzenhaus and Thomas Poole (eds), *Hobbes and the Law* (Cambridge University Press 2012) 199 footnote 41. However, here the point is not the accuracy of Hart's reconstruction of his predecessors' ideas, but merely the strength and extent of his argument against unlimited authority, meant in its broadest meaning of fully unbound authority.

104 Hart, *The Concept of Law* (n 30) chapter IV.

105 ibid chapter X. On Hart's understanding of sovereignty, see Pavlos Eleftheriadis, 'Hart on Sovereignty' in Luís Duarte d'Almeida, James Edwards and Andrea Dolcetti (eds), *Reading HLA Hart's 'The Concept of Law'* (Hart Publishing 2013); Matthew H Kramer, 'H. L.A. Hart, The Concept of Law' in Jacob T Levy (ed), *The Oxford Handbook of Classics in Contemporary Political Theory* (Oxford University Press 2015).

106 Hart, *The Concept of Law* (n 30) 69.

107 See ibid 76–77: 'The rules are constitutive of the sovereign, not merely things which we should have to mention in a description of the habits of obedience to the sovereign'.

108 ibid 220–226. Hart's theory of international law is often considered problematic, but this point seems fundamentally correct. On the problems of Hart's theory of International law, see Jeremy Waldron, 'International Law: 'A Relatively Small and Unimportant Part' of Jurisprudence?' in Luís Duarte d'Almeida, James Edwards and Andrea Dolcetti (eds), *Reading HLA Hart's 'The Concept of Law'* (Hart Publishing 2013).

109 Herbert LA Hart, *Essays on Bentham: Jurisprudence and Political Philosophy* (Oxford University Press 1982) 227.

> But the third possibility noted above and excluded by Austin's doctrine, that there might be more than one sovereign in a single political society each vested with unlimited legislative power has scarcely been discussed in the literature. No doubt this is because the idea of a constitution providing for two or more omnicompetent or sovereign legislatures seems too absurd to entertain, unlike the legal limitations and divisions of supreme legislative power which are prominent features of many modern constitutions. But a plurality of sovereigns is not logically impossible.

It is hard at this point not to imagine a connection between Hart's understanding of the sovereign as a necessarily legal concept, potentially plural, and limited in nature, and MacCormick's definition of sovereignty as near absolute normative power effectively exercised by a constituted authority.

Finally, also the idea that the foundational norm of a legal order is complex and conflictual finds some basis in Hart's jurisprudence. Hart's equivalent for the ultimate norm is the rule of recognition, a customary practice of officials which provides criteria of legal validity.[110] The wide discussion on this notion has focused on whether it can or cannot include moral principles,[111] on whether it is or not a convention,[112] on whether it confers powers or impose duties.[113] Here I am focusing on the more mundane question whether a single legal order can have more than one rule of recognition. In *The Concept of Law*, Hart's answer seems to be in the negative: although he recognizes that in developed legal orders there will be a plurality of criteria of recognition, he also states that one will work as a supreme criterion, outranking the others and solving possible conflicts. This supreme and likely unitary rule is exemplified by the paradigmatic 'what the Queen in Parliament enacts is law'.[114] However, the previously quoted lines from the *Essays on Bentham* seem to entail that, at least in later works, he may have been ready to conceive more than one sovereign institution under the same constitution. Moreover, Kent Greenwalt

110 Hart, *The Concept of Law* (n 30) 107–110.

111 For the latter option, the so-called inclusive positivism, see Wilfrid J Waluchow, *Inclusive Legal Positivism* (Oxford University Press 1994); Jules Coleman, *The Practice of Principle: In Defence of a Pragmatist Approach to Legal Theory* (Oxford University Press 2003). Eventually, Hart himself adopted this view in the Postscript to *The Concept of Law*. For the opposite view, that moral norms are by definition extra-legal standards, see exclusive positivists as Joseph Raz, 'Authority, Law, and Morality', *Ethics in the Public Domain* (Oxford University Press 1995); Scott J Shapiro, 'Was Inclusive Legal Positivism Founded on a Mistake?' (2009) 22 Ratio Juris 326.

112 Leslie Green, 'Positivism and Conventionalism' (1999) 12 Canadian Journal of Law & Jurisprudence 35; Julie Dickson, 'Is the Rule of Recognition Really a Conventional Rule?' (2007) 27 Oxford Journal of Legal Studies 373.

113 On the rule of recognition as power-conferring see Jeremy Waldron, 'Who Needs Rules of Recognition?' in Matthew Adler and Kenneth Himma (eds), *The Rule of Recognition and the U.S. Constitution* (Oxford University Press 2009). As duty-imposing, Neil MacCormick, *H.L.A. Hart* (Stanford University Press 2008). For an overview of the debate, Giorgio Pino, 'Farewell to the Rule of Recognition?' (2011) 5 Problema. Anuario de Filosofía y Teoría del Derecho 265.

114 Hart, *The Concept of Law* (n 30) 100–107.

reports of a letter from Hart written in 1986 in which he defined the reference to 'what the Queen in Parliament enacts is law' as the supreme rule of recognition as a 'slip'.[115] Thus, it is at least possible that in later stages of his life a plurality of rules of recognition seemed acceptable to Hart.

Be it as it may, we know for sure that MacCormick considered the complexification of the rule of recognition possible. Building on the customary nature of the rule of recognition, MacCormick figured that it could be plural: the practices of officials, judges in the first place, could practically diverge to some extent, and European pluralism was a case in point. Such 'evolutionary' interpretation of the rule of recognition was only a 'potentiality' in Hart's argument, but one that MacCormick was happy to develop.[116] To be fair, MacCormick's pluralism is also self-standing and based on the institutional theory of law which he developed at first together with Ota Weinberger and later autonomously.[117] Such theory, regularly recalled in the essays on European pluralism,[118] analyses societies as made of a plurality of institutions, namely human practices ordered via norms.[119] Distancing from previous forms of institutionalism which characterized all institutions as legal orders,[120] MacCormick's theory draws a line between legal and non-legal institutions and is particularly interested in the coexistence of a plurality of legal institutions modelled on the modern State with constitutional features.[121] However, despite this additional and separate theoretical basis, the complexification of the rule of recognition reminds us of Hart's influence on this aspect of MacCormick's pluralism as well.

Finally, also the conflictual character of the foundational norm has some basis in Hart. MacCormick maintains that 'the rule of recognition can be controversial or unclear on some points so long as it is not so on all' but does not elaborate further.[122] This is particularly regrettable as the risk of conflict is one of the core problems of constitutional pluralism and there are in Hart various interesting remarks to consider, especially when he discusses the 'pathology of a legal system'

115 Kent Greenwalt, 'The Rule of Recognition and the Constitution' in Matthew Adler and Kenneth Himma (eds), *The Rule of Recognition and the U.S. Constitution* (Oxford University Press 2009) 11 footnote 30.

116 MacCormick, 'Beyond the Sovereign State' (n 6) 5–11.

117 MacCormick and Weinberger (n 4); MacCormick, 'The Legal Framework' (n 4); MacCormick, *Institutions of Law* (n 4).

118 MacCormick, 'Beyond the Sovereign State' (n 6) 6; MacCormick, 'The Maastricht-Urteil' (n 7) 261–262; MacCormick, 'Sovereignty' (n 24) 5–6; MacCormick, 'Risking Constitutional Collision in Europe?' (n 8) 524–528; MacCormick, 'Juridical Pluralism and the Risk of Constitutional Conflict' (n 9) 102–104.

119 MacCormick, *Institutions of Law* (n 4) 30–33.

120 See again Santi Romano, *The Legal Order* (Routledge 2017). On the differences between Romano and MacCormick-Weinberger, see Massimo La Torre, *Law as Institution* (Springer 2010) 109–115.

121 MacCormick, *Institutions of Law* (n 4) 2: 'I make no apology for giving priority to expounding a theory about the law in its state and state-like contexts'.

122 MacCormick, 'Beyond the Sovereign State' (n 6) 5.

and the 'uncertainty on the rule of recognition'.[123] Anticipating what will be argued in the next chapter, Hart was likely right when he pointed out that even perfectly simple supreme criteria like 'what the Queen in Parliament enacts is law' cannot avoid constitutional conflicts once and for all. Radical pluralism may benefit from Hart's insights even more than his disciple figured.[124]

To sum up, there are various aspects of MacCormick's account of radical pluralism that seem fundamentally sound: besides a methodological commitment to 'sociological realism', we find a certain scepticism towards the notion of sovereignty and the idea that the foundational norm-constitution can be complex and conflictual. All of them, in turn, find some basis in Hart's theory of law.

The next two chapters of this book assert that these intuitions are correct and rely on comparative analysis to show why.

Chapter 4 argues that the constitutional complexity and conflictuality that MacCormick and Hart pictured can be documented by looking at the constitutional practice of federations and even at that of unitary States. The experience of federalism, and specifically the American case, is particularly telling, but cases of plural opinions among officials on where 'sovereignty' or 'ultimate authority' lie, are present in unitary States as well. The idea of discrete States with unitary sovereign constitutions on top, I argue, is more problematic than it may seem.

Chapter 5, finally, returns to the case of the EU and analyses the cases in which European pluralism has engendered tensed confrontations between the highest EU and national judicial institutions. I consider first one case in which the mechanisms for preventing conflicts much praised by normative pluralists worked, the *Taricco* saga, how it occurred and how it was solved. I then move to cases in which open conflict erupted, the cases of *ultra vires* judgment by national peak courts (supreme or constitutional): the Czech *Landtová*, the Danish *Ajos*, the German *PSPP*, and the Polish K-3/21 cases are scrutinized and compared. They confirm the radical pluralist view that in some cases the inevitable complexity and conflictuality of foundational norms, be them national or supranational, bring about open conflicts. These, as MacCormick suggested, are not legally solvable, but require political negotiation.

123 Hart, *The Concept of Law* (n 30) 117–123 and 147–154.

124 Despite the fact that attempts to explain European pluralism by relying on Hart's theory are indeed quite few. Mark Jones, 'The Legal Nature of the European Community: A Jurisprudential Analysis Using H.L.A. Hart's Model of Law and a Legal System' (1984) 17 Cornell International Law Journal 1; more recently, Justin Lindeboom, 'The Autonomy of EU Law: A Hartian View' (2021) 13 European Journal of Legal Studies 271.

4

CONSTITUTIONAL DISAGREEMENT

Pluralism in Composite and Unitary Legal Systems

4.1 Introduction

Constitutional pluralism is puzzling and irritating. The picture of law as a discrete system of norms with a foundational norm on top does not square with the simultaneous claims of ultimate authority which come from officials placed at the top of both the European Union (EU) and of national systems. Statements like those contained in Opinion 2/13 and the *Maastricht Urteil* which were examined in Chapter 2 are instantiations of this bifurcation.

While several pluralists have focused on the normative benefits of this scenario, seen as the most appropriate incarnation of constitutionalism in the 21st century, opponents have severely criticized the very possibility of pluralism. Sovereignty, the argument goes, means 'constitutional independence, the exercise of plenary and exclusive political authority in a legal order', as such it cannot be divided, shared, or pooled.[1] The State, on the other hand, is the result of the dialectic process through which the people identify the institution responsible for governing according to the expectations and desires of the homogeneous polity.[2] A plurality of constitutional claims means a plurality of conflicting social claims and expectations, thus no order at all.[3] Equilibrium or heterarchy between competing constitutional claims is

1 Noel Malcolm, 'Sense on Sovereignty' in Martin Holmes (ed), *The Eurosceptical Reader* (Palgrave Macmillan 1996).

2 There is an almost Schmittian view of sovereignty at play here. See Martin Loughlin, *Foundations of Public Law* (Oxford University Press 2010) 232; Martin Loughlin, 'The Concept of Constituent Power' (2014) 13 European Journal of Political Theory 218, 223–231. On Schmitt's theory of sovereignty and on its place in Loughlin's thought, David Dyzenhaus, *Legality and Legitimacy: Carl Schmitt, Hans Kelsen, and Hermann Heller in Weimar* (Oxford University Press 1999) 42–51; David Dyzenhaus, 'The Left and the Question of Law' (2004) 17 Canadian Journal of Law & Jurisprudence 7, 18–29.

3 Martin Loughlin, 'Constitutional Pluralism: An Oxymoron?' (2014) 3 Global Constitutionalism 9, 23.

DOI: 10.4324/9781003291572-4

unconceivable: either the national constitutions emerge again as the still sovereign authoritative sources of law or the latter's foundational norms turn out to be the new sovereign constitution.[4] *Tertium non datur*. Sovereignty must pass swiftly from one level to another as a unitary element, while constitutional pluralism is an empty notion, an oxymoron.[5]

Ideas like these instantiate the views on State and sovereignty that MacCormick defined 'foundationalist' and that were originally conceived to conceptualize and strengthen the construction of the unitary State in Europe during the early modernity.[6] In this chapter I will question them and argue that a certain degree of constitutional pluralism is an inevitable feature not only of a supranational organization like the EU, but also of States. Diverging claims on the site of ultimate authority take place in States as well as beyond them. Potential constitutional conflicts inevitably follow as well and the idea of an ultimate norm settling disagreements once and for all is untenable. Critics of pluralism inherit an 'absolutist' view on sovereignty that is hardly compatible with the articulated organization of modern public powers under the rule of (constitutional) law. I sustain this view by relying not on a normative political theory but rather looking at the results of several contemporary studies in comparative constitutional law. They provide evidence of the everlasting constitutional conflicts that legal orders inevitably face.

Specifically, I refer to the examination of two different forms of government.

The first is federalism, conceived as the theory and the practice of the organization of government in which constitutionalism is divided between separate levels of government. As hinted by MacCormick in his writings, federalism witnesses the everlasting emergence of competing claims of ultimate authority. This will be shown with reference to the case of American federalism before the Civil War, in which the ideas of divided constitutional government and divided sovereignty were present since the beginning. Federalism's competing claims to ultimate authority in Europe is less unique than it may seem (4.2).

The second is the State itself, even in its unitary form. Relying on theoretical arguments on the interpretation of foundational norms and on findings of comparative law, I argue that even when the single constitutional norm empowering a Queen in Parliament is clearly identified, disputes on ultimate authority can still be found because of interpretive disagreements on its content. Interpretive disagreements on the constitution generate a series of competing views that is yet another form of constitutional pluralism. A diminished constitutional complexity does not erase constitutional conflicts once and for all (4.3).

The upshot is a picture in which there is no qualitative but only quantitative difference between unitary, federal, or quasi-federal polities like the EU: sovereignty is

4 Malcolm (n 1) 23–25. See also other critics of pluralism mentioned in Chapter 2 as Grimm, Loughlin, Davies, and Kumm.

5 Loughlin, 'Constitutional Pluralism' (n 3) 9–14.

6 See the historical accounts by Daniel Philpott, 'Sovereignty: An Introduction and Brief History' (1995) 48 Journal of International Affairs 353; Lorenzo Zucca, 'A Genealogy of State Sovereignty' (2015) 16 Theoretical Inquiries in Law 399.

more and more dispersed and constitutional pluralism more and more pronounced. Constitutional disagreement is structural and not unique of the EU (4.4). Consequently, the chapter provides evidence in favour of a theory of radical pluralism: it shows how the complexity of the foundational norm works in the historical experience of legal orders and how conflict on the former is unavoidable.

4.2 Federalism and Constitutional Pluralism: On Unions of States

To show how the constitutional pluralism that features the EU is not a unicum in history, we must start by looking at federalism. Federal experiences, I argue, show competing claims to ultimate authority similar to those visible in the EU.

Providing a definition of federalism is not an easy task. Although often associated to the federal State, a specific form of State characterized by strong decentralization, federalism is conceptually separate from the latter and can be defined in various manners.[7] Indeed, various conceptualizations have been offered.[8] In Daniel Elazar's understanding, for instance, federalism is a system of government which combines shared-rule and self-rule, cooperation under common rules and autonomy.[9] Carl Friedrich defined it dynamically as a process:

> the process of federalizing a political community, that is to say, the process by which a number of separate political communities enter into arrangements for working out solutions, adopting joint policies, and making joint decisions on joint problems, and, conversely, also the process by which a unitary political community becomes differentiated into a federally organized whole.[10]

Federalism can also refer to a normative theory, a political philosophy which promises to keep together diverse constituencies by respecting their autonomy, to reconcile unity and diversity.[11] In this sense, federalism is an ethos and a political aspiration which has characterized European integration too, even before the process of constitutionalization and back into the days of the Schuman Declaration in 1950, when the Coal and Steal Community was defined as the '*first concrete foundation of a European federation* indispensable to the preservation of peace'.[12]

7 Raffaele Bifulco, 'Federalism' in Robert Schütze and Roger Masterman (eds), *The Cambridge Companion to Comparative Constitutional Law* (Cambridge University Press 2019).

8 See the review of the relevant literature by Michael Burgess, *Comparative Federalism: Theory and Practice* (Routledge 2006) 9–49.

9 Daniel Elzar, *Exploring Federalism* (University of Alabama Press 1987) 12.

10 Carl J Friedrich, *Trends of Federalism in Theory and Practice* (Pall Mall 1968) 7.

11 Thomas O Hueglin and Alan Fenna, *Comparative Federalism: A Systematic Inquiry* (University of Toronto Press 2015) 1–4.

12 Schuman Declaration in Brent F Nelsen and Alexander CG Stubb (eds), *The European Union: Readings on the Theory and Practice of European Integration* (Rienner 1994) 11–12. On the influence of federalist

Among those available, the definition of federalism that I propose in this chapter is borrowed from Daniel Halberstam. In his view, federalism is 'the coexistence within a compound polity of multiple levels of government each with constitutionally grounded claims to some degree of organizational autonomy and jurisdictional authority'.[13] Accordingly, federalism must be understood as strictly connected to constitutionalism: it refers to a particular kind of legal order in which *each* level exposes autonomous constitutional claims.[14]

This definition is inevitably at odds with the take on the nature of the European Union exposed in judgments like *Maastricht*. As we have seen in Chapter 2, the latter is based on the dichotomic distinction between *Bundesstaat* (a particularly decentralized sovereign State) and *Staatenbund* (an association of sovereign States), between organizations of constitutional law and of international law. Thus, either in an association of States' sovereignty and constitutionalism lie in the States (so that we have a confederation) or they move to the federation (so that we have a federal State). Cooperation between States must either take the form of a full-fledged federal State in which sovereignty swiftly moves to the higher level or remain a mere international organization, in which Member States are sovereign. *Maastricht* spoke of a *Staatenverbund*, instead of using the German equivalent for confederation (*Staatenbund*), but de facto it described the EU as something hardly distinguishable from a confederation.

Yet, this rigid distinction and the emphasis on sovereignty as a unitary concept are misleading.

In a recent book, Signe Rehling Larsen questioned the dichotomy between *Bundesstaat* and *Staatenbund* by showing how this was only conceived by German scholars in the late 19th century, in an era of consolidation of the previous German Confederation (1815–1866) into the Second Empire (1871–1918).[15] It was unknown before and was not fit to describe previous experiences of political unions. In this sense, Halberstam's definition allows us to recognize how a strong degree of constitutional pluralism was historically a structural feature of federalism that was only later obscured by the dichotomic view exposed by German scholarship. The conflation of federalism and federal State, specifically of rather centralized federal States in which constitutional claims of States have been significantly compressed, overshadows the previous history of political communities organized along federal lines, an history as old as that of States.[16]

thinking in the process of integration, see Michael Burgess, *Federalism and the European Union: The Building of Europe, 1950-2000* (Routledge 2000).

13 Daniel Halberstam, 'Federalism: Theory, Policy, Law' in Michel Rosenfeld and András Sajó (eds), *The Oxford Handbook of Comparative Constitutional Law* (Oxford University Press 2012) 580.

14 See also Koen Lenaerts, 'Constitutionalism and the Many Faces of Federalism' (1990) 38 American Journal of Comparative Law 205: 'As a system of divided powers, federalism proceeds from the very essence of constitutionalism, which is limited government operating under the rule of law'.

15 Signe Rehling Larsen, *The Constitutional Theory of the Federation and the European Union* (Oxford University Press 2021) 14–18. On the consolidation, see Francesco Palermo and Karl Kössler, *Comparative Federalism – Constitutional Arrangements and Case Law* (Hart Publishing 2017) 67–69.

16 Hueglin and Fenna (n 11) 73–97.

Following this anti-statist, anti-sovereigntist, and deeply pluralist line, federalism is the organizational principle of what are called, again in Larsen's vocabulary, 'federal unions of States'.[17] According to Larsen, a union of States has specific characteristics, not coincident with those of federal States. It is based on an original moment of birth (of the union) and transformation (of the States), the *foedus* or covenant.[18] It is a voluntary and intentionally permanent agreement through which States decide to constitute an organization to reach common political aims, what may be called the teleological character of unions of States.[19] The covenant is not just a treaty, but a constitutional compact, an agreement which does not bind only States, but peoples as well, joined in an ever closer union. The most evident effect of this transformation is the advent of federal citizenship: a new legal status common to all citizens is developed, featured with rights, and governed by the union. Federal citizenship entails legal rights that the union has a responsibility to enhance through its legislation.[20] Consequently, the union has a series of institutions and constituency of its own to represent, one whose rights and interests it shall preserve. In a word, it has an autonomous constitution.

While the covenant entails the advent of a new constitutional layer at the level of the union, the other side of the coin is the transformation of the States, whose constitutions are transfigured as well. In the first place, States are bound to treat subjects of other Member States not anymore as aliens, but as citizens of a common polity.[21] Moreover, the constitution of States must change to incorporate the Union's Constitution: applying its law and participating in the new institutional apparatus become binding constitutional norms of States. The most patent consequence is the system of dual representation: the union is governed by bodies which represent the citizens of the union (federal institutions) and the citizens of their States (State institutions).[22] Dual representation and constitutional change are phenomena that full-fledged federal States experience as well,[23] but in unions of States this generates a dynamic that is identical to what is defined in the context of the EU as 'constitutional pluralism': there are two sources of constitutional authority, exercised by independent institutions in the name of the *union* of States or of the union of *States*. The dual constitution entails that neither the States are subject to the union nor *vice versa*. There is no single answer to the question of ultimate authority because both States and the union have separate constitutional nature, legal authority, and

17 Larsen (n 15) 19–23.
18 ibid 23–27.
19 ibid 20 and 95–98.
20 ibid 30–36.
21 ibid 31–32 and 81–83.
22 ibid 99–101.
23 Hueglin and Fenna (n 11) 205–225; Nathalie Behnke and Arthur Benz, 'Federalism and Constitutional Change' in Xenophon Contiades and Alkmene Fotiadou (eds), *Routledge Handbook of Comparative Constitutional Change* (Routledge 2020) 170–179.

connection with citizens.[24] This differentiates unions of States and their federalism from full-fledged federal States.

What results from this picture is an organization whose form of government differs from the State because of its dual constitutional character. In Larsen's view, the discrete character of federal unions is further exacerbated by the absence of sovereignty, a concept developed as necessarily indivisible in the context of States and unfit to federal unions.[25] This is, in my opinion, an unnecessary step. Larsen's description of union of States results from the analysis of various historical experiences: the Old Swiss Confederation (1291–1798), the Restored Swiss Confederation (1815–48), the United Provinces of the Netherlands (1579–1795), the German Confederation (1815–66), and the antebellum United States of America (1777–1865).[26] However, as we will see in a moment when considering the case of the antebellum USA, there seems to be evidence of the fact that sovereignty was considered as a concept fit to define the union that was instituted, although conceived as divided and dispersed rather than united and indivisible. The self-understanding of those who built the polity shall not be discarded in the name of a dogmatic understanding of sovereignty. In principle, there is no reason to give conceptual priority to Hobbes' or Rousseau's view on sovereignty over Jefferson's or Madison's.

That unions of States examined by Larsen such as the German Confederation and the antebellum USA have later coalesced into federal States must not be taken as proof of their intrinsic instability, of the inevitable collapse into the sole organization able to provide stability, the State.[27] The mentioned cases of federal unions do not seem significantly less stable than States.[28] In fact, many of the latter have lasted less than unions of States before collapsing or experiencing seismic constitutional transformation.[29] Moreover, unions of States have not disappeared from earth. On the contrary, the EU can be understood as the last manifestation of this form of government, more than as a *sui generis* organization (a point on which I will return at the end of this paragraph). Despite various cries periodically predicting its crisis and dissolution, it does not seem close to disappear soon. There seems to be no compelling reason to think that becoming a State is the destiny of any political

24 Larsen (n 15) 36–40 and 161–162.

25 ibid 41–48.

26 ibid 13.

27 As in the characterization of federalism given by Carl Schmitt, *Constitutional Theory* (Duke University Press 2008) 388–390.

28 Using the duration of constitutions (the timespan between enactment and formal replacement) as a proxy for the stability of a constitutional regime (setting aside cases of transformation through mere amendment or interpretation), it is observed that the mean age of State constitutions is indeed just 17.2 years. See Tom Ginsburg, 'Constitutional Endurance' in Xenophon Contiades and Alkmene Fotiadou (eds), *Routledge Handbook of Comparative Constitutional Change* (Routledge 2020) 64.

29 Think about the case of France, the archetype of the unitary State, which experienced 15 written constitutions between 1789 and 1958 and an even larger number of actual deep changes of the material constitution. See Francis Hamon and Michel Troper, *Droit constitutionnel* (LGDJ-Lextenso 2014) 305.

organization. Such may eventually be the EU's future, but this depends on a variety of political, social, and cultural factors. Constitutional theory cannot forecast this outcome.

4.2.1 The Antebellum USA: Divided Sovereignty, Interposition, and Nullification

Setting aside predictions on how enduring a union of States may be, now I would like to consider in more detail one of the most interesting cases of previous unions of States, one in which the plurality of competing constitutional claims in different layers of government is particularly evident, namely the antebellum USA (1787–1865).

Comparisons between the American and EU legal experiences are certainly not new.[30] Moreover, while Europe was still bewildered by the inexplicable nature of the *sui generis* ECC (neither properly international nor fully constitutional), it was from America that some of the first conceptualizations of the Communities using the vocabulary of federalism came.[31]

The focus here, however, is not on American law in general, but on the antebellum USA, the constitutional experience from the advent of the Constitution to the Civil War. It is a particularly fruitful perspective for two reasons, one theoretical and one practical. As for the first, the theoretical thickness of American federalism is quite revealing: judicial and doctrinal debates going back to the drafting and ratification of the Constitution (1787–1789) reveal the conception of federalism held at that time in the USA and expose a particularly self-aware union of States. Moving to the practical reason, the antebellum USA experienced a series of constitutional clashes culminating into *ultra vires* declarations that resemble closely those which the EU has experienced in the last decades. Looking at the American cases of *ultra vires* helps dispelling the sense of uniqueness, of *sui generis* that surrounds the EU.

30 E.g., Lenaerts (n 14); Daniel J Elazar, 'The United States and the European Union: Models for Their Epochs', *The Federal Vision* (Oxford University Press 2001); John D Donahue and Mark A Pollack, 'Centralization and Its Discontents: The Rhythms of Federalism in the United States and the European Union', *The Federal Vision* (Oxford University Press 2001); Alberta Sbragia, 'The United States and the European Union: Comparing Two Sui Generis Systems' in Anand Menon and Martin Schain (eds), *Comparative Federalism: The European Union and the United States in Comparative Perspective* (Oxford University Press 2006); Paul Magnette and Justine Lacroix, 'EU Constitutionalism and the "American Experience"' in Gráinne de Búrca and Joanne Scott (eds), *Law and New Governance in the EU and the US* (Hart Publishing 2006).

31 See for instance Peter Hay, 'Federal Jurisdiction of the Common Market Court' (1963) 12 American Journal of Comparative Law 21; Peter Hay, 'Supremacy of Community Law in National Courts. A Progress Report on Referrals Under the EEC Treaty' (1968) 16 The American Journal of Comparative Law 524; Eric Stein, 'Treaty-Based Federalism, A.D. 1979: A Gloss on Covey T. Oliver at the Hague Academy' (1979) 127 University of Pennsylvania Law Review 897; Eric Stein, 'Lawyers, Judges, and the Making of a Transnational Constitution' (1981) 75 American Journal of International Law 1. On Hay, Stain, and in general on the pioneering American studies on European federalism, see Giuseppe Martinico, 'The Federal Language and the European Integration Process: The European Communities Viewed from the US' (2016) 53 Politique europeenne 38.

Both the theoretical and the practical reason of interest for the antebellum USA ultimately depend on its everlasting constitutional pluralism. Authors like and Steve Boom,[32] Robert Schütze,[33] and Daniel Halberstam[34] have underlined this feature of American federalism: the question of ultimate authority was not fully settled, and pluralism never completely faded away.

The first decades of American constitutional history were indeed heavily conditioned by the Madisonian theory of divided sovereignty, rather different from the European idea of indivisible and absolute sovereignty.[35] As showed by Alison LaCroix, in the years before the Revolutionary War, American lawyers and political philosophers struggled to counter the British view of sovereignty as an indivisible attribute of the supreme governmental institution, the King or Queen in Parliament.[36] Based on a line of thinking that ultimately relied on Bodin and Hobbes and was mediated by Blackstone, the unitary view of sovereignty was firmly asserted by British officials in the colonies. It was equally contested by the colonists though, who envisaged a theory of divided sovereignty. The stance of Governor Thomas Hutchinson in the 1773 debate with the General Court (colonial assembly) of Massachusetts, is telling of the British view on sovereignty. The debate regarded the salaries of colonial officials and whether it was licit that they would be henceforth paid by the Crown rather than the colonies (as it was customary). On that occasion, the Governor firmly asserted that sovereignty could not be divided or limited, but only delegated by the supreme governing institution, the King in Parliament (this way denying the claims to independent legislative power of the colonial assembly).[37] To counter such doctrine, American colonists developed the concept of divided sovereignty by relying on a vast series of materials. Some were theoretical, as the writings of Grotius, von Pufendorf, or de Vattel. Others were historical, as the experience of previous confederations between American colonies or between other fragments of the British Empire (e.g., the process of

32 Steve J Boom, 'The European Union after the Maastricht Decision: Will Germany Be the "Virginia of Europe?"' (1995) 43 The American Journal of Comparative Law 177.

33 Robert Schütze, 'On "Federal Ground": The European Union as an (Inter)National Phenomenon' (2009) 46 Common Market Law Review 1069; Robert Schütze, *From Dual to Cooperative Federalism: The Changing Structure of European Law* (Oxford University Press 2009); Robert Schütze, 'Federalism as Constitutional Pluralism: "Letter from America"' in Matej Avbelj and Jan Komárek (eds), *Constitutional Pluralism in the European Union and Beyond* (Hart Publishing 2012); Robert Schütze, *European Union Law* (Oxford University Press 2021) 41–71.

34 Daniel Halberstam, 'Pluralism in Marbury and Van Gend' in Miguel Poiares Maduro and Loïc Azoulai (eds), *The Past and Future of EU Law: The Classics of EU Law Revisited on the 50th Anniversary of the Rome Treaty* (Hart Publishing 2010); Halberstam, 'Federalism' (n 13); Daniel Halberstam, '"A People for Certain Purposes": On the History and Philosophy of Federalism(s) in the United States and Europe' (2018) University of Michigan Public Law Research Paper N. 619.

35 On Madison's impact on the debate of the time, see Halberstam, '"A People for Certain Purposes"' (n 34) 6–8.

36 Alison L LaCroix, *The Ideological Origins of American Federalism* (Harvard University Press 2011) 11–18; Akhil Reed Amar, 'Of Sovereignty and Federalism' (1987) 96 The Yale Law Journal 1425, 1430–1432.

37 LaCroix (n 36) 74–78.

union between Scotland and England).[38] Such sources of inspiration coalesced into the idea of divided governance over a polity, in which no absolute sovereign would exist. American politicians and commentators promptly used this emerging notion of divided sovereignty in their rejoinders to British officials like Hutchinson.[39] Briefly, divided sovereignty was one of the main intellectual presuppositions of the American Revolution. In turn, divided sovereignty derived from the very basic tenet of American constitutionalism, namely popular sovereignty: sovereignty belonged to the people, not to a governmental institution as the King in Parliament. The sovereign people could then act as a principal and delegate it to a series of agents, namely State and federal institutions. Then, by definition, no institution would hold indivisible and absolute authority.[40]

When the Revolutionary War ended and the new nation was born, divided sovereignty passed into the Constitution of 1787. The delegates gathered in the Philadelphia Convention set a hybrid institutional structure, a composition of both a State and a confederation.[41] The enumerated list of centralized powers, the dual system of representation with a 'national' House and a 'federal' Senate, the amendment power and the ratification of the Constitution left to a large majority, but not to the unanimity of States, all underlined the dualism of the new system of government. Moreover, no federal citizenship was originally defined by the Constitution. Finally, the Tenth Amendment, added in 1791, clarified that the 'powers not delegated to the United States by the Constitution, nor prohibited by it to the States, are reserved to the States respectively, or to the people'.

This hybrid form left a series of foundational questions unanswered. The Constitution was a compact between States, but States, as we learn from Madison's Report of 1800, had to be interpreted as referring to the 'people composing those political societies, in their highest sovereign capacity'.[42] Once the covenant was ratified, though, was the Constitution's principal *the people* of the newly constituted nation or still *the peoples* of the States? We read again in Madison, in his *Notes of Debates in the Federal Convention of 1787*, that indeed the first draft of the preamble to the Constitution enlisted all States after the renowned 'We the People', a dual reference that did not dissolve the ambiguity.[43] Given the typically American conception of popular sovereignty, then, it was not clarified whether the sovereign 'people' was unitary or a plural. In turn, this meant that the level of government holding ultimate authority (at federal or State level) remained open itself and so did the question of the entitled branch of government. The very nature of the Constitution was unclear: was it a mere compact between sovereign States or a new

38 ibid 18–29.
39 ibid 79–96.
40 Amar (n 36) 1432–1437.
41 See Madison's Federalist Paper n. 39 in Alexander Hamilton, James Madison, and John Jay, *The Federalist Papers* (Michael A Genovese ed, Palgrave Macmillan 2010) 79–83.
42 James Madison, *Selected Writings of James Madison* (Ralph Ketcham ed, Hackett 2006) 250.
43 James Madison, *The Writings of James Madison*, vol 4 (Gaillard Hunt ed, GP Putnam's Sons 1903) 91–92.

sovereign entity?[44] By splitting the atom of sovereignty, the Madisonian approach chose not to choose and left ultimate authority shared.

This fundamental ambiguity emerged in the first decades of life of the Republic as States repeatedly challenged federal authority.[45] These constitutional conflicts are particularly telling of the way in which unions of States work. Between 1787 and the Civil War, States stepped in to check on the constitutionality of federal acts to prevent initiatives beyond the constitutional limits of federal institutions. States intervened when they considered federal institutions to have acted *ultra vires* and behaved as the guardians of the federal compact. Here I focus on four cases in which American States patently denunciated federal overstep of the Constitution: the Alien and Sedition crisis of 1798–1800, the Hartford Convention of 1814–1815, the *Martin v Hunter's Lessee* case of 1816, and the South Carolina's nullification crisis of 1828–1832.

The first intervention happened at the dawn of the republic. In 1798, the legislatures of Virginia and Kentucky opposed two bills approved by the Congress, the *Alien and Sedition Acts*, perceived as a violation of the States' powers and of the Bill of Rights.[46] At the beginning of the French Revolution, relations between the USA and France rapidly deteriorated up to the point of open naval conflict in an undeclared war (the so-called Quasi-War). The ruling Federalist party in America tried to discredit the Jeffersonian Republican opposition by depicting Republicans as treacherous Jacobins and allied of the French. As European immigrants were keener to vote for the Republicans, Congress passed bills allowing the President to expel any alien 'dangerous to the peace and safety of the United States' and made naturalization longer and more difficult. Moreover, Congress also passed a *Sedition Act* criminalizing public attacks on the government, if a jury found them 'false, scandalous, and malicious'.[47] Republicans opposed the acts and prominent figures like Madison and Jefferson advised the States of Virginia and Kentucky to denounce them. Consequently, the two States approved explicit Resolutions on the matter via their legislatures.[48] The Resolution of Virginia, authored and then commented in the already mentioned Report of 1800 by Madison,[49] exposed the idea of the Constitution as a compact between States and the right of the plurality of States to step in and in extreme cases interpose between the people and the federal government by signalling 'deliberate, palpable, and dangerous' infractions of the compact. Kentucky adopted two Resolutions, one in 1798 (originally drafted by Jefferson, then moderated by the State House) and one in 1799. The Kentucky Resolutions,

44 Halberstam, '"A People for Certain Purposes"' (n 34) 12–18.

45 See the overviews by Boom (n 32) 186–195; Arthur S Miller and Ronald F Howell, 'Interposition, Nullification and the Delicate Division of Power in a Federal System' (1956) 5 Journal of Public Law 2.

46 William J Watkins, *Reclaiming the American Revolution: The Kentucky and Virginia Resolutions and Their Legacy* (Palgrave Macmillan 2004) 55–82. See the texts of the Resolutions ibid 165–177.

47 Alan Taylor, *American Revolutions – A Continental History, 1750–1804* (Norton 2016) 356–357.

48 Haywood Jefferson Powell, 'The Principles of '98: An Essay in Historical Retrieval' (1994) 80 Virginia Law Review 689, 706–727.

49 Madison (n 42) 247–269.

especially the second of 1799, were more extreme than their Virginian twin. The latter, grounded in the Madisonian idea of divided sovereignty, would allow mere *interposition*, namely the collective right of States to declare the incompatibility between the constitution as interpreted by States and the interposed provision (the *Alien and Sedition Acts*). Moreover, they would do so only in case of 'deliberate, palpable, and dangerous' violation of the compact. On the other hand, Kentucky's Resolutions would allow proper *nullification*, namely a unilateral remedy available to each State on the basis of which Kentucky assessed the *Alien and Sedition Acts* as unconstitutional in 1789 ('altogether void, and of no force'). In the more extremist 1799 ordinance, the concept of 'nullification', proposed by Jefferson already the year before, was explicitly mentioned. Madison's drafting of the Virginia Resolution was comparatively vaguer and less decided in declaring the acts unconstitutional. Even the tone and rhetoric of the Virginian text were more conciliatory and less confrontational.[50]

It is not clear what the Resolutions were exactly aimed at achieving, whether they actually intended to eventually void the *Acts* or just protest that they were unconstitutional.[51] In any case, President John Adams was advised to send troops to Virginia but refused to avoid civil war.[52] The tense constitutional conflict would eventually be solved politically in 1800, with Jefferson's ascent to the presidency: the *Sedition Act* was expiring, and the new President terminated pending prosecutions and pardoned all those previously convicted.[53] Two crucial concepts of early American constitutional theory, namely interposition and nullification, had however been exposed.

Only a few years later, well into the Jeffersoninan era, the Hartford Convention, made of representatives of various New England States, in 1814–1815 denounced as unconstitutional the congressional proposal for conscription.[54] Indeed, under President Jefferson and his successor Madison, relations between the USA and Great Britain had worsened to the point of open conflict in the War of 1812. Jefferson's and Madison's anti-British trade policies, crucial in fostering the war, were quite unpopular among New England's merchants.[55] Embargo on foreign goods had already engendered disobedience in Massachusetts and Connecticut in 1807,[56] but it was during the war, with the Eastern States exposed to the might of the British fleet, that the situation deteriorated irremediably. As a result, the Federalist Party defeated by Jefferson in 1800 and later by Madison in 1808, regained ground in New England, to the point of obtaining a resounding electoral victory for New

50 On the differences between the two States' Resolutions see Watkins (n 46) 72–76.

51 ibid 71–75.

52 Taylor (n 47) 357.

53 Watkins (n 46) 79–82.

54 Akhil Reed Amar, 'The Bill of Rights as a Constitution' (1991) 100 The Yale Law Journal 1131, 1172–1173.

55 Alison L LaCroix, 'A Singular and Awkward War: The Transatlantic Context of the Hartford Convention' (2005) 6 American Nineteenth Century History 3, 7–8.

56 Miller and Howell (n 45) 14.

England's assemblies and governors in November 1814. Legitimized by the popular vote, delegates from Massachusetts, Connecticut, Rhode Island, and a few counties in Vermont and New Hampshire, gathered in Hartford, Connecticut.[57] They were to claim more autonomy from Washington in handling a war that was damaging their States. With the federal army busy fighting the British, the States of New England were effectively in the position to ask for a revision of the constitutional compact, which they did in their *Report and Resolutions* of 4 January 1815. The Convention relied on the interposition theory framed by Madison in the Virginia Resolution (but not on the more extreme theory of nullification) to affirm the right of States to protect their sovereignty and the liberties of its citizens from violations of the Constitution by the federal government. Congressional authority to enlist citizens in a regular army by conscription (as opposed to voluntary contract) was questioned: Congress was acting *ultra vires* in conscripting New England's citizens. The Convention demanded to retain a larger share of taxes to ensure autonomously New England's security. The delegates also recommended a series of constitutional amendments to secure New England's interests within the Union. If the federal government did not agree on such requests, a new convention would convene in Boston in June 1815. If necessary, it would opt for secession from the Union: the threat of withdrawal was therefore remote, but not impossible. None of these radical constitutional changes, not to mention secession, was going to happen, though. The delegates to the Convention did not know that they were acting based on outdated information: at the end of December 1814, while the *Report* was being drafted, the Treaty of Ghent was signed to end the war with Great Britain. When New England's delegates moved to Washington to present their requests to the federal government, these had lost any reason to exist, and the crisis ended.[58] However, the Hartford Convention had instantiated for the first time the question of secession and seen again States declaring acts of federal institutions unconstitutional.

As no rest seemed possible for the Union, a new case of constitutional conflict emerged immediately after the end of the Hartford crisis. In 1816, in the *Martin v. Hunter's Lessee* case the Appellate Court of Virginia refused to obey a direct overrule by the Supreme Court. During the Revolutionary War, Virginia had enacted laws allowing for seizure of loyalists' properties. In 1781, Danny Martin inherited property from his loyalist uncle, Lord Fairfax, but the following year Virginia voided the land grant, seized Martin's property, and sold it to David Hunter. The Treaty of Paris of 1783, however, in ending the Revolutionary War nullified such confiscations. The Appellate Court upheld Virginia's law and refused to recognize the supremacy of the Treaty. The Supreme Court reversed the judgment, on the grounds that, under the Supremacy Clause in Article VII(2) of the Constitution, the federal Treaty overrode Virginia's law.[59] On remand, the Appellate Court explicitly argued that

57 For an history of the Convention, see Henry Adams (ed), 'The Hartford Convention', *History of the United States of America (1801–1817)*, vol 8 (Cambridge University Press 2011).

58 LaCroix (n 55) 23–24.

59 Fairfax's Devisee v. Hunter's Lessee, 11 U.S. (7 Cranch) 603, 628 (1813).

section 25 of the Judiciary Act (1789), granting to the Supreme Court the right to review State court decisions was unconstitutional and that the Supreme Court had no monopoly in interpreting the Constitution.[60] Thus, it had acted *ultra vires*. The Supreme Court intervened again in 1816 to claim its role of apex court within the US judiciary.[61] Yet, an example of judicial declaration of *ultra vires* action by State institutions had been experienced too.

It was in 1828, however, that the most dangerous crisis unfolded. Starting around 1820, Southern States experienced progressively growing disaffection with the Union. The Missouri controversy (1819–1820), with Northern States opposing the expansion of slavery in new States, had shown how different the two parts of the Union were becoming when it came to the 'peculiar institution' of slavery. Moreover, Southern economy needed free trade and low tariffs to competitively export cotton and other agricultural goods, while the industrial North favoured protectionist policies. While Southern discomfort grew, awareness regarding States' rights and the danger of having the Supreme Court as supreme arbiter in matters concerning the rights and powers of the States increased as well.[62] When in 1828 Congress, backed by President John Quincy Adams, imposed new tariffs, it was the final straw: political unrest spread throughout the entire South, but only South Carolina took the decisive step. South Carolina explained its opposition to the new federal tariff in the *Exposition and Protest Resolutions*.[63] The *Exposition* was the brainchild of Adams' Vice-President John C. Calhoun, fine constitutional theorist and by that time strenuous defender of Southern interests.[64] Calhoun asserted that States remained entirely sovereign within the Union, in principle even free to leave it, while federal institutions acted as mere States' agents. In the European jargon, he asserted that *kompetenz-kompetenz* belonged to States. These therefore had the right to step in and nullify federal law when it trespassed its powers.[65] In a famous address in Fort Hill (1831), Calhoun iterated the views expressed in the *Exposition* and made explicit reference to Madison's and Jefferson's ideas from the *Alien and Sedition* crisis, but this time publicly and anticipating the events of the following year.[66] Indeed, in 1832 a constitutional Convention was finally called

60 Hunter v. Martin, Devisee of Fairfax, 18 Va. (4 Munf.) 2, 3 (1815).

61 Martin v. Hunter's Lessee, 14 U.S. (1 Wheat.) 304 (1816). See the critical analysis by Boom (n 32) 186–193.

62 Donald J Ratcliffe, 'The Nullification Crisis, Southern Discontents, and the American Political Process' (2000) 1 American Nineteenth Century History 1, 1–8.

63 John C Calhoun, *Union and Liberty: The Political Philosophy of John C. Calhoun* (Ross M Lence ed, Liberty Fund 1992) 311–365.

64 Marco Luigi Bassani, 'Stati e Costituzione: Il Federalismo Autentico Di John C. Calhoun (1782–1850)' (2015) 1 Eunomia. Rivista di Studi su Pace e Diritti Umani 291.

65 In the *Exposition*, Calhoun defined the right of States to adjudicate on constitutional infringements as 'essential attribute of sovereignty – of which the States cannot be divested without losing their sovereignty itself'. See Calhoun (n 63) 348.

66 ibid 367–400. However, Madison was critical of Calhoun's interpretation of the principles of '98. See William K Bolt, 'Founding Father and Rebellious Son: James Madison, John C. Calhoun, and the Use of Precedents' (2004) 5 American Nineteenth Century History 1, 8–15.

in South Carolina and it adopted an *Ordinance of Nullification* which invalidated federal tariffs, threatening secession in case of the federal government used coercion.[67] The country was again on the brink of civil war, but the crisis deescalated once more. Adams had lost the presidency to Andrew Jackson in 1828, and the latter answered to the Convention by proclaiming the *Ordinance* illegal.[68] However, first in 1832 and then again in 1833 Congress also compromised on tariffs in a way that was acceptable for South Carolina. The South Carolina Convention repealed its own ordinance and the crisis ended for the time being. The *Exposition* and the *Ordinance* had exposed a quite extreme constitutional theory in which single States were the guardians of the constitution, had the power to nullify unconstitutional acts, and even enjoyed a right to secede. Much of these arguments would return into play decades later, when the Confederacy seceded, and the Civil War erupted.

This brief analysis of the antebellum USA shows how the story of American constitutionalism between the establishment of the new Republic and the Civil War was characterized by various clashes between States and the federal institutions. It was an era of competing claims to ultimate authority, in which different views of the constitutional compact were discussed, including Madison's and Jefferson's depiction of States as the guardians of the covenant and even Calhoun's theory that sovereignty remained in the hands of States. In the vocabulary of modern European scholars, it was a form of constitutional pluralism. Indeed, there was no doubt regarding the nature of States' constitutions, which for the most part predated the federal Constitution, encompassed autonomous catalogues of rights, and ensured the separation of powers.[69] States were seen as the original bastions of liberties which then inspired the Union's Constitution.[70] The fact that we would judge some of the justifications for States' constitutional claims as acceptable (e.g., opposition to political censorship in 1798) and others as unconceivable (the pro-slavery Convention of 1828) must not obscure the fact that at that time the controversies were as much constitutional as they were political.

It is also worth noting how, apart from *Martin v Hunter's Lessee*, all controversies involved political rather than judicial institutions. The absence of a legal answer to the question of ultimate authority forced them to look for political compromise as the only way to solve conflicts, in a manner that reminds of MacCormick's remarks on political composition of disagreements after the *Maastricht Urteil*. Even in the case of the Hartford Convention, where external events solved the crisis, it cannot

67 Paul L Ford (ed), 'South Carolina Ordinance of Nullification, 1832', *The Federalist: A Commentary on the Constitution of the United States* (Henry Holt and Co 1898) 690–691.

68 Paul L Ford (ed), 'Jackson's Nullification Proclamation, 1832', *The Federalist: A Commentary on the Constitution of the United States* (Henry Holt and Co 1898) 692–707.

69 Taylor (n 47) 299–303.

70 In the words of Thomas Jefferson, 'the true barriers of our liberty in this country are our State-governments'. Letter to Antoine-Louis-Claude Destutt de Tracy, French philosopher, commentator of Montesquieu, and friend of Jefferson. See Founders Online: Thomas Jefferson to Destutt de Tracy, 26 January 1811 http://founders.archives.gov/documents/Jefferson/03-03-02-0258.

be forgotten that what the Convention was primarily looking for negotiation in Washington. Political solutions endured and decisively solved the issues in some cases (the *Aliens and Sedition Acts*) but not in others (slavery and protectionism). The latter ultimately led to the Civil War and to a radical constitutional transformation of the country. Even so, the antebellum USA lasted for 'four score and seven years'[71] as a mostly functioning legal order, outliving many unitary constitutional regimes. The USA has existed as a union of States for decades before substantively changing.

Then the Civil War finally came. The redrafting of the US Constitution that followed resulted into the Reconstruction Amendments: the XIII Amendment was passed in 1865 to end slavery; the XIV in 1868 to establish federal citizenship, due process of law, and equal protection of the laws; the XV in 1869 to guarantee equal voting rights.[72] It is difficult to underestimate the impact of such clauses on the constitutional compact: the institution of a federal citizenship, the abolition of slavery and the pursuit of racial equality, the extension of electoral franchise, and the shift of powers in rights' regulation from States to Washington D.C., were all consequences of the Reconstruction Amendments.[73] The 'sovereign' was now the unitary American people, not the compound of State peoples; symmetrically, a constitutional compact between States became the constitution of a single State. It really was a 'second founding' for the USA, while the Madisonian view of popular sovereignty delegated to both the federation and the States faded away.[74]

From the Civil War onward, passing through the regulation of interstate commerce in the later 19th century and the New Deal, a plenary national power in the hands of the federal government emerged. Extensive interpretations of the Commerce clause of the US Constitution gave Congress the power to regulate affairs even remotely connected to interstate commerce. By incorporating the Bill of Rights into State law, the XIV Amendment conferred the power to enforce individual rights against States as well. Finally, a certain degree of fiscal centralization with the advent of the income tax in 1913, coupled with a generous interpretation of congressional spending powers, allowed Congress to influence State policies by conceding money conditioned on substantial regulatory requirements.[75]

Naturally, State constitutions are still perfectly at work but reaffirmations of the Madisonian conception of divided sovereignty after the Civil War have been

71 See Abraham Lincoln's Gettysburg address, now in Alin Fumurescu and Anna Marisa Schön, *Foundations of American Political Thought: Readings and Commentary* (Cambridge University Press 2021) 399–400.

72 Jack Fruchtman, *American Constitutional History: A Brief Introduction* (Blackwell 2016) 78–83.

73 Eric Foner, *The Second Founding: How the Civil War and Reconstruction Remade the Constitution* (Norton 2019) 22–29.

74 Stephen M Griffin, *American Constitutionalism: From Theory to Politics* (Princeton University Press 1996) 24: 'On this Madisonian understanding, sovereignty lies with the people, who then delegated power to the federal and state governments. The problem here is that Madison's carefully balanced theory did not survive the sectional stresses that led eventually to the Civil War'.

75 Mark Tushnet, *The Constitution of the United States of America* (Hart Publishing 2015) 159–179.

occasional. To name a few, when discussing the adoption of the XIV Amendment, in the immediate aftermath of the Civil War, the notion of 'sovereignty of the States' was still recalled in the 39th Congress.[76] More surprisingly, the Supreme Court has recalled such notions again several times in contemporary judgments. In 1995, in the *Term Limits* case, Justice Kennedy pointed out that the American conception of sovereignty has always been divided, while Justice Thomas remarked that sovereign consent lies in the peoples of the States.[77] Three years later, in *Alden v Maine*, the idea of American federalism as intrinsically founded on two political bodies (federal and State people), and therefore on two sovereign levels of government, was stated once again, moreover recalling the notion of 'compact' to refer to the Constitution.[78] Still in 2013, Chief Justice Roberts defined the position of States under the US Constitution as one of 'sovereign equality', in *Shelby County v Holder*.[79]

The postbellum USA has also experienced one last appearance of the doctrine of interposition. Specifically, in 1954 the overruling of the 'separate but equal' racial segregation rule in public schools in *Brown v. Board of Education*[80] provided a new moment of conflict. In 1956 a Resolution of Virginia challenged *Brown* by relying on its 1798 ancestor: the new Resolution pointed out that the federal powers were delegated, that States remained the masters of the constitutional compact, and that they retained the power to allege an *ultra vires* act. Several other Southern segregationist States passed ordinances of interposition or nullification to oppose *Brown*.[81] The postbellum constitutional environment was not particularly hospitable though: President Eisenhower sent federal troops to enforce *Brown*[82] and the Supreme Court affirmed its interpretive supremacy.[83] Southern States backed down and merely proposed a constitutional amendment introducing a new 'Court of the Union' overseeing the Supreme Court in umpiring federalism, a proposal which failed. More recently, the opposition of various liberal 'sanctuary cities' to the first attempts of the Trump administration to establish a crackdown on illegal immigration via a series of local ordinances and appeals to courts was compared to yet

76 Cong. Globe, 39th Cong., 1st Sess., Appendix, 133 (Feb. 26, 1866) now Kurt T Lash (ed), *The Reconstruction Amendments: The Essential Documents*, vol 2 (University of Chicago Press 2020) 102 Cong. Globe, 39th Cong., 1st Sess., 1083, 1087–95 (Feb. 28, 1866), ivi, 108.

77 U.S. Term Limits, Inc. v Thornton, 514 U.S. 779 (1995).

78 Alden v Maine, 527 U.S. 706 (1999).

79 Shelby County v Holder 570, US 529 (2013).

80 Brown v Board of Education, 347 U.S. 483 (1954).

81 Excerpts from the ordinances of Virginia, Georgia, South Carolina, Alabama, and Mississippi can be found in Miller and Howell (n 45) 38–42.

82 Karen Anderson, *Little Rock: Race and Resistance at Central High School* (Princeton University Press 2010) 2–4.

83 Cooper v Aaron, 358 U.S. 1 (1958): 'This decision declared the basic principle that the federal judiciary is supreme in the exposition of the law of the Constitution, and that principle has ever since been respected by this Court and the Country as a permanent and indispensable feature of our constitutional system'.

another instantiation of interposition.[84] What remains of nullification, instead, is little more than political rhetoric and propaganda.[85]

Scholars envisage in such reaffirmations of antebellum concepts a sort of persistency of American constitutional pluralism.[86] However, the much wider regulatory powers of federal government, coupled with the modest political results and resonance of the just mentioned reaffirmations, make of such claims little more than lip service to the antebellum ideas of Madisonian sovereignty, interposition, and nullification. Most importantly, none now seriously questions that the interpretation of the US Constitution, the guarding of the Supremacy Clause, and decisions on whether the federal government acted *ultra vires*, do not belong to the States. Madison's statement from the Report of 1800 that '[t]he States then being the parties to the constitutional compact, and in their sovereign capacity, it follows of necessity, that there can be no tribunal above their authority, to decide in the last resort, whether the compact made by them be violated' will hardly find supporters today.[87] If anything, the remainders of US pluralism can now be envisaged not in federalism, but in what is called in the American jargon 'departmentalism', namely the horizontal competition among federal institutions on the interpretation of the Constitution, a point on which I will return later in the chapter. By and large, the postbellum USA seems to have effectively moved from a union of States to a full-fledged federal State.

4.2.2 A View on the EU from America: A Union of States

Analysing the constitutional theory and practice of the antebellum USA cannot but ring bells for anyone interested in the European constitutional pluralism.

Before the Civil War, the question of ultimate authority was unsettled in America. Whether the birth of the Union had produced a new American people or left Virginians, New Yorkers, or Carolinians as the real principal, the 'master' of the covenant, was object of disagreement. What the *locus* of sovereignty was remained an equally open question, reinforced by the fact that Americans were committed to theory of popular, yet divided sovereignty formulated during the colonial era. Sovereignty was not expected to move from one ultimate institution swiftly and inevitably to another: it could be shared and situated in different bodies simultaneously.

Judges and especially legislatures involved in cases of interposition and nullification extrapolated from this theory the idea that the constitutional compact was to be safeguarded by its signatories, the States. They had a duty to patrol the terms of

84 Lorraine Marie A Simonis, 'Sanctuary Cities: A Study in Modern Nullification?' (2019) 8 British Journal of American Legal Studies 37.

85 Sanford Levinson, 'The Twenty-First Century Rediscovery of Nullification and Secession in American Political Rhetoric: Frivolousness Incarnate or Serious Arguments to Be Wrestled With?' (2014) 67 Arkansas Law Review 17, 17–49.

86 Schütze, 'Federalism as Constitutional Pluralism' (n 33) 201–209.

87 Madison (n 43) 251.

the contract and interpose when necessary to declare the act by the federal government *ultra vires*. The Supreme Court was not perceived as an impartial arbiter, but as a partisan institution, well suited to adjudicate over conflicts within the branches of the federal government, yet hardly trustable when it came to the relations with States.

The antebellum USA thus turns out to be quite close to the current EU in more than one regard. Indeed, when considering the discussion on the *locus* of ultimate authority in America, it is hard not to think about the paragraphs of the *Maastricht Urteil* on the absence of a European people and on the EU as a mere 'compound of States'. The fundamental disagreement between the understanding of the EU as a compound of States in *Maastricht* and the competing view that it is a legal order of a new kind, visible in cases like the Opinion 2/13, mirrors the American debates on the nature of their Union. Equally similar is the debate whether sovereign powers have been conferred to the Union or whether sovereign States ultimately retain them and merely delegated their exercise. Finally, the idea that State institutions are the guardians of the compact and may step in and declare federal acts *ultra vires* is common to the two. A thorough examination of the cases of *ultra vires* in the EU will be object of the next chapter, but we can anticipate that they follow a similar logic: in extreme circumstances of 'deliberate, palpable, and dangerous' infractions of the compact, State institutions identify and expose the violation. Truly, this function of control of the covenant is performed judicially in the EU, while it was mostly the domain of legislatures or conventions in the antebellum USA. Yet, this distinction between a juridical European constitutionalism and a more political American one does not alter the fundamentally similar dynamic. This results in both cases in a form of interpretive competition between the States and the supreme judicial body of the Union, be it the Supreme Court or the Court of Justice, and in a certain distrust of the former towards the allegedly partisan latter.

On a more general level, a comparison with the antebellum USA is useful to shed light on the legal nature of the EU: the latter, exactly as the former, is a union of States.

The EU and the antebellum USA were born out of an agreement between independent States to pursue common aims. This agreement was built with the perspective of being permanent and its nature was soon object of a conceptual metamorphosis: from a mere treaty between States, it became a constitutional compact. The newly constituted Union established in both cases a relation of direct governance with the polity, be it through bills by the American Congress or via directly effective EU provisions.

A citizenship of the Union was established, with a set of rights and duties emanating from it and institutions of the unions tasked with governing them. In Europe, the institution of the EU citizenship did not displace national citizenship, but rather was attached as an additional legal status to the latter.[88] Until the Civil War and the

88 Robert Schütze, 'Demoicracy in Europe: Some Preliminary Thoughts' (2022) 47 European Law Review 24, 31–32.

Reconstruction Amendments, in the USA too there was no paramount American citizenship supplanting that of States either.[89]

A system of dual representation, mirroring the dual polity at the basis of the union, was established in both EU and the USA, decoupling the representation of the States within the Union from that of the citizens of the Union as a whole. Truly, the body representing the American people as a whole, the House of Representatives, has always lived on a position of equality with the Senate representing States, something that is not true of the European Parliament when compared with the more powerful Council of the EU.[90] Yet, the principle of dual representation was accepted in both.

Finally, the birth of a union of States fostered a twofold constitutional transformation. On the one hand, it generated a new federal constitution and a parallel federal constitutionalism. In both the EU and antebellum USA, this gave shape to a new legal architecture which separated powers and guaranteed rights at the level of the union and was directly or indirectly legitimized by the two constituencies simultaneously (the peoples of States singularly considered and their sum of in the entire union).[91] On the other hand, State constitutions were transformed as the belonging to the new wider polity became a foundational principle. In antebellum USA, this required large 'nationalization' of powers, acceptance of a republican form of government as a requirement for participation in the Union, the supremacy of federal law, and the Supreme Court's role of umpire, to name a few. Similarly, EU States adapted to the new broader legal order via formal and informal clauses,[92] but also by accepting its primacy and direct effect, by involving their parliaments in a process of legislative dialogue as envisaged by the Protocol on subsidiarity and proportionality, by treating EU citizens as different from mere aliens, and recently even by internalizing some EU provisions as parameters of constitutional review (as in the case of the Austrian, Italian, and German constitutional courts mentioned in the Introduction).

Surely, the constitutional transformation fostered by the American Constitution of 1787 still was more profound than that occurred in Europe over the last decades. To name at least two crucial points, although reforms adopted in 2020 to face the COVID-19 crisis conferred the power to emit EU bonds to collect resources,[93] the EU never enjoyed proper taxation power, an area typically regulated by modern

89 The Supreme Court discussed *ex cathedra* the institution of a new American citizenship by the XIV Amendment in 1872, in the Slaughterhouse Cases. See 83 U.S. 16 Wall. 36 36 (1872).

90 Scholars indeed distinguish between the American 'senate model' and the European 'second chamber governance'. See Hueglin and Fenna (n 11) 205–214 and 225–230.

91 Robert Schütze, 'Constitutionalism and the European Union' in Catherine Barnard and Steve Peers (eds), *European Union Law* (Oxford University Press 2020) 82–99.

92 Monica Claes, 'Constitutionalizing Europe at Its Source: The "European Clauses" in the National Constitutions: Evolution and Typology' (2005) 24 Yearbook of European Law 81.

93 Bruno de Witte, 'The European Union's Covid-19 Recovery Plan: The Legal Engineering of an Economic Policy Shift' (2021) 58 Common Market Law Review 635.

constitutions;[94] nor it has the power to raise an army to ensure collective security, although cooperation on defence is likely to increase after the Russo-Ukrainian war started in 2022. The American Union had such powers since the beginning.

However, this only seems to point towards an internal differentiation between deeper and looser unions of States. A union will be deeper if the transfers of sovereignty are more pronounced. Constitutional pluralism endures and competing claims to ultimate guardianship of the constitutional compact are made, as they were in antebellum USA and are in the EU. Yet sovereignty, split between States and the union, is more pronouncedly assigned to the latter than in looser unions. Differentiating between forms of unions of States is probably more realistic than sticking to the dichotomy between States under constitutional law and international organizations under international law and then inevitably attaching to the EU either the label of 'State', which is clearly inappropriate, or that of international organization, which is hardly suitable as well. No international organization has engendered similar constitutional transformations on its Member States as the EU did; most importantly, not all of them combined.[95]

Conceptualizing the EU as a union of States also downplays the importance of the '*sui generis*' narrative. The difficulty to encapsulate the EU into the rigid confederation-federation dichotomy fostered intellectual puzzlement and disorientation, a sense of being in front of a 'conceptual enigma' or of a 'new kind of federal model the like of which has never before been seen'.[96] The development of the indefinite notion of a *sui generis* organization was a reaction to puzzlement: *sui generis* is a 'something else' category, a concept that does not define what the EU is, but what it is not.[97] Perhaps unsurprisingly, it is a notion contested both by those who assimilate the EU to an international organization and by those who see it as a form of federalism.[98] Understanding the EU as a union of States does not entail denying its rather unusual status, the mixture of international and State characteristics that it exposes,[99] but to realize that its features are unusual yet not unique. The EU is not an unprecedented legal experiment but an instantiation of a particular kind of political organization. Similarly, its pluralism is not a constitutional monstrosity.

94 Peter Lindseth, 'The Metabolic Constitution and the Limits of EU Legal Pluralism' in Gareth Davies and Matej Avbelj (eds), *Research Handbook on Legal Pluralism and EU Law* (Edward Elgar Publishing 2018); Cristina Fasone and Peter Lindseth, 'Europe's Fractured Metabolic Constitution: From the Eurozone Crisis to the Coronavirus Response' (2020) LUISS School of Government Working Paper N 61.

95 A point that even sceptics of the constitutional nature of the EU recognize. See Bruno de Witte, 'The European Union as an International Legal Experiment' in Grainne de Burca and JHH Weiler (eds), *The Worlds of European Constitutionalism* (Cambridge University Press 2011) 50.

96 Burgess (n 8) 226.

97 E.g. see, William Phelan, 'What Is Sui Generis About the European Union? Costly International Cooperation in a Self-Contained Regime' (2012) 14 International Studies Review 367.

98 An instance of the former contestation is contained in de Witte (n 95). For the latter, see Hueglin and Fenna (n 11) 117–121, who talk about 'treaty federalism'.

99 E.g., see the analysis of the mixed structure of the EU after Lisbon by Roger Goebel, 'Supranational? Federal? Intergovernmental? The Governmental Structure of the European Union After the Treaty of Lisbon' (2013) 20 Columbia Journal of European Law 77.

The coexistence of plural sites of constitutional authority seems de facto possible in unions of States. Following Schütze, federalism is a form of constitutional pluralism: 'the theory of constitutional pluralism speaks federal prose'.[100] This coexistence generated a constitutional environment in which conflicts between institutions claiming guardianship on the covenant were possible. Overall, the degree of conflict has not been so profound to cause the breakdown of the legal order, to compromise the ability of law to work as a well-functioning social order. The Civil War did eventually shake the foundations of the antebellum USA, fostering its transformation into a full-fledged federal State. Yet, this resulted out of one of the various constitutional conflicts which happened in those decades. Others had been eventually settled otherwise, without changing the fundamental nature of the Union. Whether consolidation into a federal State will eventually be the destiny of the EU as well we do not know, transformation out of deep constitutional conflicts does not seem a logical necessity.

What seems essential is a minimum will to keep the polity together under the same political (and legal) organization. In early America, the materials I have examined point towards a mixture of 'republicanism', meant as the ideology of popular mandate as the only legitimate source of authority (popular sovereignty), and of classic liberalism, meant as distrust towards power and willingness to limit it by dividing it both horizontally and vertically (divided sovereignty). This mixture was the basic of American constitutional ideology.[101] In the EU, the search for a common political ideology is harder, since the Union is made of relatively stable and continuous democracies, such as the Scandinavian countries; post-WWII regimes born out of transformative constitutions repudiating the authoritarian past as Germany or Italy; and Eastern European States committed to national renewal after the fall of the Berlin Wall. However, by looking at revealing clauses like Articles 2 and 7 of the Treaty on the European Union (TEU), which expose vocally the alleged values of the Union, one can grasp a common ideology at the basis of the EU too. That would be a form of liberal democracy, meant as a combination of representative democracy, modern liberalism (including some degree of welfare-state rights), rule of law, and market-based economy.[102]

Such broad ideological commitments may of course turn out to be very much indeterminate. For instance, one can disentangle several forms of liberal constitutionalism(s), quite different one another.[103] Thus, the meaning of the very basic values to agree upon to keep the union together can be hardly determinable. However, as long as disagreement remains within a relatively large area of tolerance and does not become systemic, the legal order will survive, as we will also see in the

100 Schütze, 'Federalism as Constitutional Pluralism' (n 33) 211.

101 See the epitome of these tenets of American constitutionalism in the Federalist Papers n. 39 and n. 51, in Hamilton, Madison and Jay (n 41) 79–84 and 119–122.

102 Larsen (n 15) 121–135.

103 Mark Tushnet, 'Varieties of Liberal Constitutionalism' in Xenophon Contiades and Alkmene Fotiadou (eds), *Routledge Handbook of Comparative Constitutional Change* (Routledge 2020).

next chapter considering cases of *ultra vires* in the EU. In a sense, the indeterminacy of these political and legal principles, the fact that one needs a sort of Rawlsian overlapping consensus at a high level of generality and can then to a certain extent disagree on the implementation, can even be helpful to ensure the survival of the union.[104]

What follows is a conclusion regarding the nature of organizations such as the EU and the antebellum USA. They are not federal States or confederations, nor they belong to mingled categories like 'confederal federalism' whose oxymoronic name reveals the difficulty to conceptualize organizations like the EU within the strict dichotomy *Bundesstaat-Staatenbund*.[105] They are unions of States: grounded on a voluntary and permanent constitutional compact, which generates a system of dual representation, a dual polity, and a twofold constitutional transformation. Constitutional pluralism and the degree of conflicts it entails are structural elements of such legal orders.

4.3 Constitutional Pluralism Within the State: *Harris v. Dönges* and Beyond

The argument developed in this chapter has underlined the unavoidability of a certain degree of constitutional pluralism in composite legal orders. A plurality of claims to constitutional authority are made simultaneously in the specific form of political organization that was labelled 'union of States'. Historical experiences like the antebellum USA or contemporary EU instantiate such forms of union, in which pluralism and the consequent constitutional conflicts are structural.

In the remainder of the chapter, I will push this argument one step forth and argue that constitutional pluralism is a structural feature not only of complex legal orders like unions of States, but to a certain degree of States too. I argue that the idea of States in which the question of ultimate constitutional authority has been settled once and for all by establishing a universally accepted foundational norm is unrealistic.

A clarification is immediately needed: I am not affirming that there is no difference between unitary States and unions of States in terms of constitutional pluralism. The degree of pluralism of the former is lower, even much lower. If one's goal is primarily to reduce legal uncertainty and the risk of conflicts, instead of keeping together an inhomogeneous community via a looser legal order, then opting for a more centralized legal order like a unitary State is surely the most advisable option. Still, it is important to realize that pluralism and the associated uncertainty cannot be entirely avoided, not matter how centralized is the legal order under examination.

104 John Rawls, *Political Liberalism* (Columbia University Press 1993) 133–173.
105 John Kincaid, 'Confederal Federalism and Citizen Representation in the European Union' (1999) 22 West European Politics 34.

To show why, I will first explain how the argument on pluralism in unitary States works in theory and then move to the evidence that comparative law provides us.

The theoretical explanation will be based on a series of observations that can be found in H.L.A. Hart's depiction of the rule of recognition and of the cases of 'uncertainty' and disagreement about it. As mentioned at the end of the last chapter, Hart's theory strongly inspired MacCormick's foundational works on radical pluralism (which, in turn, inspired much of this book). MacCormick did not rely on the sections of his mentor's writings I have in mind when he exposed his views on pluralism in the early 1990s, but it is my view worth doing so.

As for the comparative analysis, I rely on a body of literature that focuses on cases of deep constitutional transformation via reinterpretation of the foundational norm. Interpretive competition and disagreement on the latter within States multiply the rules of recognition and generate pluralism out of unity. These cases are explainable in the light of Hart's remarks on disagreement on the rule of recognition and tell us much about the de facto unavoidability of a certain degree of constitutional pluralism, no matter how rigidly the foundational norm is formulated.

I will start from the analysis of Hart's remarks in *The Concept of Law* before moving to cases drawn from comparative law.

4.3.1 **Harris v. Dönges*: Uncertainty on the Rule of Recognition***

As quickly discussed in Chapter 3, Hart famously introduced the notion of rule of recognition as the second order rule that allows solving problems of uncertainty about the law: it dictates whether a norm is 'law' within a certain jurisdiction. Having in mind the British tradition of parliamentary sovereignty, Hart pictures a legal system in which, in cases of doubts, we may ultimately rely on the supreme criterion 'what the Queen in Parliament enacts is law'. At the end of chapter VI of *The Concept of Law*, entirely devoted to the rule of recognition, Hart moves from the ordinary functioning of his theoretical legal order, in which the Queen in Parliament's will is respected, to discussing cases in which this does not happen. In 'pathological' cases, we learn, disagreement about the rule of recognition itself may rise.[106]

The first cases he has in mind are those of sudden and pathological alteration of the ordinary functioning of law, true 'breakdowns' caused by dramatic events such as revolutions, enemy occupation, or widespread anarchy. Another case he considers is that of a legal system, a colony of Commonwealth in his example, seceding from a wider one, either peacefully or violently. Although these cases of extreme and even violent breakdown explain the establishment of a new constitution in same circumstances,[107] they are not particularly helpful in explaining constitutional pluralism, which consists in disagreements about the ultimate authority within a legal order, not in its sudden overthrow.

106 Herbert LA Hart, *The Concept of Law* (Oxford University Press 2012) 117–123.
107 Hèctor López Bofill, *Law, Violence and Constituent Power* (Routledge 2021).

However, Hart also considers intermediate cases that are more interesting for us. What he has in mind are constitutional controversies that may arise and divide officials, so that 'unity among officials, the existence of which is normally presupposed when internal statements of law are made within the system, may partly break down'.[108] An example is given considering the South African case *Harris v. Dönges*, from the early 1950s. The case regarded the Nationalist government's attempts to disenfranchise coloured voters in the Cape Province, in one of the first steps towards consolidating apartheid. Provisions on enfranchisement in South Africa were entrenched by Section 35 of the South Africa Act, a bill passed in 1909 by the British Parliament which worked as a constitution of South Africa. It provided that only a supermajority could amend them. However, in 1931 another parliamentary bill, the Statute of Westminster, ended British rule over previous dominions like South Africa. According to the government, the supermajority requirement of the 1909 South Africa Act had been repealed by implication in the Statute of Westminster, while the Appellate Division of the South African Supreme Court, called to adjudicate on the matter, considered the supermajority as still valid. The government reacted by constituting a High Court of Parliament, with the power to overrule the Appellate Division, which in turn struck the new bill down. A few years later, the disenfranchise would be eventually implemented, but in the immediate aftermath of the judgments, the government was forced by political circumstances to back down for the time being.[109]

The reason why Hart was interested in *Harris v. Dönges* is that it shows a case in which the judiciary and the other branches disagreed on the extent of the Parliament's power: according to the former, the assembly had no power to alter the entrenched South African Act; according to the latter, it had. The disagreement regarded the *interpretation* and scope of the Statute of Westminster's repeal. A system in which the supreme authority of the British Parliament was undisputed, still allowed for disagreement among South African officials. The unity and clarity of the 'what the Queen in Parliament enacts is law' criterion was not enough to solve every conflict.

Hart also reminds us that this was not the end of South African law, nor the breakdown of law and order. The population remained united under the law, while officials themselves continued recognizing and applying a wide variety of norms: 'the great mass of legal operations not touching on this constitutional issue would go on as before'.[110]

By recalling *Harris v. Dönges*, Hart is stating that the rule of recognition, like any other norm, has an undisputable 'core', whose meaning is clear, and a more uncertain 'penumbra'. Chapter VII of *The Concept* is even more resolutely devoted to the problem of interpretation of norms and, at the very end, the penumbra of

108 Hart (n 106) 122.

109 The constitutional crisis is analysed in detail by Ian Loveland, *By Due Process of Law?: Racial Discrimination and the Right to Vote in South Africa 1855–1960* (Hart Publishing 1999).

110 Hart (n 106) 122.

the rule of recognition is discussed again and presented as an inevitable feature of law.[111] Especially after Dworkin's critique of Hart and his portrayal of the judge as an almost 'protestant' figure looking for the best possible interpretation of the (legal) scriptures, the problem of interpretation has been a major issue in contemporary jurisprudence.[112] It has been convincingly argued that the study of how officials, practitioners, scholars, and even citizens interpret the law (the interpretive methods) should be part of our effort to understand the foundations of law.[113] Inquiries into the specific methods used in constitutional interpretation have a tradition of their own.[114]

Hart's idea that the indeterminacy of norms concerns even straightforward foundational norms like 'what the Queen in Parliament enacts is law' has consequences that go even beyond cases like *Harris v. Dönges*. In *Harris*, different institutions disagreed on how to interpret the foundational norm. However, one can figure interpretive problems like those stressed by Hart even if there only is *one* institution involved, as Larry Alexander and Frederick Schauer show considering the American case.[115] Coming from a legal culture with a codified constitution and more prone to accept judicial supremacy, they imagine as the sovereign institution a 'Supreme Court in good faith' busy at interpreting the 1787 Constitution, rather than a 'Queen in Parliament'. Yet, they realize that the plurality of possible interpretive methods of the US Constitution, from originalism to strict textualism to living constitutionalism, means that different justices on the bench will not only look at the same text differently, but even adopt different materials of support in performing their task (e.g., diaries of the founding fathers, an English dictionary, works in contemporary moral philosophy).[116] Thus, 'in a very real sense, each official is interpreting a different constitution'.[117] The result is a certain pluralism of views in looking at the constitution even if there is only one body in charge of adjudicating on it.

One may imagine resorting to rules of settlement between various interpretive methods to solve the problem, but these expose the same difficulties. Disagreements

111 ibid 147–154. In the *Postscript* to *The Concept of Law*, Hart reiterates the claim that the rule of recognition itself can have an area of debatable penumbra and, more radically, that a certain degree of uncertainty may be desirable. See ibid 251–252.

112 Ronald Dworkin, 'The Model of Rules II', *Taking Rights Seriously* (Harvard University Press 1978); Ronald Dworkin, *Law's Empire* (Harvard University Press 1986). On Dworkin's 'protestant' attitude, see Postema's subtle remarks in Gerald J Postema, '"Protestant" Interpretation and Social Practices' (1987) 6 Law and Philosophy 283.

113 Scott J Shapiro, 'The "Hart–Dworkin" Debate: A Short Guide for the Perplexed' in Arthur Ripstein (ed), *Ronald Dworkin* (Cambridge University Press 2007).

114 E.g., see Jeffrey Goldsworthy, 'Constitutional Interpretation' in Michel Rosenfeld and András Sajó (eds), *The Oxford Handbook of Comparative Constitutional Law* (Oxford University Press 2012).

115 Larry Alexander and Frederick Schauer, 'Rules of Recognition, Constitutional Controversies, and the Dizzying Dependence of Law on Acceptance' in Matthew Adler and Kenneth Himma (eds), *The Rule of Recognition and the U.S. Constitution* (Oxford University Press 2009).

116 ibid 180–184.

117 ibid 181–182.

may be solved, for instance, by accepting as final what the *majority* of the sovereign institution decides (our foundational norm would then become 'what the majority of the Supreme Court in good faith decides is law'). Yet, then we would face questions like 'what is a majority of judges?', 'what to do when a judge is sick or retiring?', 'how to establish that judges are interpreting the constitution in good faith?', and so on. We would then need another layer of settlement rules, which would then be exposed to indeterminacy themselves, and so on in a *regressus ad infinitum*. Adding second or third level rules of settlement may reduce the degree of constitutional pluralism, but never fully solve it, for *every* rule is open-textured and partially undetermined in Hart's account. It is indeed turtles all the way down.[118]

4.3.2 Interpretive Pluralism in Practice

The first part of this paragraph exposed theoretical reasons explaining pluralism at the level of States too. In this second part, I argue that comparative law scholarship exhibits cases that seem to confirm the theoretical intuition of Hart and of epigones like Schauer and Alexander. Even in legal orders with a single, Queen in Parliament style foundational norm, de facto a variety of actors, well beyond constitutional courts, engage in constitutional interpretation, at times proposing radically diverging views of the foundations of the system: councils of State, parliamentary committees, heads of States, ombuds offices, legal academia, and even the public opinion participate in the process.[119] This plurality of interpretations can be analysed in the same terms that Hart used to assess *Harris v. Dönges* and amount to a form of constitutional pluralism, inevitably followed by the risk of disagreement and conflict.

Briefly looking at some of the most interesting examples considered by recent scholarship, the USA are once again an interesting case to consider. This time the horizontal rather than the vertical separation of powers in the American context needs to be considered.

Halberstam has made the case for a new form of constitutional pluralism in the postbellum USA by looking at the relations between branches of government at the federal level.[120] Remember that, after the Civil War, the USA had resolved many of its original constitutional dilemmas: creating a federal citizenship, incorporating federal rights into State law, placing constitutional supremacy firmly in the hands of the Union. In time, it moved away from being what we have defined a union of States into a full-fledged federal State. However, disagreements on the final interpreter of the Constitution re-emerged because of the persistence of a

118 ibid 192.

119 E.g., see the analysis of European systems by Maartje de Visser, *Constitutional Review in Europe: A Comparative Analysis* (Hart Publishing 2014) 11–51.

120 Daniel Halberstam, 'Constitutional Heterarchy: The Centrality of Conflict in the European Union and the United States' in Jeffrey L Dunoff and Joel P Trachtman (eds), *Ruling the World?: Constitutionalism, International Law, and Global Governance* (Cambridge University Press 2009).

doctrine known in the American jargon as 'departmentalism', namely the view that each branch has the right and indeed the duty to interpret the Constitution autonomously when a question comes before it.[121] During the course of time and well after the second foundation of the Reconstruction Amendments, the political branches have occasionally stepped in to vindicate their interpretation of the Constitution even against the Supreme Court's view:[122]

> From Andrew Jackson's constitutionally based veto of the Bank Bill and Lincoln's emancipation address to Franklin D. Roosevelt's court-packing plan and George W. Bush's frequent signing statements, presidents have asserted a right – indeed, an obligation – of independent executive branch constitutional interpretation. Congress, too, has asserted its own understanding of the Constitution, whether in supporting the president's political initiatives, as in Jefferson's and FDR's attacks on the judiciary, or in historical or contemporary efforts to strip the judiciary of jurisdiction, or by pushing for its vision of the constitutional right to equality.

Interpretive competition between the judiciary and the political branches has never fully ceased to exist in the USA, both ante and post bellum.[123] The body of literature emphasizing the role of 'popular constitutionalism' in the history of American law underlines how this tendency originated back in the founding era and stresses the active role of the people themselves in influencing constitutional interpretation.[124] The meaning of the Constitution is de facto determined in many cases by the interaction between political branches, from presidents and Congress to conventions and non-governmental organizations.[125] Traces of popular constitutionalism can be found well into the New Deal era.[126] To a certain extent, the judiciary still today adapts to the popular will in its judgments.[127]

What results is a form of constitutional pluralism within the federal government. If after the Civil War it was clear that the American postbellum equivalent of 'what the Queen in Parliament enacts is law' was 'what the Constitution as interpreted by federal institutions States is law', who should have the last word on its interpretation remained way less clear: even once the foundational norm is settled in favour of clear supremacy of the federal Constitution over States and when a specific body is identified as its interpreter, the Supreme Court, the limits and the meaning of this mandate can be questioned and disagreed upon. Yet, it is important to notice,

121 Tushnet (n 75) 134–137.

122 Halberstam, 'Constitutional Heterarchy' (n 120) 335.

123 See also Halberstam, 'Pluralism in Marbury and Van Gend' (n 34) 61–65.

124 Larry D Kramer, 'Popular Constitutionalism, circa 2004' (2004) 92 California Law Review 959; Larry D Kramer, *The People Themselves: Popular Constitutionalism and Judicial Review* (Oxford University Press 2006) 207–226.

125 Griffin (n 74) 42–46.

126 Kramer, *The People Themselves* (n 124) 219–226.

127 Kramer, 'Popular Constitutionalism, circa 2004' (n 124) 967–975.

as Halberstam does, that when conflicts arise, in most of the cases what happens is pragmatic political accommodation between the involved branches and that, by and large, this sort of pluralism does not prevent the USA from being a widely effective legal order, exactly as European constitutional pluralism does not paralyze EU law:[128]

> The United States and the European Union are both functioning legal systems. Neither the lack of settlement regarding the hierarchy of legal systems in Europe nor the lack of settlement regarding the hierarchy of institutions in the United States leads to anarchy or chaos. Instead, each system is a system of order.

Constitutional conflict is structural in contemporary legal orders and political compromise of the kind underlined in MacCormick's essays on radical pluralism is the ordinary manner to solve it. This generally does not compromise the ability of the legal order to work.

Other cases in which States, even unitary States, experience some form of constitutional pluralism can be found beyond the American borders as well.

In the Netherlands, Article 120 of the *Grondwet*, the national Constitution, explicitly prohibits judicial review of legislation. Interpretation and application of the Constitution is largely performed by the political branches through various mechanisms, including checks by governmental bodies, the Council of State's opinions, and parliamentary debate.[129] However, when it comes to international relations, the monist Dutch legal system commands judicial disapplication of domestic law if conflicting with directly applicable international treaties. These include the European Convention on Human Rights (ECHR) and the Charter of Fundamental Rights of the EU. Although these are not part of the *Grondwet*, they significantly overlap in content with the national constitutional catalogue of rights: Dutch judges are therefore under a duty to interpret and apply standards of review which instantiate the liberal prong of modern constitutionalism as much as the political branches do with the *Grondwet*. This creates a parallel system of judicial review of legislation that is constitutional in substance although not in form, and influential enough to often bring about deep reforms of the Dutch legal system.[130] This does not exactly coincide with the postbellum USA as described by Halberstam, since the ECHR and the Charter remain different from the *Grondwet* and frequently involve external institutions, the European Court of Human Rights and the Court of Justice of the EU, as interpreters of last resort. Still, it creates the conditions for de facto constitutional pluralism in a unitary State.

128 Halberstam, 'Constitutional Heterarchy' (n 120) 336.

129 Maartje de Visser, 'Nonjudicial Constitutional Interpretation: The Netherlands' in David S Law (ed), *Constitutionalism in Context* (Cambridge University Press 2022) 226–234.

130 See Elaine Mak, 'Report on the Netherlands and Luxembourg' in Giuseppe Martinico and Oreste Pollicino (eds), *The National Judicial Treatment of the ECHR and EU Laws: A Comparative Constitutional Perspective* (Europa Law Publishing 2010).

In Israel, disagreement regarding the legal status of the Basic Laws lasted for decades. The first Knesset elected in 1948 with the mandate of constituent assembly did not perform its task of drafting a constitution because of disagreement between parties. Compromise was then reached according to which the constitution-making process would evolve gradually via a series of Basic Laws to be eventually fused into a single constitution in the future. This continuous process of constitution-building engendered serious legal disagreements regarding the powers of the Knesset (a mere legislative assembly or a twofold body with constituent power as well) and regarding the rank of the Basic Laws (merely equal to legislation or superior to it), disagreements which lasted for decades. This also entailed a fundamental ambiguity regarding Israel's form of government and whether it was similar to the Westminster model of legislative sovereignty or destined to evolve into an US-inspired system of constitutional supremacy. Eventually, the Supreme Court opted for the latter with the pivotal *Mizrahi Bank* judgment of 1995, declaring that the Knesset had 'two crowns', one legislative the other constituent, and that the Basic Laws enacted while holding the latter crown were superior to ordinary legislation and judicially enforceable in front of the Court. It was a sort of constitutional revolution, a radical reorientation of the substantive content of the constitution performed interpretively. Constitutional unrest has never fully ceased even after *Mizrahi Bank*: contestation of the legality of constitutional review and proposals to reseize the Supreme Court's powers keep happening.[131]

Even in the UK, the birthplace of the 'Queen in Parliament', the interpretation of the fundamental norm turns out not to be straightforward. Penumbra recently showed up in the *Miller II* case, concerning the Queen's power, on advice of the prime minster, to prorogue Parliament.[132] Disagreement arose between the executive and the Supreme Court of the UK regarding the limits on the former's power to determine the period of prorogation. The status of the underlying rule assigning this power to the executive, whether it was a judicially enforceable legal standard or an unenforceable political convention, was object of disagreement between the courts and the executive. Perhaps what the Queen in Parliament enacts is law, but what procedures apply so that it can enact, including the prorogation period, is controversial. Equally debatable was who held the authority to determine the ordinary prorogation period: while the Supreme Court avowed the justiciability of the prorogation, the executive reacted, drafting legislation to curtail such power and assert its interpretation.[133] The result was the Dissolution and Calling of Parliament Act of March 2022, containing an ouster clause to prevent the judicial review of prerogative powers. In *Miller II*, the penumbra and the

131 Yaniv Roznai and Gary J Jacobsohn, *Constitutional Revolution* (Yale University Press 2020) 183–223.

132 Mark Elliott, 'Constitutional Adjudication and Constitutional Politics in the United Kingdom: The Miller II Case in Legal and Political Context' (2020) 16 European Constitutional Law Review 625.

133 ibid 643–646.

consequent plurality of interpretations proves to affect even perfectly straightforward foundational norms.[134]

4.4 The Grammar of Legality

We may now draw a series of conclusions from the analysis drawn in this chapter. This book is devoted to radical pluralism in Europe. Chapter 3 ended by enlisting four takeaways from MacCormick's radical phase to be developed: a descriptive stance, scepticism towards the idea of sovereignty, the view that the foundational norm is complex and its conflictual character. The aim of this chapter was to provide support to this characterization of European pluralism drawing from comparative literature. Indeed what emerges from the literature in my view fits MacCormick's intuitions.

Cases like the antebellum USA show the intricate criteria of recognition used by officials and to a certain extent even citizens in America. The uncertainty on who was the guardian of the constitutional compact in the USA resembles the uncomfortable bifurcation in the chain of validity in Europe described in Chapter 2. Disagreement on the foundational norm in America regarded the core of modern constitutionalism, namely guarantee of rights and separation of powers. For instance, the discussion in the case of the Virginia and Kentucky's ordinances did not concern who was entitled to a certain legislative power, but rather that the exercise of this power by the federal government violated the constitutional rights of citizens and stripped States of their role of rights' guardians. As in Halberstam's notion of federalism, this manifested the coexistence of autonomous sites of constitutional authority within the same polity and a form of divided and spread conception of sovereignty. MacCormick, like Hart before him, guessed that the plural and complex European rule of recognition was probably close to the experience of federations. The case of the antebellum USA seems to confirm this intuition.

The antebellum USA also shows that constitutional pluralism in unions of States at times engenders conflict, another feature that MacCormick envisaged. Indeed, the case of *ultra vires* America is an instantiation of that. Yet, in various cases they were solved through political bargain and negotiation, once it was clear that the disagreement was legally unsolvable because of the different rules of recognition held by participants. The Union survived for decades before collapsing and being rebounded by the Reconstruction Amendments.

MacCormick did not push his argument so far to imagine forms of pluralism even at the level of States, but something along this line was envisaged in Hart. Moving the argument one step forth, I relied on Hart's characterization of interpretive disagreement in cases like *Harris v. Dönges* to argue that interpretive pluralism is yet another form of constitutional pluralism that characterizes even legal orders, like unitary States,

134 Further analysis of the penumbra of UK's rule of recognition can be found in Adam Tucker, 'Uncertainty in the Rule of Recognition and in the Doctrine of Parliamentary Sovereignty' (2011) 31 Oxford Journal of Legal Studies 61.

in which a straightforward Queen-in-Parliament rule of recognition exists. Mere agreement on what counts as a legal institution and on the ordering of institutions in a hierarchy with a lonely Queen in Parliament on top is not enough to avoid pluralism. Different methods of interpretation, motivated by *lato sensu* political considerations, entail partially different rules of recognition.[135] Hart's depiction of *Harris v. Dönges* as a phenomenon deriving from the inevitable penumbra of norms, is confirmed by cases of interpretive pluralism identified by comparative constitutional lawyers. The quickly examined cases of the postbellum USA, the Netherlands, Israel, and the UK, all expose constitutional pluralism in the form of interpretive pluralism. Again, by looking at the actual functioning of legal orders, we find that pluralism and conflict are structural yet often not deadly.

What we are left with on a more general level is the idea that the foundations of legal orders, coinciding with the constitution in several modern States, is not a single and straightforward rule. Rather it is close to what we may call the 'grammar' of legality. Here I use 'grammar' in the Wittgensteinian sense of a series of criteria used by participants in a practice to distinguish between appropriate and inappropriate uses of a concept.[136] If someone wanted to talk about, say, the 'height' of 'truth' we would say that she is confused or mistaken: the 'grammar' of the concept of 'height' tells us that it is predicated of physical objects such as trees or buildings, but not of abstract concepts such as 'truth' (unless one is thinking about metaphorical and therefore secondary uses of 'height'). The grammar of 'truth', as that of any other concept, is established through the practice by the community of speakers.[137]

The rule of recognition results from the socially established criteria for the application of the concept of 'legality'. We will say that a specific norm is 'legal' or 'legally valid' if it was enacted by the specifically empowered authority, extrapolated through interpretation according to appropriate interpretive methods, and respecting the hierarchical order between the institutions. It is by following rules on what counts as a legal institution and as an appropriately enacted text, what counts as a proper method of interpretation, and how these criteria are ordered, that we recognize a norm as a 'legal' or 'valid' norm. To the extent that some of these criteria of recognition are established according to the political philosophy of modern constitutionalism (e.g., the enacting institution is an elected Parliament, the interpretive

135 Giorgio Pino, 'Farewell to the Rule of Recognition?' (2011) 5 Problema. Anuario de Filosofía y Teoría del Derecho 265, 292–293: 'Indeed, one can view some long-standing debates within the judiciary and the legal academia, such as the debate between "originalist", "textualist", and "living-tree" approaches to constitutional interpretation, exactly in this way – as attempts at implementing (and asserting the superiority of) partly different rules of recognition'.

136 Hans-Johann Glock, *A Wittgenstein Dictionary* (Blackwell 1996) 150–155; Marie McGinn, 'Grammar in the Philosophical Investigations' in Oskari Kuusela and Marie McGinn (eds), *The Oxford Handbook of Wittgenstein* (Oxford University Press 2011) 352–357.

137 Steven Holtzman and Christopher Leich, 'Introduction' in Steven Holtzman and Christopher Leich (eds), *Wittgenstein: To Follow a Rule* (Routledge 1981) 20–21.

authority is a court subject to the rule of law, and so on), we assess that a norm is 'constitutional' according to this grammar.[138]

The grammar of concepts like 'legality', here is the crucial point, is partially agreed and partially disagreed upon, it is complex and at times conflictual, it is no algorithm.[139] Officials and citizens broadly agree on a series of legal institutions, on interpretive methods, and on their ordering, but may at times hold different opinions on what institution is ultimate, on who is entitled to authoritatively interpret the constitution, on whether the elective chamber holds only legislative or also constituent power, and so on. No settlement rule, no omnipotent 'Queen in Parliament', can solve such disagreements once and for all.

When the plurality of criteria of recognition reaches the level of the constitution, what we have is some form of constitutional pluralism, more pronounced in composite systems like federal States or unions of States, but still existent even in unified legal orders. Pluralism is not a monstrosity typical of *sui generis* legal orders like the EU nor a conceptual impossibility, an oxymoron, but rather a structural feature of legal systems.

138 I am beholden to Bobbitt's idea of 'legal grammar' as the 'forms of argument' that we share and master when pointing out the 'truth' of a proposition in constitutional law. See Philip Bobbitt, *Constitutional Fate: Theory of the Constitution* (Oxford University Press 1994) 3–8.

139 Dennis Patterson, 'Theoretical Disagreement, Legal Positivism, and Interpretation' (2018) 31 Ratio Juris 260, 267–268.

5

INTERPRETIVE DISPUTES AND *ULTRA VIRES* JUDGMENTS IN EUROPEAN PLURALISM

5.1 Introduction

Radical pluralism is a descriptive enterprise, aimed at showing how the foundational norms in the context of European pluralism partly overlap and partly diverge, generating an equilibrium that only occasionally fails and originates constitutional conflicts.

In Chapter 4, I have looked for empirical support to sustain radical pluralism by looking at legal orders outside European pluralism. By relying on the existing literature in comparative law, I have noticed how partly diverging foundational norms are structural in composite legal orders characterized by federalism. The case of the antebellum USA, a union of States more than a proper federal State, was particularly instructive, as it exposes cases of *ultra vires* similar to those we experience in today's Europe. Moreover, by looking at constitutional conflicts in centralized States, it was possible to realize that a certain degree of pluralism, at least in the form of interpretive pluralism, is unavoidable in every legal system. Conflicts, as MacCormick had specified in his characterization of radical pluralism, are then tamed via political compromise and bargain, more than by relying on the law.

This chapter will finally apply these considerations to European pluralism, specifically focusing on two elements.

First, the process of constitutionalization of the European Union (EU) described in the Introduction and in Chapter 2, its gradual evolution from a merely economic organization to one also aimed at preserving human rights, has generated a large area of overlapping rights and legal principles, similar in content and textual formulation, yet at times interpreted in different manners by EU and national institutions.[1] This area is occasionally characterized by diverging interpretations

1 Here I am not entering into the details of the distinction between 'rights' and 'principles'. However, it is important to distinguish between the former and the latter at least broadly. Rights are meant as clusters of norms, specifically Hohfeldian elements, i.e. claims, liberties, powers, and immunities

DOI: 10.4324/9781003291572-5

of shared principles. These disagreements have been defined 'conflicts by convergence' and must be added to the more traditional conflicts 'by divergence', in which conflicts are the result of diverging aims of national and EU law (say, rights protection for the former and market consolidation for the latter).[2] As a result, in the case of conflicts by convergence, fundamentally similar legal materials are transformed into different rules to be applied to concrete cases; in the case of conflicts by divergence, the State reacts to the perceived interference by the Union on delicate policy areas for reasons that are alien to domestic law. Both are sources of potential conflicts.

Second, even when conflicts entail open declarations of *ultra vires*, the overall stability of EU law is usually not threatened, nor States' commitment to EU's membership questioned. Disputes are accommodated through political bargain. Only if particularly harsh disagreement arises, one that involves the commitment to the basic values of the legal order, constitutional conflicts may cause the breakdown of law. Occasional conflicts and even cases of *ultra vires* are manageable within EU pluralism.

To illustrate both points, I discuss five major cases. One, the *Taricco* saga, ended peacefully, with no declaration of *ultra vires* by national institutions. It is a rather revealing story though, since it shows how the conflict was really about the interpretation of a shared principle, legality in criminal law, and was eventually settled through a mixture of menace and persuasion by the Italian Constitutional Court (ICC). Thus, *Taricco* reveals two things: on the one hand, it illustrates well the dynamic of conflicts by convergence in European pluralism; on the other hand, it proves how careful judicial politics can be useful in avoiding escalation. This is crucial to a theory of radical pluralism, as it demonstrates how even when legal principles are agreed upon at both the national and the supranational level, still diverging interpretation may lead to conflicts and how, when we ran out of legal solutions, politics (in this case, judicial politics) remains the only viable option.

The four remaining cases involve declarations of *ultra vires* by national courts. Differently from the antebellum USA, in which a general commitment to popular constitutionalism made of elected conventions the guardians of the constitutional compact, in the EU the prominence of legal constitutionalism places the defence of the legal system mostly in the hands of the judiciary. Three of the four cases of *ultra vires* remain, however, within the physiology of constitutional conflict: the Czech *Landtová*, the Danish *Ajos*, and the German *PSPP* judgments were harsh

gathered together to safeguard specific interests. See Judith J Thomson, *The Realm of Rights* (Harvard University Press 1990) 55–56; Jeremy Waldron, 'Introduction' in Jeremy Waldron (ed), *Theories of Rights* (Oxford University Press 1985) 11–12; Pavlos Eleftheriadis, *Legal Rights* (Oxford University Press 2008) 125. Principles, on the other hand, are particularly general, indeterminate, and evaluatively thick norms that identify the safeguarded interest and the correlative right. See Joseph Raz, 'Legal Principles and the Limits of Law' (1972) 81 The Yale Law Journal 823, 836–838; Neil MacCormick, *Legal Reasoning and Legal Theory* (Oxford University Press 1994) 152.

2 On this distinction, see Giuseppe Martinico, 'The "Polemical" Spirit of European Constitutional Law: On the Importance of Conflicts in EU Law' (2015) 16 German Law Journal 1343, 1347–1351.

confrontations, but did not radically threaten the Union. Although it is not easy to draw a straight line between physiology and pathology, the last case of *ultra vires*, namely the Polish K-3/21, belongs to the latter rather than to the former. Indeed, it questions the founding values of the Union and may eventually bring about widespread disapplication of EU law in Poland. It stands apart from the other cases of *ultra vires*.

5.2 Interpretive Disputes in European Pluralism: The *Taricco* Saga

The *Taricco* saga has been widely analysed by scholars.[3] Thus, here the scrutiny will be limited to two points, namely the way in which the different interpretations of the same norm, the principle of legality in criminal law, were justified (so to illustrate a case of conflict by convergence), and to the way in which the disagreement was eventually solved through careful judicial politics.

Factually, the saga regarded VAT frauds: the defendants were charged with organizing fake trading of champagne. In particular, the company 'Planet Srl' received fake returns from shell companies, so that later it could write the VAT off. This way, Planet deceived the Italian treasury and, since part of VAT is an EU tax, the EU too.

The referring judge, the *Tribunale di Cuneo*, foresaw that the short limitation period under Italian law as reformed in 2005 would determine systematic impunity of VAT frauds in Italy and consequently also harm an EU financial interest.[4] The *Tribunale* therefore referred *ex* art. 267 of Treaty on the Functioning of the European Union (TFEU) to the Court of Justice asking whether Italian law on limitation period was compatible with EU law, specifically with Article 325 of

3 Limiting the review to works English, see Emmanouil Billis, 'The European Court of Justice: A "Quasi-Constitutional Court" in Criminal Matters? The Taricco Judgment and Its Shortcomings' (2016) 7 New Journal of European Criminal Law 20; Mikhel Timmerman, 'Balancing Effective Criminal Sanctions with Effective Fundamental Rights Protection in Cases of VAT Fraud: Taricco' (2016) 53 Common Market Law Review 779; Antonello Tancredi, 'Of Direct Effect, Primacy and Constitutional Identities: Rome and Luxembourg Enmeshed in the Taricco Case' (2017) Zoom in 37 QIL Questions of International Law 1; Davide Paris, 'Carrot and Stick. The Italian Constitutional Court's Preliminary Reference in the Case Taricco' (2017) Zoom-in 37 QIL Questions of International Law 5; Matteo Bonelli, 'The Taricco Saga and the Consolidation of Judicial Dialogue in the European Union' (2018) 25 Maastricht Journal of European and Comparative Law 357; Giovanni Piccirilli, 'The "Taricco Saga": The Italian Constitutional Court Continues Its European Journey' (2018) 14 European Constitutional Law Review 814; Clara Rauchegger, 'National Constitutional Rights and the Primacy of EU Law: M.A.S.' (2018) 55 Common Market Law Review 1521; Silvia Allegrezza, 'On Legality in Criminal Matters between Primacy of EU Law and National Constitutional Traditions. A Study of the Taricco Saga' in Valsamis Mitsilegas, Alberto di Martino and Leandro Mancano (eds), *The Court of Justice and European Criminal Law* (Hart Publishing 2019); Daniele Gallo, 'Challenging EU Constitutional Law: The Italian Constitutional Court's New Stance on Direct Effect and the Preliminary Reference Procedure' (2019) 25 European Law Journal 434; Robbert Bruggeman and Joris Larik, 'The Elusive Contours of Constitutional Identity: Taricco as a Missed Opportunity' (2020) 35 Utrecht Journal of International and European Law 20.

4 Timmerman (n 3) 780–781.

TFEU (demanding that Member States apply effective, proportionate, and dissuasive sanctions to preserve the financial interests of the EU).

In the first *Taricco* judgment, the Court of Justice commanded immediate disapplication of Italian rules on limitation periods:[5] indeed the provisions preserving EU financial interests might otherwise be deprived of their effectiveness.[6] From the point of view of the Union, the problem lied in the risk of financial loss in 'a considerable number of cases'.[7] Changes in the regulation of limitation period such to shorten it shall not, according to the Court, be considered as a lighter penalty and therefore be applied retroactively to the benefit of the convicted: the limitation period is merely *procedural*, not substantive.[8] The Court of Justice based this view on teleological reasons (the need to ensure the effective prosecution of tax frauds), on precedents,[9] and on a comparative argument,[10] namely the procedural interpretation that the Court of Strasburg gives to the twin provision (Article 7) in the European Convention on Human Rights (ECHR).[11] As a result, Article 325 TFEU and 49 of the Charter are interpreted as imposing a clear, specific, and unconditional duty on domestic authorities to disapply ineffective norms on the limitation period, even retroactively (the so-called '*Taricco* rule').

After this decision, a response from the ICC was inevitable.[12] In 2017, the response took the form of a preliminary reference to the Court of Justice in which the ICC asked for a new interpretation of Article 325 TFEU, subtly inviting the Court of Justice to reconsider its position. Specifically, the Constitutional Court underlined the vagueness of the 'significant number of cases' requirement and how in Italy a substantive and non-retroactively applicable *in peius* limitation period was considered as an instantiation of the principle of legality in criminal law and part of the country's constitutional identity. The *Taricco* rule, the Court underlined, may therefore be objectionable under the Italian Constitution: implicitly, this threatened application of the counter-limits doctrine to the case.[13] Besides this

5 C-105/14 Taricco and others EU:C:2015:555.

6 This solution was proposed by Advocate General Kokott in her Opinion (paras.74–76) too. See Allegrezza (n 3) 166–167.

7 C-105/14 para. 47.

8 C-105/14 paras. 54–55.

9 The recalled precedent in at para. 56 is C-457/02 Criminal proceedings against Antonio Niselli ECLI:EU:C:2004:707.

10 C-105/14 para. 57. Article 7 ECHR was looked at in drafting Article 49 of the Charter and is expressly referred to in the Explanations. See Valsamis Mitsilegas, 'The Principles of Legality and Proportionality of Criminal Offences and Penalties' in Steve Peers and others (eds), *The EU Charter of Fundamental rights: A Commentary* (Hart Publishing 2014) 1354–1355.

11 Although with slight variations, the taxonomy on interpretive arguments employed here is borrowed from Neil MacCormick and Robert S Summers, *Interpreting Statutes: A Comparative Study* (Routledge 1991) 512–515.

12 Some scholars not only predicted this outcome, but also wished for the Constitutional Court to be rather caustic. See Massimo Luciani, 'Il Brusco Risveglio. I Controlimiti e La Fine Mancata Della Storia Costituzionale' (2016) 2 Rivista AIC 1, 17–20.

13 Corte costituzionale, order 24/2017, paras. 2–9.

threat of triggering the counter-limits, though, it is crucial to also recall that the Constitutional Court relied heavily on EU law to suggest how it was possible to reinterpret Article 325 TFEU to make it compatible with Italian constitutional law. Articles 2, 4(2), 4(3) of the Treaty on the European Union (TEU), and 49 and 53 of the Charter were explicitly recalled,[14] as well as paragraphs 53 and 55 of the *Taricco I* judgment, in which the Court of Justice stated that, in disapplying internal provisions, judges still had to safeguard individual rights.[15] Finally, the ICC mentioned the *Omega* judgment by the Court of Justice, in which room was left for Member States' to specify the constitutional interpretations of fundamental rights.[16] The extensive reliance on rules and principles of EU law, including carefully selected paragraphs of *Taricco I*, was designed to make easier for the Court of Justice rethinking its previous statements: order 24/2017 offered a way out to the colleagues in Luxembourg.

This decision fostered a quite restrained reaction by the Court of Justice, which delivered its meagre and austere *Taricco II* judgment on 5 December 2017.[17] The Court immediately paved the way for a reform of the *Taricco I* judgment by asserting that only part of the factual and legislative context was brought to its attention by the *Tribunale di Cuneo* in the first referring order.[18] At paragraph 44, the Court of Justice recognized that the protection of financial interests was a shared competence, and that partial harmonization only came in 2017 (Directive 2017/1371): the Italian Republic was therefore free to deploy a substantive conception of limitation period to frauds committed before that date.[19] As for later cases, instead, the Court allowed an exception to the *Taricco* rule when fundamental rights were concerned.[20] Domestic judges were exempted from applying the *Taricco* rule if they found that it would be excessively undetermined (the 'significant number of cases' criterion) or entail retroactive application *in malam partem* of criminal punishment.[21] *Taricco II* never explicitly accepted a substantive interpretation of the principle of legality, yet it allowed domestic judges to de facto disapply the *Taricco* rule. As a result, it decisively deescalated tensions.

The ICC ultimately marked the end of the saga with its decision 115/2018. The Constitutional Court accepted the reasoning of the Court of Justice but reasserted some of the points already stressed in order 24/2017. In particular, it clarified that

14 Ivi para. 6. See also Rauchegger (n 3) 1524–1525; Giacomo Rugge, 'The Italian Constitutional Court on Taricco: Unleashing the Normative Potential of "National Identity"?' (2017) Zoom-In 37 QIL Questions of International Law 21, 24–27; Pietro Faraguna, 'Constitutional Identity in the EU–A Shield or a Sword?' (2017) 18 German Law Journal 1617, 1630–1631.

15 Ivi para. 7.

16 C-36/02 Omega Spielhallen- und Automatenaufstellungs GmbH v. Oberbürgermeisterin der Bundesstadt Bonn ECLI:EU:C:2004:614.

17 C-42/17 M.A.S. and M.B. EU:C:2017:935. I will stick to the *Taricco II* wording to underline the continuity within the saga.

18 Rauchegger (n 3) 1539–1541.

19 ibid 1532–1537.

20 C-42/17 paras. 55–57.

21 ibid paras. 59–62.

no matter the circumstances of the case at stake, there would never be space for the *Taricco* rule in the Italian legal order:[22] the concept of limitation period must be substantive, and a civil law jurisdiction could never allow for the judicial branch to oversee specifying the 'significant number of cases' requirement.[23] The counter-limits could be lifted if necessary.[24]

Besides its undeniable relevance to the development of European criminal law, here *Taricco* was recalled, as anticipated, to illustrate two points.

First, the saga shows how conflicts by convergence occur in European pluralism. Both courts agreed on legality in criminal law as a binding constitutional principle but diverged on its interpretation (whether it encompassed or not the limitation period). It would be difficult to explain this divergence by looking at texts the two courts work on: Article 25, par. 2 of the Italian Constitution, enshrining the principle of legality in criminal law, points out that:

> No punishment may be inflicted except by virtue of a law in force at the time the offence was committed.

On the other hand, Article 49, par. 1 of the Charter of Fundamental Rights of the European Union, runs as follows:

> No one shall be held guilty of any criminal offence on account of any act or omission which did not constitute a criminal offence under national law or international law at the time when it was committed. Nor shall a heavier penalty be imposed than that which was applicable at the time the criminal offence was committed. If, subsequent to the commission of a criminal offence, the law provides for a lighter penalty, that penalty shall be applicable.

Despite some differences in textual formulation, it is hard to imagine how one could infer any meaningful theory of limitation period from these provisions: the raw legal materials allow both a procedural and a substantive conception.

The diverging results were reached because of the different teleology adopted: the equal protection of EU and national financial interests for the Court of Justice, the preservation of constitutional identity for the Italian Court. None of the two different interpretive criteria eventually depended on strictly legal considerations, but rather on diverging 'political' aims. At this depth in the chain of justification of a norm's legality, we reach the limits of law and the beginning of politics. No *legal* solution could be offered in the case because no clear specification of the abstract (and shared) legal principle was strictly required by the law.

22 Corte costituzionale, judgment 115/2018, para. 10.
23 Corte costituzionale judgment 115/2018, para. 11.
24 As pointed out, here dialogue is only apparent. See Fabio Ferraro, 'Il conflitto reale e il dialogo apparente della Corte di giustizia e della Corte costituzionale in merito al principio di legalità e alla riserva di legge in materia penale' (2018) 18 Federalismi 1, 6–9.

As for the second point, and consequently, *Taricco* shows the potential of careful judicial politics. The ICC chose a mixture of threatening and persuasion when referring to the Court of Justice. On the one hand it explained why the rather idiosyncratic understanding of the limitation period under the Italian constitutional tradition may eventually lead to lifting the counter-limits and declare the *Taricco* rule *ultra vires*; that was the threat, the stick. On the other hand, the Italian Court also relied on provisions from the Treaties to persuade the Court of Justice that backing down was legally feasible from the perspective of EU law. The *Corte costituzionale* was not required nor particularly expected to do so. Indeed, before 2017 it had remained quite passive in its role of judge under Article 267 TFEU and only referred twice before to Luxembourg.[25] The large reliance on EU law in order 24/2017 was a clever manoeuvre of judicial politics which eventually paid off and was subsequently iterated in later cases like *Consob*.[26] Conflict was avoided by proposing a compromise that the Court of Justice could justify under EU law. Provisions like Articles 2 and 4(2) TEU and 53 of the Charter have no single interpretation, they are wide enough to leave a blanket of EU legality and at the same time save the Italian constitutional identity. Clever judicial politics rather than rigorous legal reasoning saved the day.

5.3 *Ultra Vires* Judgments in Europe

As we have seen, *Taricco* did not end with direct and open constitutional conflict, but rather with the Court of Justice backing down and accepting a compromise with the ICC. The rest of the chapter is instead devoted to analysing cases in which no compromise was found by judges and national supreme or constitutional courts openly declared EU provisions to be authority-exceeding, *ultra vires*. Judgments declaring *ultra vires* an act of EU institutions or of domestic institutions applying EU law are the ultimate weapon in the hands of domestic courts and may force disapplication of EU law by national judges. Here I will consider how the controversies unfolded and also how *ultra vires* cases were subsequently handled by the political branches, namely executives and parliaments.

While three of the cases of European *ultra vires* were contained, did not threaten escalation, and therefore belong to the physiology of conflicts (*Landtová*, *Ajos*, *PSPP*), the Polish K-3/21 case of October 2021 seems different and way more dangerous.

25 The use of the preliminary reference was advocated before. E.g., Marta Cartabia, 'Europe and Rights: Taking Dialogue Seriously' (2009) 5 European Constitutional Law Review 5. However, its use came quite late. See Piccirilli (n 3) 823 on the rare previous applications of the mechanism by the Italian Court, namely orders 103/2008 and 207/2013.

26 On the 'seductive' approach of the Italian Constitutional Court see Daniel Sarmiento, 'Long Read: "The Consob Way – or How the Corte Costituzionale Taught Europe (Once Again) a Masterclass in Constitutional Dispute Settlement"' (*EU Law Live*, 16 April 2021) https://eulawlive.com/long-read-the-consob-way-or-how-the-corte-costituzionale-taught-europe-once-again-a-masterclass-in-constitutional-dispute-settlement-by-daniel-sarmiento/.

At the end of the analysis, I compare the first three to the fourth and try differentiating cases of physiological conflict from cases of pathology.

5.3.1 Landtová – Holubec

The first judgment to consider is *Landtová*. The case derived from the dissolution of Czechoslovakia in 1992.[27] The new-born States, the Czech Republic and Slovakia, reached an agreement to divide pension claims and other social securities issues.[28] The agreement used as a selection criterion the domicile of the citizen's employer on the date of the dissolution or the last known one prior to this date. This allowed people who worked for long periods in one State but ended their careers in the other to receive pension from the latter, not the former. Since Slovak pensions were generally lower than the Czech, a series of complaints was raised by Czech citizens. Within the Czech judiciary, the Constitutional Court (*Ústavní soud*, hereinafter ÚS) was generally favourable to accept the complaints, allowing for special economic supplements to citizens destined to Slovak pensions, while the Supreme Administrative Court (*Nejvyšší správní soud*, hereinafter NSS) refused this opinion, backed by the executive and the administration in general. This led to a harsher and harsher confrontation in 17 cases between 2003 and 2012, culminating in threat of disciplinary proceedings and State liability on the rebel administrative justices by the ÚS.[29]

In the meantime, both countries accessed the European Union (2004), and the original agreement became part of the framework of Regulation 1408/71 on the application of social security schemes in the Union. At Point 9 of Annex III(A) to the Regulation, it was stated that Articles 12, 20 and 33 of the Social Security Treaty shall remain applicable as *lex specialis* within the regulation system. This way they would become part of EU law, which famously includes a general prohibition of discrimination on the basis of nationality. Special supplements destined to Czech nationals only could be seen as discriminatory under EU law and the NSS invited the ÚS to revise its position in the light of the new legal framework. The ÚS refused.

When facing the issue in 2011, the Court of Justice in the *Landtová* judgment confirmed that the jurisprudence of the Czech Constitutional Court in the matter of Slovak pensions conflicted with the principle of non-discrimination on the basis of nationality.[30] It would be acceptable under EU law only if supplements were

27 For a detailed explanation of the entire saga and beyond, see Jan Komárek, 'Czech Constitutional Court Playing with Matches: The Czech Constitutional Court Declares a Judgment of the Court of Justice of the EU Ultra Vires; Judgment of 31 January 2012, Pl. ÚS 5/12, Slovak Pensions XVII' (2012) 8 European Constitutional Law Review 323; Michal Bobek, 'Landtová, Holubec, and the Problem of an Uncooperative Court: Implications for the Preliminary Rulings Procedure' (2014) 10 European Constitutional Law Review 54.

28 Treaty between the Czech Republic and the Slovak Republic on Social Security, 29 October 1992.

29 Komárek (n 27) 325–326; Bobek (n 27) 57–61.

30 Case C-399/09 Landtová ECR I-5573.

extended to all migrant citizens of other Member States.[31] The decision was however prospective and had no effect on already conferred pensions.[32]

Although this decision by the Court of Justice was relatively mild and tolerant, the previously accumulated tensions with other Czech authorities, coupled with the frustrating denial of any possible hearing for the ÚS in Luxembourg, finally brought about the ultimate reaction available to the Czech Constitutional Court. In *Holubec*, the ÚS declared the *Landtová* judgment *ultra vires*, exceeding the powers transferred by the Czech Republic to the EU.[33] Regulation No. 1408/71 would not be applicable to the cases of Czechoslovak pensions, governed instead by the agreement between Czech Republic and Slovakia signed in 1992. According to the ÚS, the *Landtová* decision treats them as transnational, while they are purely internal: periods of employment in a country cannot be retroactively treated as periods abroad. Consequently, the ÚS declared explicitly an EU provision, as interpreted by the Court of Justice, inapplicable within its jurisdiction.[34]

What happened then? The NSS bowed to the authority of the Constitutional Court and the Regulation was not applied: primacy and direct effect of EU law, fundamental constitutional principles of the Union, were set aside in that occasion.[35] The NSS also prepared a second preliminary reference to the Court of Justice, but the case was struck out of register thanks to the intervention of the Czech legislature in December 2013 which introduced special supplements to Slovak pensions.[36] The question was solved through legislative compromise and the conflict ceased, although in another couple of judgments the NSS reaffirmed the *Landtová* doctrine over *Holubec*. The ÚS itself started distinguishing and reducing *Holubec*'s scope little by little. Moreover, after a while the composition of the Constitutional Court changed. The judicial war was over, and no further escalation followed. In the *Landtová* saga, an EU regulation was disapplied, but EU law remained widely effective and the authority of the Court of Justice recognized.

31 Lenka Pítrová, 'The Judgment of the Czech Constitutional Court in the "Slovak Pensions" Case and Its Possible Consequences (In Light of the Fortiter In Re Suaviter In Modo Principle)' (2013) 3 The Lawyer Quarterly 86, 88.

32 Bobek (n 27) 61–62.

33 ÚS, plenary judgment of 31 Jan. 2012, Pl. ÚS 5/12. See Komárek (n 27) 328–332.

34 It is worth noting that the ÚS widely employed the narrative of the German Constitutional Court on *ultra vires* review. Cases such as *Solange I* and *Maastricht* were relied on in 'steps and terminology'. Julio Baquero Cruz, 'Another Look at Constitutional Pluralism in the European Union' (2016) 22 European Law Journal 356, 367; Tomas Dumbrovsky, 'Federal Solution to the EU Internal Sovereignty Conundrum: The European Doctrine of the Czech Constitutional Court and the U.S. Compact Theory' in Tomas Dumbrovsky and Tichý Luboš (eds), *Sovereignty and Competences of the European Union* (Charles University 2010) 86–87. However, it has been argued that this resemblance was purely instrumental, for the Czech Court selectively picked only part of the German reasoning. For instance, the limits of *ultra vires* review established by the German Constitutional Court were omitted. See Leonardo Pierdominici, 'The Theory of EU Constitutional Pluralism: A Crisis in a Crisis?' (2017) 9 Perspectives on Federalism 119, 140–141.

35 Bobek (n 27) 63–68.

36 ibid 67–70.

Similarly, Czech constitutional authorities remained still. Disagreement and conflict disappeared after legislative intervention and Czech integration in the EU was not significantly harmed.

5.3.2 Dansk Industri-Ajos

The second case of *ultra vires* came from Denmark. In the *Ajos* case, in 2016, the Danish Supreme Court (Højesteret) set aside a decision by the Court of Justice on the prohibition of discrimination on basis of age, pointing out that it conflicted with the Danish principles on labour legislation.[37] The judicial rebellion came after an unsuccessful attempt of dialogue between the two courts. The case concerned the dismissal in May 2009 of a Danish citizen aged 60. Having accepted a new job, he asked the former employer, the private company Ajos, for the severance allowance normally destined to dismissed employees (Article 2a(1) of the Salaried Employees Law). However, the company refused to pay, claiming that, since he had already reached pensionable age and could retire, there was no duty to pay the allowance (Article 2a(3) of the Salaried Employees Law). The case was first brought to the Danish Maritime and Commercial Court, which in 2014 asserted that Danish law consenting Ajos not to pay the allowance was in violation of Directive 2000/78 (the Employment Directive) and of the EU general principle of non-discrimination on grounds of age. Ajos appealed to the Supreme Court which, in turn, referred to the Court of Luxembourg. It asked whether the principle of non-discrimination prevented exceptions for citizens who already reached pensionable age and whether the same principle had to be balanced against the competing principles of legal certainty and protection of legitimate expectations in such cases.

Danish law was found in contrast with the Employment Directive. According to the Court of Justice, salaried workers who did not intend retiring and were denied the allowance, were directly discriminated based on age.[38] It is worth mentioning that this issue was not per se questioned by Danish institutions: indeed, amendment of the Salaried Employees Law was adopted to make it consistent with

37 For the decision by the Court of Justice, see Case 441/14, Dansk Industri (DI), acting on behalf of Ajos A/S, v. Estate of Karsten Eigil Rasmussen, ECLI:EU:C:2016:278. As for the Danish decision, see SCDK, Case no. 15/2014 Dansk Industri (DI) acting for Ajos A/S vs. The estate left by A. For detailed commentaries on *Ajos*, see Urška Šadl and Sabine Mair, 'Mutual Disempowerment: Case C-441/14 Dansk Industri, Acting on Behalf of Ajos A/S v Estate of Karsten Eigil Rasmussen and Case No. 15/2014 Dansk Industri (DI) Acting for Ajos A/S v The Estate Left by A' (2017) 13 European Constitutional Law Review 347; Mikael Rask Madsen, Henrik Palmer Olsen and Urška Šadl, 'Competing Supremacies and Clashing Institutional Rationalities: The Danish Supreme Court's Decision in the Ajos Case and the National Limits of Judicial Cooperation' (2017) 23 European Law Journal 140; Helle Krunke and Sune Klinge, 'The Danish Ajos Case: The Missing Case from Maastricht and Lisbon' (2018) 3 European Papers 157; Rass Holdgaard, Daniella Elkan, and Gustav Krohn Schaldemose, 'From Cooperation to Collision: The ECJ's Ajos Ruling and the Danish Supreme Court's Refusal to Comply' (2018) 55 Common Market Law Review 17.

38 C-441/14 Dansk Industri (DI), acting on behalf of Ajos A/S v Estate of Karsten Eigil Rasmussen ECLI:EU:C:2016:278.

EU law, although reform did not enter into force before February 2015.[39] However, since EU Directives have no horizontal effects,[40] the key parameter in *Ajos* was the general principle of non-discrimination.[41] Therefore, it was the general principle that Luxembourg considered as the legal basis to state that Danish law had to be either disapplied or applied consistently with the Directive.[42] As for the second question, it was established that the principle of legal certainty could not override the plaintiff's protections under the principle of non-discrimination and the balancing between legal certainty and the principle of discrimination on the basis of age could not be left to national judges: the latter option would infringe the effectiveness of EU law and engender more rather than less uncertainty on the application of the general principle.[43]

The problematic issue in *Ajos* was not the substantive conflict between Danish labour law and EU law, which was unquestionable. Rather, the legal basis for the Court of Justice to establish the infringement was debated: could the Court of Justice apply the principle of non-discrimination on the basis of age horizontally? The Danish Supreme Court reacted by stating that no consistent interpretation was available (especially considering the *travaux préparatoires* on the Salaried Employees Law) and that the unwritten principle of non-discrimination was not applicable either. The Højesteret argued that neither the Accession Act, nor the *travaux préparatoires* mentioned the validity of the unwritten principle of non-discrimination: when the accession was signed, the Danish Parliament knew of the Court of Justice's case law on general principles, but it was assumed that they were not going to have any horizontal effect. Indeed, in the preliminary reference the Danish Supreme Court had insisted on the problems for legal certainty that would derive from giving direct horizontal effect to general principles.[44] As a result, the Supreme Court pointed out that it would be beyond its competences to grant applicability to the general principle of non-discrimination and disapplied the preliminary ruling.[45]

There are three points worth making in the perspective of this chapter on *Ajos*.

First, the decision lies in the line of cases which ultimately rely on the *Maastricht Urteil*, and, as discussed in Chapter 2, witness the difficulties of national officials in accepting the complexity of the European foundational norms. In the specific case of Denmark, there also are reasons of judicial politics and legal culture beneath the surface of this decision.[46] But one cannot overlook the fact that, according to the Danish Supreme Court, the applicability of EU law was governed by the Accession

39 Šadl and Mair (n 37) 351.

40 On the no-horizontal direct effect rule of directives see C-152/84 M. H. Marshall v Southampton and South-West Hampshire Area Health Authority ECLI:EU:C:1986:84 para. 48; C-91/02 Paola Faccini Dori v Recreb Srl ECLI:EU:C:1994:292 paras. 22–25.

41 C-144/04 Werner Mangold v Rüdiger Helm ECLI:EU:C:2005:709 paras. 76-78. C-555/07 Seda Kücükdeveci v Swedex GmbH & Co. KG ECLI:EU:C:2010:21 para. 43.

42 On the duty of consistent interpretation, see C-14/83 Sabine von Colson and Elisabeth Kamann v Land Nordrhein-Westfalen ECLI:EU:C:1984:153 para. 26.

43 Rass Holdgaard, Daniella Elkan, and Gustav Krohn Schaldemose (n 37) 36–41.

44 ibid 21.

45 Helle Krunke and Sune Klinge (n 37) 160–162.

46 Šadl and Mair (n 37) 358–368; Madsen, Olsen and Šadl (n 37) 148–150.

Act of Denmark to the Union, not by EU law itself. The Supreme Court refers widely to the Act and to the way it was explained and interpreted by domestic political bodies like the Ministries of Justice and Foreign Affairs. The idea that powers ultimately grounded in the Danish Constitution have been conferred to the Union through the Act is recalled several times. In the context of the challenge of constitutional pluralism, this means upholding a rule of recognition whose peak is constituted by the Danish Constitution, denying the Treaties' autonomy.[47] It shows once again the bifurcation of European pluralism.

Second, two hardly reconcilable interpretive methodologies are at stake.[48] The Danish Supreme Court is moved by a conception of the principle of democracy and judicial review that prevents the judiciary to go beyond strict application of the law. This brings about a rather detailed examination of the relevant legislation and a literal method of interpretation. Judicial self-restraint is therefore at the basis of the Court's interpretation and does not allow for the application of a doubtful non-written principle.[49] The Court of Justice, on the other hand, has often been way more 'activist' in its history and mostly forged the main principles of a new legal order on its own, with the aim of ensuring an even closer union between Europe's States and peoples. National institutions, especially courts, are expected to loyally cooperate in reaching such aim. This perspective entails a less deferent style of argumentation, based more on teleology than on literalism, and a broader conception of the judiciary's powers. This is particularly well revealed in the refusal by the Danish Supreme Court in engaging in consistent interpretation of Article 2a(3) of the Salaried Employees Law, something that the Court of Justice found perfectly feasible. Consequently, a change in the method of interpretation adopted by the Danish judiciary was possible and even due under the principle of loyal cooperation from the perspective of the Court of Justice.[50] Yet, from that of the Danish Supreme Court, interpreting statutes beyond the legislature's will once the latter was clarified was simply impossible, as it would betray the traditional deference of Danish judges towards the original intent of the democratically elected legislature. This difference in attitude is exacerbated by the fact that *Ajos*, as *Landtová* and differently from *Taricco* and from the later *PSPP* case, is motivated by divergence between EU and national law: the principle of non-discrimination on the basis of nationality (*Landtová*) and the horizontally applicable principle of non-discrimination on the basis of age (*Ajos*) are alien to Denmark and potentially harm competing interests recognized under national law. Divergence as well as convergence can foster conflicts under EU pluralism.

Last, and as in *Landtová*, legislative intervention, specifically the entry into force of the reformed Salaried Employees Law in February 2015, reduced the likelihood

47 Danish Supreme Court, judgment, no. 15/2014, 44–48. Madsen, Olsen and Šadl (n 37) 149–150.

48 See extensively Šadl and Mair (n 37) 360–362.

49 Helle Krunke and Sune Klinge (n 37) 164–169. *Ajos* is perfectly in line with the Danish tradition of judicial self-restraint towards the national legislature.

50 Rass Holdgaard, Daniella Elkan, and Gustav Krohn Schaldemose (n 37) 31–36.

of future conflicts on the same issue and in any case the reversal of the primacy of EU law in a single case did not entail any dramatic change. In the end, the Danish Supreme Court had only pointed its finger on the horizontal effects of general principles, leaving most of EU law perfectly binding and operative in its legal system. As a result, the consequences of the judgment were quite limited, EU law remained widely applied in Denmark, and the authority of the Court of Justice on its validity and interpretation undisputed.

5.3.3 Weiss-PSPP

The third *ultra vires* decision is the *PSPP* judgment by the German Constitutional Court.[51] The German Court challenged the principle of primacy by declaring the *Weiss* decision of the Court of Justice *ultra vires*.[52] The Court in Karlsruhe harshly criticized the way in which the colleagues in Luxembourg assessed the compatibility of the Public Sector Asset Purchase Programme (PSPP) by the European Central Bank with the Treaties. The programme, established in the first place in ECB's Decision 2015/774, allowed for purchase of public sector securities on the secondary market. Complainants challenged the Decision in Karlsruhe and claimed that German constitutional authorities (the Federal Parliament, the Federal Government, and the German Federal Bank) were constitutionally bound to take steps against the implementation of the programme in Germany. In particular, the massive purchase might hide beneath the mantle of monetary policy some kind of de facto fiscal measure (a power still belonging to the Member States). Moreover, it could be used to circumvent the ban imposed by Article 123 TFEU on monetization of public debts. In July 2017, the Second Senate of the German Constitutional Court referred to the Court of Justice *ex* Article 267 TFEU and asked five questions regarding the possible violation of Articles 123(1) TFEU (preventing direct monetization of public debt), 119 and 127(1 and 2) TFEU (restricting ECB's competences to monetary policy only), 125 TFEU (preventing mutualization of Member States' public debts), 4(2) TEU (preserving Member States' national identity), 5(1) TEU (principle of conferral), and 5(4) TEU (principle of proportionality).

The Court of Justice issued its *Weiss* decision on 11 December 2018. No violation of the Treaties was identified, although the Court engaged in an assessment of the proportionality of the PSPP. The German Constitutional Court received the ruling and published its final decision on 5 May 2020: the *Weiss* judgment was explicitly deemed *ultra vires*. In particular, in the view of the German Constitutional Court, the proportionality assessment performed by the Court of Justice manifestly failed to hold the PPSP programme accountable. A series of competing economic interests affected by the programme were not adequately considered and

51 BVerfG, 2 BvR 859/15.
52 C-493/17 *Weiss and Others* ECLI:EU:C:2018:1000.

balanced: the monetary measures de facto had wide economic impact and the Court of Justice failed to ask the ECB adequate justification for their sacrifice. As a result, Karlsruhe decided that it could not rely on the interpretation provided by the Court of Justice and that the German institutions could no longer participate to the PSPP unless a sufficiently detailed proportionality assessment was provided within three months by the Governing Council of the ECB, showing the necessity and overall proportionality of the PSPP. In the previous *Honeywell* case[53] the *Bundesverfassungsgericht* claimed that it would consider an EU provision *ultra vires* only in cases of 'manifest and structurally significant exceeding of EU competences' and only after the Court of Justice had the possibility to clarify its interpretation of EU law, a position the German Court kept asserting in *PSPP*.[54] Yet, the allegedly meagre assessment by the Court in Luxembourg in *Weiss* was considered a manifest violation of proportionality. By failing to do hold the ECB accountable, the German Court argued, the Court of Justice acted *ultra vires* as it legitimized decisions by the ECB potentially beyond its mandate under the Treaties. In turn, this meant that the ECB might be violating the principle of conferral by usurping States' powers on economic policy and therefore infringing their budgetary responsibility, the effectiveness of the popular will expressed through ballots (in turn an element of the broader principle of democracy), and the constitutional identity of Germany itself. Once more, the German Constitutional Court relied on the idea that States remain the masters of the Treaties and the EU a mere association of States.[55]

There is no doubt that the *PSPP* judgment was the most dangerous for EU law of all the cases of *ultra vires* up to that point, if only because of the prestige and influence of the German Constitutional Court and because of Germany's economic role in sustaining the ECB's monetary programs.[56] Differently from *Landtová* and *Ajos*, *PSPP* engendered an EU wide discussion: this is hardly surprising, since the 'object' of the latter judgment, namely the unconventional quantitative easing (QE) program, potentially had a large impact on the Union and originated in a long-lasting conflict on economic governance,[57] one started

53 BVerfG, 2 BvR 2661/06, paras. 55–61.

54 BVerfG, 2 BvR 859/15, paras. 105 and 110–113.

55 BVerfG, 2 BvR 859/15, paras. 111 and 157.

56 Early commentators immediately noticed the potentially wide impact of the judgment for the monetary union. See Paul Dermine, 'The Ruling of the Bundesverfassungsgericht in PSPP – An Inquiry into Its Repercussions on the Economic and Monetary Union: Bundesverfassungsgericht 5 May 2020, 2 BvR 859/15 and Others, PSPP' (2020) 16 European Constitutional Law Review 525, 535–544.

57 Dieter Grimm, 'A Long Time Coming' (2020) 21 German Law Journal 944. The point that the *PSPP* judgment was to a certain extent 'a story of a clash foretold' is clearly made by Teresa Violante, 'Bring Back the Politics: The PSPP Ruling in Its Institutional Context' (2020) 21 German Law Journal 1045, 1046–1050. Annunziata traces back the *PSPP* judgment to the previous *Gauweiler* and *Landeskreditbank-Banking Union* cases in Karlshrue. See Filippo Annunziata, 'Cannons over the EU Legal Order: The Decision of the BVerfG (5 May 2020) in the Weiss Case' (2021) 28 Maastricht Journal of European and Comparative Law 123. For a detailed discussion of the PSPP judgment in the context of the historical relations between Karlsruhe and the EU, see Franz C Mayer, 'The

already in 2012 with the *Pringle* decision on the European Stability Mechanism and continued with the *Gauweiler* saga on the *Outright Monetary Transactions (OMT)* programme.[58] Moreover, while in *Landtová* and *Ajos* the national legislature could step in and solve the issue through the law-making process modifying internal provisions applying EU law, in *PSPP* the *ultra vires* decision regarded measures directly issued by EU institutions (the ECB and the Court) in an area of EU competence (monetary policy). In this sense, the *PSPP* case is the *ultra vires* decision which resembles the most the American cases of nullification.[59]

However, the consequences of the judgment were limited, and a political solution was found thanks to the cooperative behaviour of EU and German institutions.

The latter found themselves in an embarrassing position, starting from the question of what to do with the *PSPP* judgment. Indeed, the duties of German institutions after the judgment seemed unclear: the three months period to get further illustration on the programme's proportionality had no clear addressee, as the most natural candidate, the *Bundesbank*, was not even mentioned in the dispositive part of the judgment (the *Tenor*). German institutions seemed willing to cooperate with their EU counterparts to avoid further institutional conflict. In June 2020, asked for by the *Bundesbank*, the ECB Council disclosed a series of documents showing the continuous monitoring on the effects of the PSPP. In July the German Federal Parliament, Government, and Central Bank took them as sufficient evidence of the proportionality of the programme.[60] On 29 April 2021, the German Constitutional Court itself dismissed two complaints aimed at preventing further participation to the PSPP: the Court considered that the German government and *Bundestag* had followed up sufficiently on the *PSPP* judgment of the previous year and recognized that they enjoyed a wide margin of appreciation in taking political responsibility for Germany's participation to the programme.[61]

As for EU institutions, immediately after *PSPP*, both the ECB and the Court of Justice issued press releases, claiming that they took note of the judgment, but

Ultra Vires Ruling: Deconstructing the German Federal Constitutional Court's PSPP Decision of 5 May 2020' (2020) 16 European Constitutional Law Review 733, 739–747; Peter Hilpold, 'So Long Solange? The PSPP Judgment of the German Constitutional Court and the Conflict between the German and the European "Popular Spirit"' (2021) 23 Cambridge Yearbook of European Legal Studies 159, 162–175.

58 See Annelieke AM Mooij, 'The Weiss Judgment: The Court's Further Clarification of the ECB's Legal Framework: Case C-493/17 Weiss and Others, EU:C:2018:1000' (2019) 26 Maastricht Journal of European and Comparative Law 449, 450–452. On Gauweiler see extensively Alicia Hinarejos, 'Gauweiler and the Outright Monetary Transactions Programme: The Mandate of the European Central Bank and the Changing Nature of Economic and Monetary Union' (2015) 11 European Constitutional Law Review 563; Paul Craig and Menelaos Markakis, 'Gauweiler and the Legality of Outright Monetary Transactions' (2016) 41 European Law Review 4.

59 On nullification outside the USA (and with a special focus on European integration) see Ran Hirschl, 'Opting Out of "Global Constitutionalism"' (2018) 12 Law & Ethics of Human Rights 1, 18–33.

60 Mayer (n 57) 762–764.

61 2 BvR 1651/15 and 2 BvR 2006/15, paras. 89-111. See Hilpold (n 57) 185–186.

that they still considered the PSPP programme lawful under EU law in the light of *Weiss*.[62] In June 2020, the ECB Council's adopted six decisions and discussed, among other things, the macroeconomic impact of the PSPP.[63] After a long hesitance and pressured by the European Parliament, in June 2021 the European Commission launched an infringement procedure against Germany.[64] The Commission was clearly moved by the desire to fix a precedent on what it would do in case of other declarations of *ultra vires* by national courts in the future. However, the Commission also recognized the renewed German commitment to the programme in the answer to the letter of formal notice and dropped the procedure in December 2021.[65] Even this harsh conflict, in other words, did not entail a dramatic collapse of the European legal order but was rather solved through bargain and negotiation by political institutions: both the German and the EU institutions did what they could to reach an acceptable political compromise and eventually succeeded in de-escalating the conflict.

To the aims of this chapter, it is also important to notice that the *Weiss-PSPP* saga, as *Taricco* a few years before, can be seen as another case of diverging interpretations of a shared legal principle, namely proportionality. In *Weiss*, the Court of Justice interpreted proportionality as a broad review of the reasons provided for by the ESCB (European System of Central Banks) to justify the programme, while leaving a wide margin of appreciation to the central banks. In other words, it merely reviewed manifest errors in appreciating the suitability, necessity, and proportionality *stricto sensu* of the PSPP.[66] The German Constitutional Court, on the other hand, required a much stricter evaluation of the necessity of the measures and an analysis of the wider economic impact. When an ECB's programme is at the edges of its mandate, the scrutiny must be stringent. This view about the role of institutions at the constitutional level instantiates to a certain extent a vision of political philosophy in Karlsruhe, but this also has a direct impact on the law when it conditions the interpretation of proportionality. Although there are doubts regarding the existence of a proper method to perform the proportionality assessment (so that a more deferent approach turns out to be 'not comprehensible' from a methodological perspective[67]) and even more doubts on how to reconcile this with *Honeywell*,[68] the disagreement on the appropriate method to specify

62 European Central Bank, Press Release of 5 May 2020 and Court of Justice of the European Union, Press Release No 58/20.

63 European Central Bank, Press Release of 4 June 2020.

64 European Commission, June 2021 infringements package: Key Decisions, available at https://ec.europa.eu/commission/presscorner/detail/en/inf_21_2743.

65 European Commission, December 2021 infringements package: Key Decisions, available at https://ec.europa.eu/commission/presscorner/detail/en/inf_21_6201.

66 Case 493/17, paras. 71–100. See in particular paras. 78, 79, 81, 86, 91, 92, 93 for the Court of Justice repeatedly recalling a 'manifest error' standard of review.

67 BVerfG, 2 BvR 859/15, paras. 11, 133, and 141. See the discussion by Sven Simon and Hannes Rathke, '"Simply Not Comprehensible." Why?' (2020) 21 German Law Journal 950, 952–955.

68 I discuss the difficulties in identifying a clear method on proportionality and the debatable compatibility of *PSPP* with *Honeywell* more extensively in my own Orlando Scarcello, 'Proportionality in

the abstract principle of proportionality remains the key to understand *Weiss-PSPP*. In a sense, this divergence is the by-product of a different understanding of the separation of powers itself: while the Court of Justice opts for deference towards administrative discretion, especially in areas where technical expertise is crucial, and to review decisions only to when manifestly mistaken, the German Constitutional Court endorses a stronger idea of judicial review, in which courts actually are the embodiment of public reason and the right place to scrutinize in detail public policies, even those enacted by independent agencies and even in rather technical matters.[69] Briefly, the two Courts cannot agree on the proper scope of judicial review, though in this case it is the Court of Justice that opts for self-restraint.[70] Although this stringent review is justified by the need to verify whether the conferral of powers was duly respected, results is a substantive evaluation of the ECB's policies by the German Court.

5.3.4 K-3/21

Decided on 7 October 2021, judgment K-3/21 of the Polish Constitutional Tribunal is the last case of *ultra vires* in the EU at the time of writing. It is also an anomaly: judgment K-3/21 stands alone from the three other judgments. While all other cases of *ultra vires* were in the end solved through compromise by the political branches, the Polish case is quite different especially because no such solution is available.

The case must be understood in the light of profound transformation that the legal orders of Eastern Europe in general and of Poland in particular have experienced after the fall of the Berlin Wall. The post-1989 constitutional change in Central and Eastern European States was depicted as a form of 'return to Europe', a reprise of a common path temporarily interrupted by the experience of Soviet rule.[71] The returning States adopted constitutions inspired to the liberal-democratic commitment of Western European States, ideally restoring the previous political unity of Europe, and rectifying a twisted history. The return to Europe also implied a constitutional transformation inspired by the model of legal constitutionalism and towards the rule of law dominating in the West.[72]

the PSPP and Weiss Judgments: Comparing Two Conceptions of the Unity of Public Law' (2021) 13 European Journal of Legal Studies 45. On the questionable relation between *PSPP* and *Honeywell* see also Mayer (n 57) 750–755.

69 Mattias Wendel, 'Paradoxes of Ultra-Vires Review: A Critical Review of the PSPP Decision and Its Initial Reception' (2020) 21 German Law Journal 979, 989 casts doubt on the compatibility of this strong approach to judicial review and the understanding of proportionality in German legal history.

70 The Court of Justice, however, has typically applied proportionality in a looser manner when dealing with EU institutions rather than with Member States. See Gráinne de Búrca, 'The Principle of Proportionality and Its Application in EC Law' (1993) 13 Yearbook of European Law 105, 115–126 and 145.

71 Signe Rehling Larsen, *The Constitutional Theory of the Federation and the European Union* (Oxford University Press 2021) 92–95.

72 Sergio Bartole, *The Internationalisation of Constitutional Law: A View from the Venice Commission* (Hart Publishing 2020) 33–42.

Between 1945 and 1989, however, Western Europe had largely integrated and joining the Union immediately became the goal of the returning States as well. In June 1993, the European Council specified membership criteria for the EU, the so-called Copenhagen criteria, a mixture of economic, legal, and political standards for any applicant. The reforms, including a drive towards market economies, legal changes to incorporate the vast *acquis Communautaire*, and the commitment to the rule of law and to respecting the rights of individuals and of minorities, were quickly launched in Central and Eastern Europe to join the EU as soon as possible. The process was completed in the early 2000s and ten new States joined in 2004.[73]

However, the results of this adhesion were mixed and problematic. The reforms approved to meet the Copenhagen criteria were perceived as obviously necessary by the political elites of the Eastern States and overall implemented successfully. Yet, approval and implementation were hasty and accomplished for the most part by the executives, with limited involvement of legislative assemblies. A sense of insufficient democratic legitimacy of the reforms was at times perceived.[74] Most importantly, this happened to States recently freed from decades of foreign rule and therefore understandably jealous of their reacquired national independence.[75] Constitutionalism and rule of law required by the EU, with their emphasis on counter-majoritarianism and on independent institutions holding in check the will of the majority, were perceived by some as illegitimate constraints on the popular will and eventually object of what Blokker has defined 'legal resentment'.[76]

This resentment manifested in the most extreme form in Hungary and Poland, two of the States which joined the Union in 2004. Different as they may be, these two countries share a particularly strong sense of victimhood and injustice connected to previous occupations or repressions, be they in the form of the disposal of Hungary by the Treaty of Trianon or in that of the partitions of Poland, not to mention the trauma of Soviet rule in both. These dynamics have generated a particularly strong worry against foreign control and, in the end, the search for strongmen and identarian policies as coping mechanisms.[77]

The ascent of Viktor Orbán's *Fidesz* in Hungary (2010) and of Jarosław Kaczyński's *Prawo i Sprawiedliwość* or PiS in Poland (2015) determined a series of formal and unformal constitutional changes rejecting the principles of legal constitutionalism and the rule of law. Inspired by an extremist form of political constitutionalism, populist politics, alleged anti-elitism, and nationalism, the two countries

73 Paul Craig and Gráinne de Búrca, *EU Law: Texts, Cases, and Materials* (Oxford University Press 2011) 19.

74 Jiří Přibáň, 'Constituting the Heterarchy of European Constitutionalism in the EU's New Member States' in Alberto Febbrajo and Wojciech Sadurski (eds), *Central and Eastern Europe After Transition* (Routledge 2016) 16–20.

75 ibid 20–25.

76 Paul Blokker, *New Democracies in Crisis?: A Comparative Constitutional Study of the Czech Republic, Hungary, Poland, Romania and Slovakia* (Routledge 2014) 136–160.

77 Timea Drinoczi and Agnieszka Bień-Kacała, *Illiberal Constitutionalism in Poland and Hungary: The Deterioration of Democracy, Misuse of Human Rights and Abuse of the Rule of Law* (Routledge 2021) 46–60.

experienced strong pressure on any kind of counter-majoritarian institution, dismantling the check-and-balances typical of legal constitutionalism. The result was a form of 'illiberal' or 'authoritarian' constitutionalism,[78] etiquettes that some scholars consider nonsensical and self-contradictory[79] and others as useful conceptualizations of cases in which typically authoritarian or illiberal practices live side by side with institutions of liberal democracies, giving birth to mixed constitutional orders.[80]

Be that as it may, what is relevant for us is that both Hungary and Poland experienced such transformation. Hungary's transformation was swifter and deeper, also because of the wide parliamentary majority sustaining Orbán since the beginning. The unilateral adoption of a new Constitution in 2011 sealed a sort of legal revolution in the country.[81]

The transformation of Poland, which concerns us here, was slower, but equally characterized by a strong rejection of counter-majoritarian institutions. Since 2015, PiS repeatedly followed a pattern of limiting the scope of counter-powers, packing them, purging nonloyal members, and using the 'reformed' institutions as enablers for its own policies. Such pattern affected in various ways several institutions, including parliamentary opposition, professional civil service, free media, and the civil society.[82]

Nowhere, however, it was as disrupting as in the case of the judiciary. The PiS majority effectively dismantled the judicial counter-power, systematically packing first the Constitutional Tribunal and later ordinary courts. This relentless dismantling was aimed at neutralizing a possible check on the majority and transforming it into pro-majoritarian, supportive institutions.

The Constitutional Tribunal was targeted first. During the 1990s and then again after the enactment of the 1997 Constitution, the Constitutional Tribunal had established itself as an active institution in Poland, a respected guardian of the constitution.[83] Moreover, during the first and short-lived PiS government between 2005 and 2007, the Tribunal had often stepped in to repair breaches of the Constitution by the government, a lesson that would not be forgotten.[84] As soon as in late 2015, just after winning both the presidential and the parliamentary elections, the PiS majority started a two-pronged offensive. The first prong was aimed at paralysing the Tribunal by preventing the appointment of three legitimately chosen judges, at packing it with loyal ones, at keeping it busy with a bombardment of unconstitutional statutes concerning the functioning of the Tribunal itself, and at denying the

78 Tímea Drinóczi and Agnieszka Bień-Kacała, 'Illiberal Constitutionalism: The Case of Hungary and Poland' (2019) 20 German Law Journal 1140.

79 An 'oxymoron', in the view of Gábor Halmai, 'Populism, Authoritarianism and Constitutionalism' (2019) 20 German Law Journal 296.

80 Mark Tushnet, 'Authoritarian Constitutionalism: Some Conceptual Issues' in Alberto Simpser and Tom Ginsburg (eds), *Constitutions in Authoritarian Regimes* (Cambridge University Press 2013).

81 Yaniv Roznai and Gary J Jacobsohn, *Constitutional Revolution* (Yale University Press 2020) 59–101.

82 Wojciech Sadurski, *Poland's Constitutional Breakdown* (Oxford University Press 2019) 132–149.

83 ibid 42–43.

84 ibid 50–52.

publication of unwelcome judgments.[85] By 2017, the Constitutional Tribunal was packed enough with loyal judges to become an effective enabler of the government, not a counter-power. The second prong then begun, with the government and the parliamentary majority withdrawing the measures aimed at paralysing the Tribunal and frequently referring to it themselves to legitimize their reforms with a blanket of constitutional legality.[86]

The second target was the judiciary at large. After the capture of the Constitutional Tribunal, regular courts had become the de facto guardians of the Constitution, applying it themselves in ordinary proceedings. They were countered through a campaign of anti-judicial propaganda and the usual mixture of neutralization and packing. Three crucial reforms regarded the National Council of the Judiciary (Krajowa Rada Sądownictwa, KRS), the Supreme Court, and the common courts. Combined, such reforms ensured that the KRS, the Supreme Court, and the presidents of ordinary courts were purged of previous members and filled with judges loyal to PiS. Self-rule of the judiciary, including promotions, internal discipline, mobility, appointments to the highest bodies, was effectively dismantled and put under direct control of PiS members, such as the President of the Republic and the Minister of Justice. As a result, most of the judicial counter-power was successfully silenced.[87]

This systematic and relentless dismantling of the judiciary's independence could not remain unnoticed. As mentioned in Chapter 4, when discussing the core normative commitments of the EU, the rule of law stands as one of the main tenets. The rule of law is mentioned among the basic values in Article 2 TEU and was identified as a foundational principle of EU law by the Court of Justice since *Les Verts*.[88] The dismantling of an independent judiciary could only be seen as a direct assault on the rule of law in Poland and eventually determined a reaction.

After an initial and significantly long phase of hesitation,[89] EU institutions were progressively more involved after the *Associação Sindical dos Juízes Portugueses* (*ASJP*) judgment by the Court of Justice, which I have already mentioned in the Introduction.[90] *ASJP* adopted an 'institutional' conception of the rule of law, one that requires the separation of powers and an independent judiciary to check on the political branches as preconditions for the rule of law.[91] The Court indeed clarified that Article 19 TEU, read in the light of Article 47 of the Charter of Fundamental Rights of the EU, requires Member States to establish an independent judiciary and that this gives substance to the value of the rule of law mentioned in

85 ibid 61–79.
86 ibid 79–84.
87 ibid 96–131.
88 C-294/83 Parti écologiste 'Les Verts' v European Parliament ECLI:EU:C:1986:166, para. 23.
89 Melanie Smith, 'Staring into the Abyss: A Crisis of the Rule of Law in the EU' (2019) 25 European Law Journal 561.
90 See Introduction, 1.2 and the literature mentioned there.
91 Renáta Uitz and András Sajó, *The Constitution of Freedom: An Introduction to Legal Constitutionalism* (Oxford University Press 2017) 308–323.

Article 2 TEU.[92] A series of actions launched both by the European Commission as infringement proceedings and by ordinary judges in Poland via Article 267 TFEU followed.[93] As a consequence, the Court of Justice repeatedly adjudicated on the reforms of the Polish judiciary by stating that these violated Article 19 TEU as interpreted in *ASJP*.[94] In the meanwhile, the Court of Human Rights in Strasburg too was involved in the controversy and in the *Xero Flor* judgment of 7 May 2021 stated explicitly that the Constitutional Tribunal was unlawfully composed and violated the right to a tribunal established by law under Article 6 of the ECHR.[95]

K-3/21 must be understood in the light of this long-lasting, deep, and systemic conflict between supranational and Polish institutions. After one of the most relevant cases on the rule of law in Poland was decided in April 2021, *A.B. and Others v KRS*,[96] the Polish government decided to exploit the Constitutional Tribunal's new role as an enabler to discredit the Court of Justice's judgments. On 31 March 2021, the Prime Minister of Poland filed an application to the Constitutional Tribunal asking about the compatibility Articles 1, 2, 4(3), and 19(1) TEU concerning primacy of EU law and effective judicial protection with the Polish Constitution.[97] The Tribunal issued its decision on 7 October 2021, by a majority vote and with two dissenting opinions.[98] In the only available section of the judgment, the operative part, the Constitutional Tribunal stated that:

92 C-64/16 Associação Sindical dos Juízes Portugueses v Tribunal de Contas (*ASJP*) EU:C:2018:117, paras. 29–37.

93 By the end of 2021, more than 30 preliminary references connected to the rule of law crisis had been issued by Polish judges and four actions for infringement were lodged by the Commission. See Laurent Pech and Dimitry Kochenov, *Respect for the Rule of Law in the Case Law of the European Court of Justice: A Casebook Overview of Key Judgments since the Portuguese Judges Case* (Swedish Institute for European Policy Studies 2021) 191 www.sieps.se/en/publications/2021/respect-for-the-rule-of-law-in-the-case-law-of-the-european-court-of-justice/.

94 E.g., C-192/18 European Commission v Poland ECLI:EU:C:2019:924; Joined Cases C-558/18 and C-563/18 Miasto Łowicz ECLI:EU:C:2020:234; Joined cases C-585/18, C-624/18 and C-625/18 A. K. and Others v Sąd Najwyższy ECLI:EU:C:2019:982; C-619/18 European Commission v Poland ECLI:EU:C:2019:531; C-824/18 A.B. and Others v Krajowa Rada Sądownictwa and Others (A.B.) EU:C:2021:153; C-487/19 W.Ż., EU:C:2021:798; C-791/19 European Commission v Poland ECLI:EU:C:2021:596.

95 ECtHR 7 May 2021, No. 4907/18, Xero Flor w Polsce sp. z o.o. v Poland. See Marcin Szwed, 'The Polish Constitutional Tribunal Crisis from the Perspective of the European Convention on Human Rights: ECtHR 7 May 2021, No. 4907/18, Xero Flor w Polsce Sp. z o.o. v Poland' (2022) European Constitutional Law Review 1.

96 C-824/18 A.B. and Others v Krajowa Rada Sądownictwa and Others (A.B.) EU:C:2021:153.

97 'PM Action to Review Constitutionality of EU Treaty Now in English – Rule of Law' https://ruleoflaw.pl/pm-action-to-review-constitutionality-of-eu-treaty-now-in-english/ accessed 25 April 2022. Among other things, the application widely relies on the case law of other national courts stressing the relative character of EU primacy in their jurisdiction (e.g., *Solange* and counter-limits doctrines) and on the other *ultra vires* judgments (*Landtová*, *Ajos*, and *PSPP*). The judicial treatment of EU law in Germany, Italy, the Czech Republic, and Denmark is therefore discussed.

98 Ref. K-3/21, assessment of the conformity to the Polish Constitution of selected provisions of the Treaty on European Union, 'Trybunał Konstytucyjny: Ocena Zgodności z Konstytucją RP Wybranych Przepisów Traktatu o Unii Europejskiej' https://trybunal.gov.pl/en/hearings/judgments/art/11662-ocena-zgodnosci-z-konstytucja-rp-wybranych-przepisow-traktatu-o-unii-europejskiej.

a) Article 1 TEU, read together with Article 4(3) TEU, is incompatible with the Polish Constitution insofar as the EU has entered a 'new stage' aimed at ever closer union among the peoples of Europe, in which it acts beyond its conferred powers, the Polish Constitution is no more the supreme law of the land, and Poland may not work anymore as a sovereign State.
b) Article 19(1) second paragraph TEU is incompatible with the Polish Constitution if interpreted so that it empowers domestic courts to disapply the Constitution or apply provisions declared unconstitutional or repealed by the Parliament.
c) Article 19(1) second paragraph and 2 TEU are incompatible with the Polish Constitution insofar as they allow domestic courts to review the procedures to appoint judges under Polish law or refuse to recognize the legitimacy of judges' appointments for the sake of preserving the principle of effective judicial protection under EU law.

The judgment is not connected to a specific controversy and does not have individual parties whose rights depend on the outcome. It is an abstract review of constitutionality, adjudicating on the hypothetical interpretation of a series of TEU articles.[99] Indeed, it is an interpretive decision, which concerns the *norms*, not the *sources of law*.[100] The first paragraph, in particular, is extremely abstract and theoretical, so much so that it was commented upon more like a sort of political declaration than as a proper legal proposition.[101] This sense of abstractness is naturally reinforced by the lack of clear motivation, detailing on the factual context that led to the judgment.

Of course, abstractness is dispelled when thinking about the political context. The Tribunal is referring to the interpretation of the Treaty provisions that the Court of Justice has been upholding in the last few years and that directly conflict with the reforms aimed at by PiS, a contextualization that is significantly eased once the application to the Tribunal is considered. The Constitutional Tribunal declaring *ultra vires* the mentioned Treaty provisions insofar as they are interpreted as the Court of Justice did in its judgments on effective judicial protection. That EU law has a say on the internal reorganization of the judiciary is contested and that ordinary Polish judges may refuse to look at other judges as lawfully established courts is questioned too. Finally, that EU law has primacy over the Polish Constitution is not accepted as well.

K-3/21, directly and blatantly challenging the primacy of EU law as such and the Court's interpretation of effective judicial protection, inevitably fostered harsh reactions. Only two weeks after the judgment, on 21 October 2021 the European

99 Wojciech Brzozowski, 'C'è Del Marcio in Polonia? Il Significato Autentico Della Sentenza Costituzionale 7 Ottobre 2021' (2021) Quaderni costituzionali 965.

100 Fábio Perin Shecaira, 'Sources of Law Are Not Legal Norms' (2015) 28 Ratio Juris 15.

101 Jakub Jaraczewski, 'Gazing into the Abyss' (*Verfassungsblog*, 12 October 2021) https://verfassungsblog.de/gazing-into-the-abyss/

Parliament adopted a Resolution which openly defined the Constitutional Tribunal 'illegitimate', criticized the government's use of the judiciary as a tool to accomplish a political agenda, and stated that the Treaties could not unilaterally be modified by national courts. It also urged the Commission and the Council to take action against the Polish reforms of the judiciary by launching an infringement proceeding and by withholding EU funds.[102] On 22 December 2021, the European Commission launched an infringement procedure against Poland for violation of EU law by the Constitutional Tribunal, also expressing serious doubts on the independence and impartiality of the Court.[103]

Briefly, the constitutional conflict seems far from being settled and, differently from what happened in *Landtová*, *Ajos*, and *PSPP*, national institutions have little incentive in cooperating with the EU to solve the issue. On the contrary, they have appealed to the captured Constitutional Tribunal to receive a blanket of legality on their reforms of the judiciary and to counter with it the bombardment of judgments by the Court of Justice declaring the reforms illicit under EU law. Having actively looked for conflict, it is unlikely that they may operate to solve it.

Future evolution is hard to predict. PiS marches towards dismantling the judicial counter-power and may be eventually able to obtain the loyalty or at least the obedience of the vast majority of Polish judges. Should this happen, appeals to the Court of Justice via Article 267 TFEU would likely end. On the other hand, the EU has developed new tools for pressuring recalcitrant Member States. In particular, after the Court of Justice's judgment on February 2022 regarding the so-called Rule of Law Conditionality Regulation (Regulation 2020/2092), the Council of the EU, on proposal of the Commission, can now suspend payments of EU funds if breaches of the rule of law at the State level affect or seriously risk affecting the sound financial management of the Union budget or the protection of the financial interests of the Union in a sufficiently direct way.[104] In practice, this gives EU institutions financial leverage which might be used to reverse the rule of law backsliding in the years to come. As in June 2022, this is still to happen for most of the EU funding of Poland, but remains a possibility for the future.

As we have seen examining the nullification crisis in the antebellum USA, it took more than three decades before the conflict already manifest in the South Carolinian ordinances became the legal basis for the secession of the Confederacy and later for the transformation of the Union with the Reconstruction Amendments. The constitutional crisis in Eastern Europe may drag on for a long time too before reaching a conclusion.

102 European Parliament Resolution of 21 October 2021 on the Rule of Law Crisis in Poland and the Primacy of EU Law (2021/2935(RSP))' (21 October 2021) www.europarl.europa.eu/doceo/document/TA-9-2021-10-21_EN.html

103 Rule of Law: Commission Launches Infringement Procedure' (*European Commission - European Commission*) https://ec.europa.eu/commission/presscorner/detail/en/ip_21_7070

104 C-156 and 157/21 Hungary and Poland v Parliament and Council ECLI:EU:C:2022:97.

5.3.5 Comparative Assessment

Cases of *ultra vires* in the EU are not bizarre juridical singularities, never to happen again, but a structural manifestation of constitutional pluralism. As in the case of antebellum USA examined in the last chapter, pooled sovereignty and multi-layered constitutionalism entail the possibility of disagreement on the interpretation and application of constitutional norms and, consequently, that of open conflicts. Whether it will be a constitutional convention (USA) or a court (EU) to declare it is a matter of institutional organization that does not change the structural character of this phenomenon. As in MacCormick's remarks on radical pluralism, in these circumstances political negotiation is what will eventually settle the dispute.

If this analysis is correct, constitutional conflicts both in the mild form of *Taricco*, in which no declaration of *ultra vires* was eventually issued, and in that of *Landtová*, *Ajos*, and *PSPP*, are part of the physiology, not of the pathology of EU law: these are disagreements bound to happen without threatening the overall functioning of the legal system, the breakdown of law. After *PSPP* was issued, scholars discussed whether it marked the end of constitutional pluralism as a theory of European law.[105] However, later events proved that such worry was excessive: disagreement on the application of the proportionality assessment to the ECB's PSPP programme was overcome by political institutions and no dramatic event followed. The overall agreement on a series of underlying legal principles and political values, coupled with cooperative political institutions, was enough to prevent further escalation of the constitutional conflict in *PSPP* as it had been enough in *Taricco*, *Landtová*, and *Ajos*. All these cases still belong to the physiology of constitutional pluralism.

Moving to the last discussed case, K-3/21, we find that it is fundamentally different from the others. It moves us from physiology to pathology of pluralism as the likelihood that conflict may escalate until the breakdown of (EU) law in Poland here is significantly higher. The other cases of *ultra vires* are not actually comparable to it. I ground this statement on a series of observations.

First, debatable as they may be, *Landtová*, *Ajos*, and *PSPP* were judicial statements issued by lawfully established and independent courts, busy at interpreting the law. There can be no doubt that what they were doing was attempting to interpret the law and that the Czech, Danish, and German peak courts were the legitimate body to perform such task in their respective jurisdictions. Of course, political considerations inevitably play a role in judicial interpretation, yet what we see is anyway an exercise in jurisdiction, in the ancient sense of *ius dicere*, stating the content of the law independently from the political power (*gubernaculum*).[106]

105 Annegret Engel, Julian Nowag and Xavier Groussot, 'Is This Completely M.A.D.? Three Views on the Ruling of the German FCC on 5th May 2020' (2020) 3 Nordic Journal of European Law 128, 145–150.

106 Gianluigi Palombella, 'The Rule of Law and Its Core' in Jan Klabbers and Gianluigi Palombella (eds), *Relocating the Rule of Law* (Hart Publishing 2009) 27–30. The mentioned analysis relies on McIlwain's famous distinction between *gubernaculum* and *iurisdictio*. See Charles H McIlwain, *Constitutionalism: Ancient and Modern* (Liberty Fund 1947).

This task may naturally be performed poorly or ideologically, as judges blunder and have political views as anyone else, but it remains a *bona fide* attempt to state the content of the law. The case of the Constitutional Tribunal is indeed quite different. For reasons we have already discussed, there are serious doubts on the lawfulness of its establishment and there is little doubt that it acts not as a counter-power, but as an enabler of the political branches.[107] The Tribunal has become yet another body within the *gubernaculum* and has abandoned its task to state content of the law. This crucial difference is corroborated by the simple observation that in *Landtová*, *Ajos*, and *PSPP*, as well as in *Taricco*, national institutions tried to cooperate with the Court of Justice. In *Taricco*, *Ajos*, and *PSPP*, the national courts referred to the Court of Justice and asked for a ruling to avoid conflict, successfully in the first case, unsuccessfully in the Danish and German cases. Even in *Landtová*, the Czech Constitutional Court tried to explain its position to the Court of Justice, although the chosen channel (a hearing in Luxembourg) was deemed inappropriate. K-3/21 is completely different: the Polish government asked for a blanket of legality to justify its reforms and obtained it: the stamp of constitutional legality was aimed at discrediting the EU judgments. No possible cooperation was possible from the beginning. Thus, while in the other cases national courts looked for the appropriate interpretation of EU law and involved the specialized institution in Luxembourg in the process, in K-3/21 the Constitutional Tribunal simply delivered on the government's request.

A second key difference lies in the motivation of the judgments. One can disagree with the *Landtová*, *Ajos*, and *PSPP*, but it is undeniable that the Czech, Danish, and German courts published judgments with clearly visible and accessible justifications. This is not true of the Polish case, in which only the operative part was quickly made available. The closest thing one has to a motivation is the Prime Minister's application, yet it is clearly anomalous that the Tribunal's reasoning must be guessed by looking at the applicant's plea, even more so considering the discussed problems with the Tribunal's independency. As previously mentioned, in Poland the government denied publishing constitutional judgments when the Tribunal was still not packed as a tool to restrict its influence.[108] In K-3/21, the same tool obscures the possibility to publicly assess the Tribunal's motivation for such judgment. This may seem a minor point, but it is not. The influence of constitutional and supreme courts is frequently criticized on the ground that institutions with low democratic credentials take extremely important political decisions.[109] One of the key instruments to mitigate such problem of legitimacy is for judges to compensate through the transparency and completeness of the motivation what they lack in democratic credentials. The emphasis on explanation and motivation of decisions by public powers as a tool to increase legitimacy is not limited to the

107 Sadurski (n 82) 79–84.

108 ibid 75–79.

109 Among many, see Jeremy Waldron, 'The Core of the Case against Judicial Review' (2006) 115 The Yale Law Journal 1346.

judiciary, it also applies to other branches and particularly to the executive. It is common to speak about a 'culture of justification' replacing a 'culture of authority' to clarify how in contemporary public law legitimacy does not derive purely from the pedigree of a decision, that is, having been enacted by the appropriate institution, but also from its substantive rationality and reasonableness.[110] In pluralist contexts, in which the judge is required to address independent normative claims originating in autonomous legal orders, the complexity of the involved legality makes an exhaustive justification of the judgment even more necessary.[111] Thus, the lack of available motivation in K-3/21 is far from a minor difference in relation to the other cases of *ultra vires*.

Third, the object of the conflict is rather different. *Landtová*, *Ajos*, and *PSPP*, as well as *Taricco*, were concerned with the specific application of EU principles in concrete controversies, be they the application of proportionality to the PSPP programme or the limitation period applied to VAT frauds. These are certainly extremely important issues, but even if they led to disapplication of EU provisions on the matter, that would simply entail the ineffectiveness of some specific EU norms. This is not particularly uncommon, since all legal orders have some degree of infectiveness, nor particularly threatening for EU law, since most of it remains broadly in place. K-3/21, on the other hand, concerns essential principles of EU law, namely primacy and effective judicial protection, in a larger and way more threatening manner.[112] Indeed, it affirms the supremacy of Polish law on the matter of the organization of the judiciary, to the point of possibly establishing in the future a judicial power that is for the most part loyal to the ruling party and hostile towards EU law. This might lead to systematic disapplication of EU law and to the marginalization of the Court of Justice which, because of the structure of the preliminary ruling mechanism, is heavily dependent on the cooperation of national judges. That would indeed signal the breakdown of EU law in Poland. The level of threat for the stability of the composite European legality is way higher in K-3/21 than in any other case before.[113]

Last, there is a difference in the context of the four *ultra vires* cases. *Landtová*, *Ajos*, and *PSPP* are cases in which the *ultra vires* judgment was followed quickly by the

110 Etienne Mureinik, 'A Bridge to Where? Introducing the Interim Bill of Rights' (1994) 10 South African Journal on Human Rights 31; Moshe Cohen-Eliya and Iddo Porat, 'Proportionality and the Culture of Justification' (2011) 59 American Journal of Comparative Law 463.

111 Jan Klabbers, 'Judging Inter-Legality' in Jan Klabbers and Gianluigi Palombella (eds), *The Challenge of Inter-Legality* (Cambridge University Press 2019); Gianluigi Palombella, 'Theory, Realities, and Promises of Inter-Legality: A Manifesto' in Gianluigi Palombella and Jan Klabbers (eds), *The Challenge of Inter-Legality* (Cambridge University Press 2019).

112 Enzo Cannizzaro, 'Sovereign Within the Union? The Polish Constitutional Tribunal and the Struggle for European Values' (2021) 6 European Papers 1117, 1117–1118.

113 Similarly, from a political theory perspective, see Cormac S Mac Amhlaigh, 'Eppur Esiste!: Legitimacy and Longevity in the EU's Long Decade of Crisis.' (2022) University of Edinburgh School of Law Research Paper Series N 8 20–21.

stepping in of the political branches, ready to find a solution to the controversy. By legislative intervention in *Landtová* and *Ajos* or by acquiring the necessary information from the ECB in *PSPP*, the Czech, Danish, and German authorities proved themselves committed to settle the conflict peacefully.

From the perspective of radical pluralism, this is particularly important: as long as there is a common will and commitment to the same broad political values, specific conflicts are solved thought bargain and negotiation. In Poland, on the other hand, the behaviour of the political branches is quite the opposite. As previously mentioned, K-3/21 was decided upon request of the Prime Minister and in a context of conflictuality between PiS and EU institutions, especially the Court of Justice: there is virtually no hope of negotiated political solution. This is highly instructive, as it shows that what really troubles the stability of a legal order, especially that of a union of States like the EU, is not that much the existence of constitutional conflicts which, as stated in the last chapter, are inevitable even in unitary States, but rather the political will to compose them.

5.4 Conclusion

In this chapter I have considered a series of conflicts within EU constitutional pluralism: *Taricco*, *Landtová*, *Ajos*, and *PSPP*. In a context dominated by legal constitutionalism like contemporary Europe, the main actors are naturally constitutional and supreme courts rather than legislatures as in the antebellum USA considered in the last chapter.

All these cases expose severe conflicts between the EU and national law, often involving very basic constitutional principles of the Member State. The successful management of conflicts required willing political branches to step in and cooperate. Indeed, it was the inclination to negotiate and mediate of political branches that ultimately solved *Landtová*, *Ajos*, and even *PSPP*. In *Taricco*, courts too showed a certain ability to engage in judicial politics and find bargained solutions. All in all, these cases expose how appropriate MacCormick's remarks were back in 1995 when commenting on the *Maastricht Urteil*. Radical pluralism is the theory that correctly anticipated the dynamics that we see at play in the examined cases: a certain degree of conflict is inevitable and physiological within European pluralism, and it is solved more through political bargain rather than through legal reasoning. There is no one right legal answer dictated by an overarching legality, but various possible interpretations of shared principles that are then reconciled politically.

Last, the K-3/21 case was examined, a judgment which instead shows what happens when the minimum degree of willingness to participate in the political bargaining is lacking and when the very basic values on which a union of States is founded are not shared anymore. The differences with the other cases of *ultra vires* are too many and too pronounced to be ignored: the capture of the Constitutional Tribunal and its transformation into an enabler of the political branches, the lack of motivation in the judgment, the danger to the effectiveness of EU law, and the political context of the case in K-3/21 clearly separate it from *Landtová*, *Ajos*, and *PSPP*. These differences are so deep to make the comparison rather difficult and, most importantly, they explain why it makes sense to talk about *Landtová*, *Ajos*, and *PSPP* as cases of physiological conflict in a union of States, while leaving K-3/21 in the field of constitutional pathology.

6

EPILOGUE

The Limits of Jurisprudence

We come now to the end of our journey. Throughout this book, I have tried to answer the question how it is possible that independent claims of ultimate authority coexist in the European legal order. Even more, how it is possible that multiple independent *constitutional* claims coexist, given the normatively demanding characters of modern constitutionalism. This is the riddle of constitutional pluralism.

In answering this question, some have denied the possibility of pluralism and asserted that it is necessarily an oxymoron, a *contradictio in adiecto*. Others, the main body of contemporary pluralists, have not only accepted pluralism as a perfectly logical possibility, but even celebrated it as the finest incarnation of constitutionalism in the contemporary post-statist world. I have tried to find a middle way, navigating between categorical anti-pluralism and an openly normative pluralism by accepting as a matter of fact the coexistence of several claims and trying to explain it without celebrating.

In doing so, I followed the path traced by Neil MacCormick in his first essays on the problem, when the Scottish scholar was illustrating his theory of radical pluralism. Commitment to a minimalist definition of legal positivism lies beneath the book, namely the idea, visible in MacCormick's radical phase, that pluralism consists of a series of ascertainable social facts and that it is possible to investigate them without committing to direct approval or disapproval. Comparative law has provided much of the empirical evidence used to sustain the main thesis of the book, namely that a plurality of claims to ultimate authority, even of constitutional kind, can coexist within a single and well-functioning legal order. As a matter of fact, the foundational norm of any legal system never consists of the simple and straightforward obedience to a sovereign Queen in Parliament: various claims to ultimate authority can coexist either in the form of various 'sovereigns' operating simultaneously, as in the case of the European constitutional pluralism, or in that of interpretive disagreement on the meaning of the obedience to the 'Queen in

DOI: 10.4324/9781003291572-6

Parliament'. The consequent risk of conflict is structural in the law and does not necessarily entail the breakdown of the legal system. Most conflicts are handled through political negotiation and ultimately solved peacefully: as long as they do not concern the very basic values that keep together a political community and as long as they do not become long-lasting and structural, conflicts belong to the physiology of law. Only when such conditions occur, we move form physiology to pathology and conflicts become unsustainable.

Briefly, pluralism is a structural feature of law in general and of constitutional law in particular. Partly overlapping and partly diverging rules of recognition lie at the basis of any legal order. Not even in case a single, legally omnipotent Queen in Parliament was empowered, it would be possible to settle constitutional controversies once and for all. However, such unbound sovereign is hardly identifiable in legal orders featured by the separation of powers typical of modern constitutionalism, be it vertical, horizontal, or both. To quote Judith Shklar commenting on Rousseau's unitary and unlimited concept of sovereignty: '[t]he word sovereignty has scarcely any meaning at all apart from absolute monarchy. It is the chief attribute of the man who can say *tel est mon plaisir*, and make it stick'.[1] The organization of public powers in modern constitutionalism is inevitably prone to articulating into different bodies, and this makes disagreement and conflict even more likely. A union of States like the European Union (EU) is especially exposed to controversy.

These claims were articulated in four substantive chapters.

In Chapter 2, the riddle of constitutional pluralism is explained by presenting both the judicial and the academic formants. As for the first, I focus on three crucial cases that illustrate how judges have coped with the coexistence of several claims of ultimate authority in Europe. Two of them are opposite and specular. Opinion 2/13 by the Court of Justice of the EU is the epitome of a series of cases that since *Van Gend en Loos* and *Costa* has insisted on the autonomy of EU law. The Opinion not only illustrates this narrative, in which the EU *grundnorm* is separated from those of the Member States and originates directly in the Treaties, but fills it with the typical content of modern constitutionalism, namely the separation of powers and the guarantee of rights. The second judgment, the *Maastricht Urteil* by the German Constitutional Court, upholds the opposite thesis: it denies EU's autonomy and defines it as an association of States, an agent whose principal rests in the Member States, and an organization deprived of constitutional character. The ideas of *kompetenz-kompetenz*, no-*demos* thesis, and *ultra vires* review are brainchildren of this judgment with a huge impact on other supreme and constitutional courts. Finally, the third examined judgment, the *Granital* case by the ICC, tries to find an authentically pluralist path by recognizing the autonomy of EU law and its independent operation within Italian law, with the latter refraining from adjudicating on EU law's validity except in the case of a threat to the essential principles

1 Judith N Shklar, *Men and Citizens – A Study of Rousseau's Social Theory* (Cambridge University Press 1985) 168.

of the Italian Republic (counter-limits). The rest of the chapter introduces the two opposite factions in legal academia on pluralism: those who openly defy pluralism and dismiss it as oxymoronic and those who instead espouse it as the finest incarnation of constitutionalism in the 20th century. This academic formant of constitutional pluralism is constantly active in either justifying or criticizing it.

Chapter 3 moves to directly examining the theory of pluralism of Neil MacCormick that inspires much of the work. It can be divided into two main phases. The first, from 1993 to 1997, shapes the main lines of radical pluralism, a theory fundamentally based on the jurisprudence of H.L.A. Hart. It criticizes the idea of the modern State as the only possible legal order of the modernity, elaborates on the idea that the rule of recognition can be complex (made of partly overlapping, partly diverging beliefs hold by officials), and accepts that conflicts are inevitable and handled through political negotiation rather than legal reasoning. The second phase, covering the 1998–1999 timespan, goes under the etiquette of pluralism under international law, and it takes an overtly normative turn, with MacCormick's emphasis moving to the risk of conflicts. The proposal is to handle them through legal obligations coming from international law. I sustain that the latter theory is mistaken, as it tries to reconcile a Hartian basis with Kelsen's theory of international law, an impossible task that ultimately generates an is-ought fallacy. Moreover, it inevitably leads to the normative side of pluralism, aimed at handling the possible conflicts through legal obligations and reasoning rather than politically, a path that has been tried frequently in the last decades. Instead, 30 years after MacCormick's path-breaking essay *Beyond the Sovereign State*, I argue that it is time to resume radical pluralism to explain EU constitutional pluralism. A methodological commitment to positivism and realism, the idea that sovereignty can be shared, the view that the foundational norm of a legal order is complex and potentially controversial, and that conflicts are mostly handled politically, are the main tenets of such theory.

Chapter 4 elaborates on these ideas by comparatively looking at States which experienced simultaneous claims to ultimate authority. First, I look at federalism, defined by Halberstam as the coexistence within a compound polity of multiple levels of government, each with constitutionally grounded claims to some degree of organizational autonomy and jurisdictional authority. Federalism characterizes not only full-fledged States, but also looser organizations lying in the middle between federations and confederations which are defined 'unions of States' by Larsen. These forms of integrations are based on a constitutional compact, institute a federal citizenship, directly provide their citizens with rights, and substantively change the constitutions of their Member States. The case of one of these looser orders, namely the antebellum USA, is examined in the chapter and particular attention is devoted to those circumstances in which American States, relying on the theories of interposition and nullification, stepped in as guardians of the compact and declared provisions by the federal government *ultra vires*. These conflicts were mostly the result of the activity of States' legislatures and were then handled politically. This state of constitutional affairs lasted for several decades, more than many unitary

States survived. Showing various similarities with the EU experience, the antebellum USA proves, as scholars like Schütze have argued, that federalism is a form of constitutional pluralism, and the EU is way less *sui generis* than one may imagine. I then move to the case of States in which a Queen in Parliament is instead clearly identifiable and show how even in such cases a certain amount of constitutional pluralism persists in the form of interpretive pluralism. Relying on Hart's idea of the penumbra of the rule of recognition and on Alexander's and Schauer's remarks, I argue that no ultimate settling rule can eradicate pluralism once and for all. A series of cases coming from comparative law are then examined to show this point practically, including the postbellum USA and its departmentalism, the Netherlands and its decentralized judicial review through the European Convention on Human Rights and the Charter of Fundamental Rights of the EU, Israel and its long history of indecision between a model of parliamentary or judicial supremacy, and even the UK and its controversies on the limits of the executive's powers in *Miller II*.

Chapter 5, finally, reverts to the EU and focuses on cases of conflicts which unfolded in the last years. I argue that in most cases politics, either by courts or by the legislative and executive branches, solves conflicts when they arise in Europe. The *Taricco* saga is the first considered case, one in which the Italian Constitutional Court and the Court of Justice came close to open confrontation on the interpretation of the principle of legality in criminal law. This was eventually avoided, but *Taricco* remains instructive on the role of interpretive pluralism in fostering conflicts and of the capacity of judicial politics to solve them. I then move to the four cases of *ultra vires* in Europe pronounced by national supreme or constitutional courts until today. The Czech *Landtová*, the Danish *Ajos*, the German *PSPP*, and the Polish K-3/21 cases are examined. I argue that the first three must be divided form the latter: *Landtová*, *Ajos*, and *PSPP* can be analysed stressing the role of political negotiation in handling the tensions after the *ultra vires* statement was issued. Indeed, the political branches, especially parliaments, played a key role in all three of them and ultimately solved the conflict. Besides this cooperative attitude of the political branches, the courts too tried to engage in dialogue with the Court of Justice, although unsuccessfully. Moreover, the very basic values of the Union were never questioned. Under these conditions, we can consider them as cases of physiological conflict, that do not threaten the overall stability of EU law. The Polish K-3/21 case stands alone, instead, because of the capture of the Constitutional Tribunal by political powers and the sheer opposition of Polish institutions to some of the EU's value, witnessed by the unfolding rule of law crisis. The Tribunal does not behave as a court of law but as an enabler of the political branches, simply putting a stamp of alleged legality upon governmental request in K-3/21. Moreover, it makes the ascertainment of the reasons of the *ultra vires* declarations impossible to grasp by not publishing the motivation. This entails a context of confrontation between Poland and the EU which may threaten the foundations of the legal order and ultimately entail the breakdown of EU law in Poland. Forecasts are hard to make, but the comparison between *Landtová*, the *Ajos*, and *PSPP* on the one hand and K-3/21 on the other, illustrates the difference between the physiology and the pathology of conflicts, between those which happen without threatening the breakdown of law and those which do.

Altogether, the arguments exposed in the book make for a theory of radical pluralism in Europe. A plurality of constitutional claims de facto exist and this is not inexplicable, but part of the essentially conflictual character of law, even on the very basic norms of the legal system. Europe is not special in that regard, although the union of States it is made of today exposes such feature in a remarkably clear manner. The future of such union is uncertain, whether it will eventually consolidate into a federal State, dissolve into a looser confederacy, or remain suspended as a union of States for a long time.

I would like to make one last remark on the role of politics in constitutional pluralism as a departure.

One of the key tenets of radical pluralism is the emphasis on the role of politics in solving conflicts. There are cases, the argument goes, in which no legal principle or obligation can solve the disagreements that judges, practitioners, and even scholars face. As exposed in chapter 2, constitutional pluralists in Europe have devoted much attention to identifying overarching principles to guide legal reasoning and avoid conflicts: proportionality, subsidiarity, or loyal cooperation are cases in point. This search for principles to prevent conflict is of course remarkable in its attitude, its willingness to provide a legal answer in every possible case, to avoid conflicts because indeed the law requires one outcome, and no disagreement is allowed. There is a certain degree of Dworkinism beneath this search for a legal answer. Judges in particular are required to identify a legal answer, extrapolating it from the overarching principles previously mentioned, as judge Hercules looking for the one-right answer. The relative authority of EU and national constitutions is a question to be determined by striking the appropriate balance between these competing principles of constitutionalism.

Radical pluralism stresses the limits of jurisprudence, meant both as the abstract theory of law that guides adjudication and as the outcome of judgments, the judicial formant of law. There are cases in which simply no one-right-answer is available, in which various outcomes are justifiable on the basis of reasonable legal arguments. Difference in interpretation depends on methods which, in turn, are functions of different political preferences. Legal reasoning per se cannot solve such controversies: at some point law must leave room for political deliberation. The attempt to use sound legal reasoning to reconcile different interests in the context of European pluralism is understandable and, as long as we move in the area of plain law, probably destined to succeed too. Yet, once we are in the inevitable penumbra of law, where various interpretations are justifiable, one cannot hide behind a curtain of alleged neutral legal reasoning but is required to expose sincerely the political commitments of her decision. This may be frustrating but remains necessary to preserve intellectual honesty.

Radical pluralism is the theory that openly recognizes the effect of the penumbra of legal norms in EU pluralism and points the finger at the ability of political deliberation to find compromises and solve conflicts beyond the reach of legal principles. Much of the analysis of Chapter 5 proves, I believe, that in many of the most extreme cases of confrontation this is what political branches in Europe were indeed able to accomplish. Examining the practical unfolding of constitutional conflicts is informative of this remarkable role of politics in European law.

In his posthumous *Realism and Moralism in Political Argument*, the philosopher Bernard Williams extrapolated a motto from Goethe's Faust. When trying to translate the first line of the Gospel of John, Faust struggles to convey the Greek word *logos*. After a great deal of thinking, he moves from 'word' to 'mind', then to 'force' and, finally, overturns the original: 'in the beginning was the deed'. In recalling Faust's axiom, as he calls it, Williams was trying to state the independency of contingent politics from abstract morality, defend a realistic version of the former, and underline the inadequacy of the Rawlsian view of politics as applied morality. In a somehow similar manner, when considering the field of law, we must look at its conflictual practice over its dreamt harmony. There we will always find a certain amount of conflict, and in the middle of the storm legal reason will help us only to a certain extent. In the beginning is the deed.[2]

2 Bernard Williams, *In the Beginning Was the Deed* (Princeton University Press 2005) 14.

BIBLIOGRAPHY

Adams H (ed), 'The Hartford Convention', *History of the United States of America (1801–1817)*, vol 8 (Cambridge University Press 2011)

Alexander L and Schauer F, 'Rules of Recognition, Constitutional Controversies, and the Dizzying Dependence of Law on Acceptance' in Matthew Adler and Kenneth Himma (eds), *The Rule of Recognition and the U.S. Constitution* (Oxford University Press 2009)

Allegrezza S, 'On Legality in Criminal Matters between Primacy of EU Law and National Constitutional Traditions. A Study of the Taricco Saga' in Valsamis Mitsilegas, Alberto di Martino and Leandro Mancano (eds), *The Court of Justice and European Criminal Law* (Hart Publishing 2019)

Alter KJ, 'Explaining National Court Acceptance of European Court Jurisprudence: A Critical Evaluation ofTheories of Legal Integration' in Anne Marie Slaughter, Alec Stone Sweet and Joseph HH Weiler (eds), *The European Court and National Courts: Doctrine and Jurisprudence: Legal Change in Its Social Context* (Hart Publishing 1998)

———, *Establishing the Supremacy of European Law: The Making of an International Rule of Law in Europe* (Oxford University Press 2003)

Amar AR, 'Of Sovereignty and Federalism' (1987) 96 The Yale Law Journal 1425

———, 'The Bill of Rights as a Constitution' (1991) 100 The Yale Law Journal 1131

Anderson K, *Little Rock: Race and Resistance at Central High School* (Princeton University Press 2010)

Annunziata F, 'Cannons over the EU Legal Order: The Decision of the BVerfG (5 May 2020) in the Weiss Case' (2021) 28 Maastricht Journal of European and Comparative Law 123

Arena A, 'From an Unpaid Electricity Bill to the Primacy of EU Law: Gian Galeazzo Stendardi and the Making of Costa v. ENEL' (2019) 30 European Journal of International Law 1017

Avbelj M, 'Questioning EU Constitutionalisms' (2008) 9 German Law Journal 1

———, 'Constitutional Pluralism and Authoritarianism' (2020) 21 German Law Journal 1023

Avbelj M and Komárek J, 'Four Visions of Constitutional Pluralism Symposium Transcript' (2008) 2 European Journal of Legal Studies 323

Baquero Cruz J, 'The Legacy of the Maastricht-Urteil and the Pluralist Movement' (2008) 14 European Law Journal 389

———, 'Another Look at Constitutional Pluralism in the European Union' (2016) 22 European Law Journal 356

Barber N, *The Constitutional State* (Oxford University Press 2010)

———, *The Principles of Constitutionalism* (Oxford University Press 2018)

Barents R, *The Autonomy of Community Law* (Kluwer 2004)

Barile P, 'Il Cammino Comunitario Della Corte' *Giurisprudenza costituzionale* (1973) 2406

Barsotti V and others, *Italian Constitutional Justice in Global Context* (Oxford University Press 2015)

Bartole S, *The Internationalisation of Constitutional Law: A View from the Venice Commission* (Hart Publishing 2020)

Bassani ML, 'Stati e Costituzione: Il Federalismo Autentico Di John C. Calhoun (1782–1850)' (2015) 1 Eunomia. Rivista di Studi su Pace e Diritti Umani 291

Behnke N and Benz A, 'Federalism and Constitutional Change' in Xenophon Contiades and Alkmene Fotiadou (eds), *Routledge Handbook of Comparative Constitutional Change* (Routledge 2020)

Berman PS, 'Global Legal Pluralism' (2007) 80 Southern California Law Review 1155

Besselink L, *A Composite European Constitution* (Europa Law Publishing 2007)

———, 'National and Constitutional Identity before and after Lisbon' (2010) 6 Utrecht Law Review 36

Bifulco R, 'Federalism' in Robert Schütze and Roger Masterman (eds), *The Cambridge Companion to Comparative Constitutional Law* (Cambridge University Press 2019)

Billis E, 'The European Court of Justice: A "Quasi-Constitutional Court" in Criminal Matters? The Taricco Judgment and Its Shortcomings' (2016) 7 New Journal of European Criminal Law 20

Blokker P, *New Democracies in Crisis?: A Comparative Constitutional Study of the Czech Republic, Hungary, Poland, Romania and Slovakia* (Routledge 2014)

Bobbio N, *Teoria dell'ordinamento giuridico* (Giappichelli 1960)

Bobbitt P, *Constitutional Fate: Theory of the Constitution* (Oxford University Press 1994)

Bobek M, 'Landtová, Holubec, and the Problem of an Uncooperative Court: Implications for the Preliminary Rulings Procedure' (2014) 10 European Constitutional Law Review 54

Bobić A, 'Constitutional Pluralism Is Not Dead: An Analysis of Interactions Between Constitutional Courts of Member States and the European Court of Justice' (2017) 18 German Law Journal 1395

———, 'Constructive Versus Destructive Conflict: Taking Stock of the Recent Constitutional Jurisprudence in the EU' (2020) 22 Cambridge Yearbook of European Legal Studies 60

Bolt WK, 'Founding Father and Rebellious Son: James Madison, John C. Calhoun, and the Use of Precedents' (2004) 5 American Nineteenth Century History 1

Bonelli M, 'The Taricco Saga and the Consolidation of Judicial Dialogue in the European Union' (2018) 25 Maastricht Journal of European and Comparative Law 357

Bonelli M and Claes M, 'Judicial Serendipity: How Portuguese Judges Came to the Rescue of the Polish Judiciary: ECJ 27 February 2018, Case C-64/16, *Associação Sindical Dos Juízes Portugueses*' (2018) 14 European Constitutional Law Review 622

Boom SJ, 'The European Union after the Maastricht Decision: Will Germany Be the "Virginia of Europe?"' (1995) 43 The American Journal of Comparative Law 177

Bruggeman R and Larik J, 'The Elusive Contours of Constitutional Identity: Taricco as a Missed Opportunity' (2020) 35 Utrecht Journal of International and European Law 20

Brzozowski W, 'C'è Del Marcio in Polonia? Il Significato Autentico Della Sentenza Costituzionale 7 Ottobre 2021' (2021) Quaderni costituzionali 965

Buratti A, *Western Constitutionalism: History, Institutions, Comparative Law* (Springer 2019)

Burgess M, *Federalism and the European Union: The Building of Europe, 1950–2000* (Routledge 2000)

———, *Comparative Federalism: Theory and Practice* (Routledge 2006)

Calhoun JC, *Union and Liberty: The Political Philosophy of John C. Calhoun* (Ross M Lence ed, Liberty Fund 1992)

Canihac H, 'Is Constitutional Pluralism (Il)Liberal? On the Political Theory of European Legal Integration in Times of Crisis' (2021) 22 German Law Journal 491

Cannizzaro E, 'Sovereign Within the Union? The Polish Constitutional Tribunal and the Struggle for European Values' (2021) 6 European Papers 1117

Cartabia M, 'The Italian Constitutional Court and the Relationship Between the Italian Legal System and the European Community' (1990) 12 Michigan Journal of International Law 173

———, 'Europe and Rights: Taking Dialogue Seriously' (2009) 5 European Constitutional Law Review 5

Claes M, 'Constitutionalizing Europe at Its Source: The "European Clauses" in the National Constitutions: Evolution and Typology' (2005) 24 Yearbook of European Law 81

———, *The National Courts' Mandate in the European Constitution* (Hart Publishing 2006)

Cohen-Eliya M and Porat I, 'Proportionality and the Culture of Justification' (2011) 59 American Journal of Comparative Law 463

Coleman J, *The Practice of Principle: In Defence of a Pragmatist Approach to Legal Theory* (Oxford University Press 2003)

Conway G, 'Recovering a Separation of Powers in the European Union: Separation of Powers in the EU' (2011) 17 European Law Journal 304

Craig P and de Búrca G, *EU Law: Texts, Cases, and Materials* (Oxford University Press 2011)

Craig P and Markakis M, 'Gauweiler and the Legality of Outright Monetary Transactions' (2016) 41 European Law Review 4

Crawford J, *Brownlie's Principles of Public International Law* (Oxford University Press 2012)

Culver K and Giudice M, *Legality's Borders* (Oxford University Press 2010)

———, 'Not a System but an Order: An Inter-Institutional View of European Union Law' in Keith Culver and Michael Giudice (eds), *Philosophical Foundations of European Union Law* (Oxford University Press 2012)

d'Aspremont J, 'International Law-Making by Non-State Actors: Changing the Model or Putting the Phenomenon into Perspective?' in Cedric Ryngaert and Noortmann Math (eds), *Non-State Actor Dynamics in International Law: From Law-Takers to Law-Makers* (Routledge 2010)

Davies B, *Resisting the European Court of Justice: West Germany's Confrontation with European Law, 1949–1979* (Cambridge University Press 2012)

Davies G, 'Constitutional Disagreement in Europe and the Search for Pluralism' in Matej Avbelj and Jan Komárek (eds), *Constitutional Pluralism in the European Union and Beyond* (Hart Publishing 2012)

de Búrca G, 'The Principle of Proportionality and Its Application in EC Law' (1993) 13 Yearbook of European Law 105

———, 'Sovereignty and the Supremacy Doctrine of the European Court of Justice' in Neil Walker (ed), *Sovereignty in Transition* (Hart Publishing 2003)

———, 'The Evolution of EU Human Rights Law' in Paul Craig and Gráinne de Búrca (eds), *The Evolution of EU Law* (Oxford University Press 2021)

de Visser M, *Constitutional Review in Europe: A Comparative Analysis* (Hart Publishing 2014)

———, 'Nonjudicial Constitutional Interpretation: The Netherlands' in David S Law (ed), *Constitutionalism in Context* (Cambridge University Press 2022)

de Witte B, 'The European Union as an International Legal Experiment' in Grainne de Burca and JHH Weiler (eds), *The Worlds of European Constitutionalism* (Cambridge University Press 2011)

———, 'Direct Effect, Primacy, and the Nature of the Legal Order' in Paul Craig and Gráinne de Búrca (eds), *The Evolution of EU Law* (Oxford University Press 2021)

———, 'The European Union's Covid-19 Recovery Plan: The Legal Engineering of an Economic Policy Shift' (2021) 58 Common Market Law Review 635

Dermine P, 'The Ruling of the Bundesverfassungsgericht in PSPP – An Inquiry into Its Repercussions on the Economic and Monetary Union: Bundesverfassungsgericht 5 May 2020, 2 BvR 859/15 and Others, PSPP' (2020) 16 European Constitutional Law Review 525

Dickson J, 'Is the Rule of Recognition Really a Conventional Rule?' (2007) 27 Oxford Journal of Legal Studies 373

———, 'Towards a Theory of European Union Legal Systems' in Julie Dickson and Pavlos Eleftheriadis (eds), *Philosophical Foundations of European Union Law* (Oxford University Press 2012)

Dinan D, *Europe Recast: A History of the European Union* (Lynne Rienner Publishers 2014)

Donahue JD and Pollack MA, 'Centralization and Its Discontents: The Rhythms of Federalism in the United States and the European Union', *The Federal Vision* (Oxford University Press 2001)

Drinóczi T and Bień-Kacała A, 'Illiberal Constitutionalism: The Case of Hungary and Poland' (2019) 20 German Law Journal 1140

———, *Illiberal Constitutionalism in Poland and Hungary: The Deterioration of Democracy, Misuse of Human Rights and Abuse of the Rule of Law* (Routledge 2021)

Dumbrovsky T, 'Federal Solution to the EU Internal Sovereignty Conundrum: The European Doctrine of the Czech Constitutional Court and the U.S. Compact Theory' in Tomas Dumbrovsky and Tichý Luboš (eds), *Sovereignty and Competences of the European Union* (Charles University 2010)

Dworkin R, 'Comments on the Unity of Law Doctrine (a Response)' in Howard Evans Kiefer and Milton Karl Munitz (eds), *Ethics and Social Justice* (State University of New York Press 1968)

———, *Taking Rights Seriously* (Harvard University Press 1978)

———, 'The Model of Rules II', *Taking Rights Seriously* (Harvard University Press 1978)

———, *Law's Empire* (Harvard University Press 1986)

Dyzenhaus D, *Legality and Legitimacy: Carl Schmitt, Hans Kelsen, and Hermann Heller in Weimar* (Oxford University Press 1999)

———, 'The Left and the Question of Law' (2004) 17 Canadian Journal of Law & Jurisprudence 7

———, 'Hobbes on the Authority of Law' in David Dyzenhaus and Thomas Poole (eds), *Hobbes and the Law* (Cambridge University Press 2012)

———, 'The Janus-Faced Constitution' in David Dyzenhaus, Jacco Bomhoff and Thomas Poole (eds), *The Double-Facing Constitution* (Cambridge University Press 2020)

Elazar D, *Exploring Federalism* (University of Alabama Press 1987)

———, 'The United States and the European Union: Models for Their Epochs', *The Federal Vision* (Oxford University Press 2001)

Eleftheriadis P, *Legal Rights* (Oxford University Press 2008)

———, 'Pluralism and Integrity: Pluralism and Integrity' (2010) 23 Ratio Juris 365

———, 'Hart on Sovereignty' in Luís Duarte d'Almeida, James Edwards and Andrea Dolcetti (eds), *Reading HLA Hart's 'The Concept of Law'* (Hart Publishing 2013)
———, *A Union of Peoples* (Oxford University Press 2020)
Elliott M, 'Constitutional Adjudication and Constitutional Politics in the United Kingdom: The Miller II Case in Legal and Political Context' (2020) 16 European Constitutional Law Review 625
Engel A, Nowag J, and Groussot X, 'Is This Completely M.A.D.? Three Views on the Ruling of the German FCC on 5th May 2020' (2020) 3 Nordic Journal of European Law 128
Fabbrini F and Larik J, 'The Past, Present and Future of the Relation between the European Court of Justice and the European Court of Human Rights' (2016) 35 Yearbook of European Law 145
Faraguna P, 'Constitutional Identity in the EU – A Shield or a Sword?' (2017) 18 German law journal 1617
Fasone C, Gallo D, and Wouters J, 'Re-Connecting Authority and Democratic Legitimacy in the EU: Introductory Remarks' (2020) 5 *European Papers* 175
Fasone C and Lindseth P, 'Europe's Fractured Metabolic Constitution: From the Eurozone Crisis to the Coronavirus Response' (2020) LUISS School of Government Working Paper N 61
Ferrares Comella V, 'The European Model of Constitutional Review of Legislation: Toward Decentralization?' (2004) 2 International Journal of Constitutional Law 461
Ferraro F, 'Il conflitto reale e il dialogo apparente della Corte di giustizia e della Corte costituzionale in merito al principio di legalità e alla riserva di legge in materia penale' (2018) 18 Federalismi 1
Ferrone V, *The Enlightenment and the Rights of Man* (Liverpool University Press 2019)
Flynn T, 'Constitutional Pluralism and Loyal Opposition' (2021) 19 International Journal of Constitutional Law 241
Foner E, *The Second Founding: How the Civil War and Reconstruction Remade the Constitution* (Norton 2019)
Ford PL (ed), 'Jackson's Nullification Proclamation, 1832', *The Federalist: A Commentary on the Constitution of the United States* (Henry Holt and Co 1898)
——— (ed), 'South Carolina Ordinance of Nullification, 1832', *The Federalist: A Commentary on the Constitution of the United States* (Henry Holt and Co 1898)
Friedrich CJ, *Trends of Federalism in Theory and Practice* (Pall Mall 1968)
Fritz V, 'The First Member State Rebellion? The European Court of Justice and the Negotiations of the "Luxembourg Protocol" of 1971: The ECJ and the Luxembourg Protocol of 1971' (2015) 21 European Law Journal 680
Fruchtman J, *American Constitutional History: A Brief Introduction* (Blackwell 2016)
Fumurescu A and Schön AM, *Foundations of American Political Thought: Readings and Commentary* (Cambridge University Press 2021)
Gaja G, 'Constitutional Court (Italy), Decision No. 170 of 8 June 1984, S.p.a. Granital v. Amministrazione Delle Finanze Dello Stato' (1984) 21 Common Market Law Review 756
Gallie WB, 'Essentially Contested Concepts' (1955) 56 Proceedings of the Aristotelian Society 167
Gallo D, 'Challenging EU Constitutional Law: The Italian Constitutional Court's New Stance on Direct Effect and the Preliminary Reference Procedure' (2019) 25 European Law Journal 434
Gardbaum S, 'The New Commonwealth Model of Constitutionalism' (2001) 49 The American Journal of Comparative Law 707

———, *The New Commonwealth Model of Constitutionalism* (Cambridge University Press 2013)

Gardner J, 'Legal Positivism: 5 1/2 Myths' (2001) 46 American Journal of Jurisprudence 199

Gattini A, 'Joined Cases C–402/05 P & 415/05 P, Yassin Abdullah Kadi, Al Barakaat International Foundation v. Council and Commission, Judgment of the Grand Chamber of 3 September 2008' (2009) 46 Common Market Law Review 213

Ginsburg T, 'Constitutional Endurance' in Xenophon Contiades and Alkmene Fotiadou (eds), *Routledge Handbook of Comparative Constitutional Change* (Routledge 2020)

Giudice M, 'Hart and Kelsen on International Law' in Leslie Green and Brian Leiter (eds), *Oxford Studies in Philosophy of Law: Volume 2* (Oxford University Press 2013)

Glock H-J, *A Wittgenstein Dictionary* (Blackwell 1996)

Goebel R, 'Supranational? Federal? Intergovernmental? The Governmental Structure of the European Union After the Treaty of Lisbon' (2013) 20 Columbia Journal of European Law 77

Goldoni M and Wilkinson MA, 'The Material Constitution' (2018) 81 The Modern Law Review 567

Goldsworthy J, 'Constitutional Interpretation' in Michel Rosenfeld and András Sajó (eds), *The Oxford Handbook of Comparative Constitutional Law* (Oxford University Press 2012)

Gordley J, 'Comparative Legal Research: Its Function in the Development of Harmonized Law' (1995) 43 American Journal of Comparative Law 555

Green L, 'Positivism and Conventionalism' (1999) 12 Canadian Journal of Law & Jurisprudence 35

———, 'Introduction' in Herbert LA Hart, *The Concept of Law* (Oxford University Press 2012)

———, 'Positivism, Realism and Sources of Law' in Torben Spaak and Patricia Mindus (eds), *The Cambridge Companion to Legal Positivism* (Cambridge University Press 2021)

Greenwalt K, 'The Rule of Recognition and the Constitution' in Matthew Adler and Kenneth Himma (eds), *The Rule of Recognition and the U.S. Constitution* (Oxford University Press 2009)

Griffin SM, *American Constitutionalism: From Theory to Politics* (Princeton University Press 1996)

Griffiths J, 'What Is Legal Pluralism?' (1986) 18 The Journal of Legal Pluralism and Unofficial Law 1

Grimm D, 'Does Europe Need a Constitution?' (1995) 1 European Law Journal 282

———, *Constitutionalism: Past, Present, and Future* (Oxford University Press 2016)

———, 'A Long Time Coming' (2020) 21 German Law Journal 944

Habermas J, 'Remarks on Dieter Grimm's "Does Europe Need a Constitution?"' (1995) 1 European Law Journal 303

Halberstam D, 'Constitutional Heterarchy: The Centrality of Conflict in the European Union and the United States' in Jeffrey L Dunoff and Joel P Trachtman (eds), *Ruling the World?: Constitutionalism, International Law, and Global Governance* (Cambridge University Press 2009)

———, 'Pluralism in Marbury and Van Gend' in Miguel Poiares Maduro and Loïc Azoulai (eds), *The Past and Future of EU Law: The Classics of EU Law Revisited on the 50th Anniversary of the Rome Treaty* (Hart Publishing 2010)

———, 'Federalism: Theory, Policy, Law' in Michel Rosenfeld and András Sajó (eds), *The Oxford Handbook of Comparative Constitutional Law* (Oxford University Press 2012)

———, '"It's the Autonomy, Stupid!" A Modest Defense of Opinion 2/13 on EU Accession to the ECHR, and the Way Forward' (2015) 16 German Law Journal 105

———, 'Joseph Weiler, Eric Stein, and the Transformation of Constitutional Law' in Marlene Wind and Miguel Poiares Maduro (eds), *The Transformation of Europe: Twenty-Five Years On* (Cambridge University Press 2017)

———, '"A People for Certain Purposes": On the History and Philosophy of Federalism(s) in the United States and Europe' (2018) University of Michigan Public Law Research Paper N. 619

Halberstam D and Möllers C, 'Special Section: The Federal Constitutional Court's Lisbon Case' 10 German Law Journal 18

Halmai G, 'Populism, Authoritarianism and Constitutionalism' (2019) 20 German Law Journal 296

Hamilton A, Madison J, and Jay J, *The Federalist Papers* (Michael A Genovese ed, Palgrave Macmillan 2010)

Hamon F and Troper M, *Droit constitutionnel* (LGDJ-Lextenso 2014)

Hancox E, 'The Relationship Between the Charter and General Principles: Looking Back and Looking Forward' (2020) 22 Cambridge Yearbook of European Legal Studies 233

Harbo T-I, 'The Function of the Proportionality Principle in EU Law' (2010) 16 European Law Journal 158

Hart H.L.A., *Essays on Bentham: Jurisprudence and Political Philosophy* (Oxford University Press 1982)

———, *Essays in Jurisprudence and Philosophy* (Oxford University Press 1983)

———, *The Concept of Law* (Oxford University Press 2012)

Hay P, 'Federal Jurisdiction of the Common Market Court' (1963) 12 American Journal of Comparative Law 21

———, 'Supremacy of Community Law in National Courts. A Progress Report on Referrals Under the EEC Treaty' (1968) 16 The American Journal of Comparative Law 524

Helle Krunke and Sune Klinge, 'The Danish Ajos Case: The Missing Case from Maastricht and Lisbon' (2018) 3 European Papers 157

Herdegen M, 'Maastricht and the German Constitutional Court: Constitutional Restraints for an "Ever Closer Union" and Document "Extracts from: Brunner v. The European Union"' (1994) 31 Common Market Law Review 235

Hilpold P, 'So Long Solange? The PSPP Judgment of the German Constitutional Court and the Conflict between the German and the European "Popular Spirit"' (2021) 23 Cambridge Yearbook of European Legal Studies 159

Hinarejos A, 'Gauweiler and the Outright Monetary Transactions Programme: The Mandate of the European Central Bank and the Changing Nature of Economic and Monetary Union' (2015) 11 European Constitutional Law Review 563

Hirschl R, 'Opting Out of "Global Constitutionalism"' (2018) 12 Law & Ethics of Human Rights 1

———, 'Comparative Methodologies' in Roger Masterman and Robert Schütze (eds), *The Cambridge Companion to Comparative Constitutional Law* (Cambridge University Press 2019)

Holtzman S and Leich C, 'Introduction' in Steven Holtzman and Christopher Leich (eds), *Wittgenstein: To Follow a Rule* (Routledge 1981)

Hueglin TO and Fenna A, *Comparative Federalism: A Systematic Inquiry* (University of Toronto Press 2015)

Imamovic Š, *The Architecture of Fundamental Rights in the European Union* (Hart Publishing 2022)

Isiksel T, *Europe's Functional Constitution: A Theory of Constitutionalism Beyond the State* (Oxford University Press 2016)

Itzcovich G, 'Sovereignty, Legal Pluralism and Fundamental Rights: Italian Jurisprudence and European Integration (1964–73)' (2004) 10 European Public Law 28

———, *Teorie e ideologie del diritto comunitario* (Giappichelli 2006)

———, 'Legal Order, Legal Pluralism, Fundamental Principles. Europe and Its Law in Three Concepts: Legal Order, Legal Pluralism, Fundamental Principles' (2012) 18 European Law Journal 358

———, 'The European Court of Justice' in András Jakab, Arthur Dyevre and Giulio Itzcovich (eds), *Comparative Constitutional Reasoning* (Cambridge University Press 2017)

Jackson V, 'Comparative Constitutional Law: Methodologies' in Michel Rosenfeld and András Sajó (eds), *The Oxford Handbook of Comparative Constitutional Law* (Oxford University Press 2012)

Jacobson A and Schlink B (eds), *Weimar: A Jurisprudence of Crisis* (2002)

Jaklic K, *Constitutional Pluralism in the EU* (Oxford University Press 2014)

Jaroszyński T, 'National Parliaments' Scrutiny of the Principle of Subsidiarity: Reasoned Opinions 2014–2019' (2020) 16 European Constitutional Law Review 91

Jefferson Powell H, 'The Principles of '98: An Essay in Historical Retrieval' (1994) 80 Virginia Law Review 689

Jones M, 'The Legal Nature of the European Community: A Jurisprudential Analysis Using H.L.A. Hart's Model of Law and a Legal System' (1984) 17 Cornell International Law Journal 1

Kalypso Nicolaidis, 'The Idea of European Demoicracy' in Julie Dickson and Pavlos Eleftheriadis (eds), *Philosophical Foundations of European Union Law* (Oxford University Press 2012)

Kelemen RD, 'On the Unsustainability of Constitutional Pluralism: European Supremacy and the Survival of the Eurozone' (2016) 23 Maastricht Journal of European and Comparative Law 136

Kelemen RD and Pavone T, 'Where Have the Guardians Gone? Law Enforcement and the Politics of Supranational Forbearance in the European Union' (Social Science Research Network 2021) SSRN Scholarly Paper 3994918 https://papers.ssrn.com/abstract=3994918

Kelemen RD and Pech L, 'The Uses and Abuses of Constitutional Pluralism: Undermining the Rule of Law in the Name of Constitutional Identity in Hungary and Poland' (2019) 21 Cambridge Yearbook of European Legal Studies 59

Kelsen H, *General Theory of Norms* (Oxford University Press 1991)

———, 'Sovereignty' in Stanley Paulson (ed), *Normativity and Norms: Critical Perspectives on Kelsenian Themes* (Oxford University Press 1999)

———, *Pure Theory of Law* (The Lawbook Exchange 2003)

———, *General Theory of Law and State* (Transaction Publishers 2005)

———, *The Essence and Value of Democracy* (Rowman & Littlefield 2013)

Kincaid J, 'Confederal Federalism and Citizen Representation in the European Union' (1999) 22 West European Politics 34

Klabbers J, 'Judging Inter-Legality' in Jan Klabbers and Gianluigi Palombella (eds), *The Challenge of Inter-Legality* (Cambridge University Press 2019)

Klabbers J and Palombella G (eds), *The Challenge of Inter-Legality* (Cambridge University Press 2019)

Komárek J, 'Czech Constitutional Court Playing with Matches: The Czech Constitutional Court Declares a Judgment of the Court of Justice of the EU Ultra Vires; Judgment of 31 January 2012, Pl. ÚS 5/12, Slovak Pensions XVII' (2012) 8 European Constitutional Law Review 323

———, 'The Place of Constitutional Courts in the EU' (2013) 9 European Constitutional Law Review 420

Kramer LD, 'Popular Constitutionalism, circa 2004' (2004) 92 California Law Review 959

———, *The People Themselves: Popular Constitutionalism and Judicial Review* (Oxford University Press 2006)

Kramer MH, 'H.L.A. Hart, The Concept of Law' in Jacob T Levy (ed), *The Oxford Handbook of Classics in Contemporary Political Theory* (Oxford University Press 2015)

Krisch N, *Beyond Constitutionalism: The Pluralist Structure of Postnational Law* (Oxford University Press 2010)

———, 'Who Is Afraid of Radical Pluralism? Legal Order and Political Stability in the Postnational Space' (2011) 24 Ratio Juris 386

——— (ed), *Entangled Legalities Beyond the State* (Cambridge University Press 2021)

Kumm M, 'Who Is the Final Arbiter of Constitutionality in Europe?: Three Conceptions of the Relationship Between the German Federal Constitutional Court and the European Court of Justice' (1999) 36 Common Market Law Review 351

———, 'The Jurisprudence of Constitutional Conflict: Constitutional Supremacy in Europe before and after the Constitutional Treaty' (2005) 11 European Law Journal 262

———, 'The Moral Point of Constitutional Pluralism: Defining the Domain of Legitimate Institutional Civil Disobedience and Conscientious Objection' in Julie Dickson and Pavlos Eleftheriadis (eds), *Philosophical Foundations of European Union Law* (Oxford University Press 2012)

La Torre M, *Law as Institution* (Springer 2010)

———, 'Reform and Tradition: Changes and Continuities in Neil MacCormick's Concept of Law' in Agustín José Menéndez and John Erik Fossum (eds), *Law and Democracy in Neil MacCormick's Legal and Political Theory* (Springer 2011)

———, 'Institutionalism as Alternative Constitutional Theory: On Santi Romano's Concept of Law and His Epigones' (2020) 11 Jurisprudence 92

Lacey N, *A Life of H.L.A. Hart: The Nightmare and the Noble Dream* (Oxford University Press 2006)

———, 'Analytical Jurisprudence Versus Descriptive Sociology Revisited' in Maksymilian Del Mar and Michael Giudice (eds), *Legal Theory and the Social Sciences*, vol II (Routledge 2010)

LaCroix AL, 'A Singular and Awkward War: The Transatlantic Context of the Hartford Convention' (2005) 6 American Nineteenth Century History 3

———, *The Ideological Origins of American Federalism* (Harvard University Press 2011)

Larsen SR, *The Constitutional Theory of the Federation and the European Union* (Oxford University Press 2021)

Lash KT (ed), *The Reconstruction Amendments: The Essential Documents*, vol 2 (University of Chicago Press 2020)

Lavranos N, 'The Solange-Method as a Tool for Regulating Competing Jurisdictions among International Courts and Tribunals' (2008) 30 Loyola of Los Angeles International and Comparative Law Review 275

Lawrence JC, 'Constitutional Pluralism's Unspoken Normative Core' (2019) 21 Cambridge Yearbook of European Legal Studies 24

Leczykiewicz D, 'The Charter of Fundamental Rights and the EU's Shallow Constitutionalism' in Nicholas Barber, Maria Cahill and Richard Ekins (eds), *The Rise and Fall of the European Constitution* (Hart Publishing 2019)

Leiter B, 'Legal Positivism as a Realist Theory of Law' in Torben Spaak and Patricia Mindus (eds), *The Cambridge Companion to Legal Positivism* (Cambridge University Press 2021)

Lenaerts K, 'Constitutionalism and the Many Faces of Federalism' (1990) 38 American Journal of Comparative Law 205
Levinson S, 'The Twenty-First Century Rediscovery of Nullification and Secession in American Political Rhetoric: Frivolousness Incarnate or Serious Arguments to Be Wrestled With?' (2014) 67 Arkansas Law Review 17
Leyland P, *The Constitution of the United Kingdom* (Hart Publishing 2016)
Lindeboom J, 'Why EU Law Claims Supremacy' (2018) 38 Oxford Journal of Legal Studies 328
———, 'The Autonomy of EU Law: A Hartian View' (2021) 13 European Journal of Legal Studies 271.
Lindseth P, 'The Metabolic Constitution and the Limits of EU Legal Pluralism' in Gareth Davies and Matej Avbelj (eds), *Research Handbook on Legal Pluralism and EU Law* (Edward Elgar Publishing 2018)
López Bofill H, *Law, Violence and Constituent Power* (Routledge 2021)
Loughlin M, *Foundations of Public Law* (Oxford University Press 2010)
———, 'Constitutional Pluralism: An Oxymoron?' (2014) 3 Global Constitutionalism 9
———, 'The Concept of Constituent Power' (2014) 13 European Journal of Political Theory 218
———, *Political Jurisprudence* (Oxford University Press 2017)
Loveland I, *By Due Process of Law?: Racial Discrimination and the Right to Vote in South Africa 1855–1960* (Hart Publishing 1999)
Luciani M, 'Il Brusco Risveglio. I Controlimiti e La Fine Mancata Della Storia Costituzionale' (2016) 2 Rivista AIC 1
Mac Amhlaigh CS, 'The Anatomy of Constitutional Pluralism in the European Union' in Gareth Davies and Matej Avbelj (eds), *Research Handbook on Legal Pluralism and EU Law* (Edward Elgar 2018)
———, 'Eppur Esiste!: Legitimacy and Longevity in the EU's Long Decade of Crisis' (2022) University of Edinburgh School of Law Research Paper Series N 8
MacCormick N, 'Beyond the Sovereign State' (1993) 56 The Modern Law Review 1
———, 'Beyond the Sovereign State' (1993) 56 The Modern Law Review 1
———, *Legal Reasoning and Legal Theory* (Oxford University Press 1994)
———, 'Sovereignty: Myth and Reality' (1995) 11 (First Series) Scottish Affairs 1
———, 'The Maastricht Urteil: Sovereignty Now' (1995) 1 European Law Journal 259
———, 'Democracy, Subsidiarity, and Citizenship in the "European Commonwealth"' (1997) 16 Law and Philosophy 331
———, 'Risking Constitutional Collision in Europe?' (1998) 18 Oxford Journal of Legal Studies 517
———, 'Juridical Pluralism and the Risk of Constitutional Conflict', *Questioning Sovereignty* (Oxford University Press 1999)
———, 'On Sovereignty and Post-Sovereignty', *Questioning Sovereignty* (Oxford University Press 1999)
———, 'The Legal Framework: Institutional Normative Order', *Questioning Sovereignty* (Oxford University Press 1999)
———, *Questioning Sovereignty* (Oxford University Press 1999)
———, *Institutions of Law: An Essay in Legal Theory* (Oxford University Press 2007)
———, *H.L.A. Hart* (Stanford University Press 2008)
MacCormick N and Summers RS, *Interpreting Statutes: A Comparative Study* (Routledge 1991)
MacCormick N and Weinberger O, *An Institutional Theory of Law* (Springer 1986)

Madison J, *The Writings of James Madison*, vol 4 (Gaillard Hunt ed, GP Putnam's Sons 1903)
———, *Selected Writings of James Madison* (Ralph Ketcham ed, Hackett 2006)
Madsen MR, Olsen HP and Šadl U, 'Competing Supremacies and Clashing Institutional Rationalities: The Danish Supreme Court's Decision in the Ajos Case and the National Limits of Judicial Cooperation' (2017) 23 European Law Journal 140
Magnette P and Lacroix J, 'EU Constitutionalism and the "American Experience"' in Gráinne de Búrca and Joanne Scott (eds), *Law and New Governance in the EU and the US* (Hart Publishing 2006)
Mak E, 'Report on the Netherlands and Luxembourg' in Giuseppe Martinico and Oreste Pollicino (eds), *The National Judicial Treatment of the ECHR and EU Laws: A Comparative Constitutional Perspective* (Europa Law Publishing 2010)
Malcolm N, 'Sense on Sovereignty' in Martin Holmes (ed), *The Eurosceptical Reader* (Palgrave Macmillan 1996)
Mancini GF, 'The Making of a Constitution for Europe' (1989) 26 Common Market Law Review 595
Marquand D, *Parliament for Europe* (J Cape 1979)
Martinico G, *The Tangled Complexity of the EU Constitutional Process: The Frustrating Knot of Europe* (Routledge 2013)
———, 'The Autonomy of EU Law – A Joint Celebration of Kadi II and Van Gend En Loos' in Matej Avbelj, Filippo Fontanelli and Giuseppe Martinico (eds), *Kadi on trial: a multifaceted analysis of the Kadi judgment* (Routledge 2014)
———, 'The "Polemical" Spirit of European Constitutional Law: On the Importance of Conflicts in EU Law' (2015) 16 German Law Journal 1343
———, 'The Federal Language and the European Integration Process: The European Communities Viewed from the US' (2016) 53 Politique europeenne 38
Martinico G and Repetto G, 'Fundamental Rights and Constitutional Duels in Europe: An Italian Perspective on Case 269/2017 of the Italian Constitutional Court and Its Aftermath' (2019) 15 European Constitutional Law Review 731
Mayer FC, 'The Ultra Vires Ruling: Deconstructing the German Federal Constitutional Court's PSPP Decision of 5 May 2020' (2020) 16 European Constitutional Law Review 733
McGinn M, 'Grammar in the Philosophical Investigations' in Oskari Kuusela and Marie McGinn (eds), *The Oxford Handbook of Wittgenstein* (Oxford University Press 2011)
McIlwain CH, *Constitutionalism: Ancient and Modern* (Liberty Fund 1947)
Menéndez AJ, 'From Constitutional Pluralism to a Pluralistic Constitution? Constitutional Synthesis as a MacCormickian Constitutional Theory of European Integration' in Agustín José Menéndez and John Erik Fossum (eds), *Law and Democracy in Neil MacCormick's Legal and Political Theory* (Springer 2011)
Merry SE, 'Legal Pluralism' (1988) 22 Law & Society Review 869
Michaels R, 'The Functional Method of Comparative Law' in Mathias Reimann and Reinhard Zimmermann (eds), *The Oxford Handbook of Comparative Law* (Oxford University Press 2019)
Miller AS and Howell RF, 'Interposition, Nullification and the Delicate Division of Power in a Federal System' (1956) 5 Journal of Public Law 2
Mitsilegas V, 'The Principles of Legality and Proportionality of Criminal Offences and Penalties' in Steve Peers and others (eds), *The EU Charter of Fundamental rights: A Commentary* (Hart Publishing 2014)
Moellers C, *The Three Branches: A Comparative Model of Separation of Powers* (Oxford University Press 2013)

Mooij AA, 'The Weiss Judgment: The Court's Further Clarification of the ECB's Legal Framework: Case C-493/17 Weiss and Others, EU:C:2018:1000' (2019) 26 Maastricht Journal of European and Comparative Law 449
Mortati C, *L'ordinamento del governo nel nuovo diritto pubblico italiano* (Giuffrè 2000)
Mureinik E, 'A Bridge to Where? Introducing the Interim Bill of Rights' (1994) 10 South African Journal on Human Rights 31
Nelsen BF and Stubb AC-G (eds), *The European Union: Readings on the Theory and Practice of European Integration* (Rienner 1994)
Öberg M-L, *The Boundaries of the EU Internal Market: Participation without Membership* (Cambridge University Press 2020)
Oliver PC, 'Sovereignty in the Twenty-First Century' (2003) 14 King's Law Journal 137
Palermo F and Kössler K, *Comparative Federalism – Constitutional Arrangements and Case Law* (Hart Publishing 2017)
Palombella G, 'Arguments in Favour of a Functional Theory of Fundamental Rights' (2001) 14 International Journal for the Semiotics of Law 299
———, 'The Rule of Law and Its Core' in Jan Klabbers and Gianluigi Palombella (eds), *Relocating the Rule of Law* (Hart Publishing 2009)
———, 'The Rule of Law beyond the State: Failures, Promises, and Theory' (2009) 7 International Journal of Constitutional Law 442
———, 'Theory, Realities, and Promises of Inter-Legality: A Manifesto' in Gianluigi Palombella and Jan Klabbers (eds), *The Challenge of Inter-Legality* (Cambridge University Press 2019)
Paris D, 'Carrot and Stick. The Italian Constitutional Court's Preliminary Reference in the Case Taricco' (2017) Zoom-in 37 QIL Questions of International Law 5
———, 'Constitutional Courts as European Union Courts: The Current and Potential Use of EU Law as a Yardstick for Constitutional Review' (2017) 24 Maastricht Journal of European and Comparative Law 792
Patterson D, 'Explicating the Internal Point of View' (1999) 52 Southern Methodist University Law Review 67
———, 'Theoretical Disagreement, Legal Positivism, and Interpretation' (2018) 31 Ratio Juris 260
Pech L and Kochenov D, *Respect for the Rule of Law in the Case Law of the European Court of Justice: A Casebook Overview of Key Judgments since the Portuguese Judges Case* (Swedish Institute for European Policy Studies 2021) www.sieps.se/en/publications/2021/respect-for-the-rule-of-law-in-the-case-law-of-the-european-court-of-justice/
Pech L and Scheppele KL, 'Illiberalism Within: Rule of Law Backsliding in the EU' (2017) 19 Cambridge Yearbook of European Legal Studies 3
Pech L, Wachowiec P and Mazur D, 'Poland's Rule of Law Breakdown: A Five-Year Assessment of EU's (In)Action' (2021) 13 Hague Journal on the Rule of Law 1
Pergola AL and Duca PD, 'Community Law, International Law and the Italian Constitution' (1985) 79 American Journal of International Law 598
Pernice I, 'Multilevel Constitutionalism and the Treaty of Amsterdam: European Constitution-Making Revisited?' (1999) 36 Common Market Law Review 48
Peters A, 'Compensatory Constitutionalism: The Function and Potential of Fundamental International Norms and Structures' (2006) 19 Leiden Journal of International Law 579
Phelan W, 'What Is Sui Generis About the European Union? Costly International Cooperation in a Self-Contained Regime' (2012) 14 International Studies Review 367
Philpott D, 'Sovereignty: An Introduction and Brief History' (1995) 48 Journal of International Affairs 353

Piccirilli G, 'The "Taricco Saga": The Italian Constitutional Court Continues Its European Journey' (2018) 14 European Constitutional Law Review 814

Pierdominici L, 'The Theory of EU Constitutional Pluralism: A Crisis in a Crisis?' (2017) 9 Perspectives on Federalism 119

———, *The Mimetic Evolution of the Court of Justice of the EU: A Comparative Law Perspective* (Palgrave Macmillan 2020)

Pino G, 'Farewell to the Rule of Recognition?' (2011) 5 Problema. Anuario de Filosofía y Teoría del Derecho 265

Pirker BH and Reitemeyer S, 'Between Discursive and Exclusive Autonomy – Opinion 2/13, the Protection of Fundamental Rights and the Autonomy of EU Law' (2015) 17 Cambridge Yearbook of European Legal Studies 168

Pítrová L, 'The Judgment of the Czech Constitutional Court in the "Slovak Pensions" Case and Its Possible Consequences (In Light of the Fortiter In Re Suaviter In Modo Principle)' (2013) 3 The Lawyer Quarterly 86

'PM Action to Review Constitutionality of EU Treaty Now in English – Rule of Law' https://ruleoflaw.pl/pm-action-to-review-constitutionality-of-eu-treaty-now-in-english/ accessed 25 April 2022

Poiares Maduro, Miguel, 'The Importance of Being Called a Constitution: Constitutional Authority and the Authority of Constitutionalism' (2005) 3 International Journal of Constitutional Law 332

Poiares Maduro, Miguel M, 'Contrapunctual Law: Europe's Constitutional Pluralism in Action' in Neil Walker (ed), *Sovereignty in Transition* (Hart Publishing 2003)

———, 'Three Claims of Constitutional Pluralism' in Matej Avbelj and Jan Komárek (eds), *Constitutional Pluralism in the European Union and Beyond* (Hart Publishing 2012)

Poiares Maduro, Miguel MP, 'Interpreting European Law: Judicial Adjudication in a Context of Constitutional Pluralism' (2008) 1 European Journal of Legal Studies 137

Polzin M, 'Constitutional Identity, Unconstitutional Amendments and the Idea of Constituent Power: The Development of the Doctrine of Constitutional Identity in German Constitutional Law' (2016) 14 International Journal of Constitutional Law 411

Postema GJ, '"Protestant" Interpretation and Social Practices' (1987) 6 Law and Philosophy 283

Přibáň J, 'Constituting the Heterarchy of European Constitutionalism in the EU's New Member States' in Alberto Febbrajo and Wojciech Sadurski (eds), *Central and Eastern Europe After Transition* (Routledge 2016)

———, *Constitutional Imaginaries: A Theory of European Societal Constitutionalism* (Routledge 2022)

Rasmussen M, 'From Costa v ENEL to the Treaties of Rome: A Brief History of a Legal Revolution' in Miguel Poiares Maduro and Loïc Azoulai (eds), *The Past and Future of EU Law: The Classics of EU Law Revisited on the 50th Anniversary of the Rome Treaty* (Hart Publishing 2010)

———, 'Revolutionizing European Law: A History of the Van Gend En Loos Judgment' (2014) 12 International Journal of Constitutional Law 136

———, 'Law Meets History: Interpreting the Van Gend En Loos Judgment' in Fernanda Nicola and Bill Davies (eds), *EU Law Stories* (Cambridge University Press 2017)

Rass Holdgaard, Daniella Elkan, and Gustav Krohn Schaldemose, 'From Cooperation to Collision: The ECJ's Ajos Ruling and the Danish Supreme Court's Refusal to Comply' (2018) 55 Common Market Law Review 17

Ratcliffe DJ, 'The Nullification Crisis, Southern Discontents, and the American Political Process' (2000) 1 American Nineteenth Century History 1

Rauchegger C, 'National Constitutional Rights and the Primacy of EU Law: M.A.S.' (2018) 55 Common Market Law Review 1521

———, 'National Constitutional Courts as Guardians of the Charter: A Comparative Appraisal of the German Federal Constitutional Court's *Right to Be Forgotten* Judgments' (2020) 22 Cambridge Yearbook of European Legal Studies 258

Rawls J, *Political Liberalism* (Columbia University Press 1993)

Raz J, 'Legal Principles and the Limits of Law' (1972) 81 The Yale Law Journal 823

———, *The Authority of Law* (Oxford University Press 1979)

———, 'Authority, Law, and Morality', *Ethics in the Public Domain* (Oxford University Press 1995)

Romano S, *The Legal Order* (Routledge 2017)

Roznai Y, *Unconstitutional Constitutional Amendments: The Limits of Amendment Powers* (Oxford University Press 2019)

Roznai Y and Jacobsohn GJ, *Constitutional Revolution* (Yale University Press 2020)

Rubinelli L, *Constituent Power: A History* (Cambridge University Press 2020)

Rugge G, 'The Italian Constitutional Court on Taricco: Unleashing the Normative Potential of "National Identity"?' (2017) Zoom-In 37 QIL Questions of International Law 21

Sacco R, 'Legal Formants: A Dynamic Approach to Comparative Law (Installment I of II)' (1991) 39 The American Journal of Comparative Law 1

———, 'Legal Formants: A Dynamic Approach to Comparative Law (Installment II of II)' (1991) 39 The American Journal of Comparative Law 343

Šadl U and Mair S, 'Mutual Disempowerment: Case C-441/14 Dansk Industri, Acting on Behalf of Ajos A/S v Estate of Karsten Eigil Rasmussen and Case No. 15/2014 Dansk Industri (DI) Acting for Ajos A/S v The Estate Left by A' (2017) 13 European Constitutional Law Review 347

Sadurski W, *Poland's Constitutional Breakdown* (Oxford University Press 2019)

Sbragia A, 'The United States and the European Union: Comparing Two Sui Generis Systems' in Anand Menon and Martin Schain (eds), *Comparative Federalism: The European Union and the United States in Comparative Perspective* (Oxford University Press 2006)

Scarcello O, 'Proportionality in the PSPP and Weiss Judgments: Comparing Two Conceptions of the Unity of Public Law' (2021) 13 European Journal of Legal Studies 45

Schilling T, 'The Autonomy of the Community Legal Order: An Analysis of Possible Foundations' (1996) 37 Harvard International Law Journal 389

Schmidt VA, 'Democracy and Legitimacy in the European Union Revisited: Input, Output and "Throughput"' (2013) 61 Political Studies 2

Schmitt C, *Constitutional Theory* (Duke University Press 2008)

Schönberger C, 'Lisbon in Karlsruhe: Maastricht's Epigones At Sea' (2009) 10 German Law Journal 1201

Schütze R, *From Dual to Cooperative Federalism: The Changing Structure of European Law* (Oxford University Press 2009)

———, 'On "Federal Ground": The European Union as an (Inter)National Phenomenon' (2009) 46 Common Market Law Review 1069

———, *European Constitutional Law* (Cambridge University Press 2012)

———, 'Federalism as Constitutional Pluralism: "Letter from America"' in Matej Avbelj and Jan Komárek (eds), *Constitutional Pluralism in the European Union and Beyond* (Hart Publishing 2012)

———, 'Constitutionalism(s)' in Roger Masterman and Robert Schütze (eds), *The Cambridge Companion to Comparative Constitutional Law* (Cambridge University Press 2019)

———, 'Constitutionalism and the European Union' in Catherine Barnard and Steve Peers (eds), *European Union Law* (Oxford University Press 2020)
———, *European Union Law* (Oxford University Press 2021)
———, 'Demoicracy in Europe: Some Preliminary Thoughts' (2022) 47 European Law Review 24
Shapiro S, 'What Is the Internal Point of View?' (2006) 75 Fordham Law Review 1157
Shapiro SJ, 'The "Hart–Dworkin" Debate: A Short Guide for the Perplexed' in Arthur Ripstein (ed), *Ronald Dworkin* (Cambridge University Press 2007)
———, 'Was Inclusive Legal Positivism Founded on a Mistake?' (2009) 22 Ratio Juris 326
Shecaira FP, 'Sources of Law Are Not Legal Norms' (2015) 28 Ratio Juris 15
Shklar JN, *Men and Citizens – A Study of Rousseau's Social Theory* (Cambridge University Press 1985)
Shuibhne NN, 'What Is the Autonomy of EU Law, and Why Does That Matter?' (2019) 88 Nordic Journal of International Law 9
Sieyès EJ, 'What Is the Third Estate?' in Oliver W Lembcke and Florian Weber (eds), *Emmanuel Joseph Sieyès: The Essential Political Writings* (Brill 2014)
Simon S and Rathke H, '"Simply Not Comprehensible." Why?' (2020) 21 German Law Journal 950
Simoncini A, 'The Success of a Constitutional Experiment: When History Matters. The Italian Constitutional Court in Global Context' (2016) 8 The Italian Journal of Public Law 79
Simonis LMA, 'Sanctuary Cities: A Study in Modern Nullification?' (2019) 8 British Journal of American Legal Studies 37
Smith M, 'Staring into the Abyss: A Crisis of the Rule of Law in the EU' (2019) 25 European Law Journal 561
Somek A, 'Monism: A Tale of the Undead' in Matej Avbelj and Jan Komárek (eds), *Constitutional Pluralism in the European Union and Beyond* (Hart Publishing 2012)
Stein E, 'Treaty-Based Federalism, A.D. 1979: A Gloss on Covey T. Oliver at the Hague Academy' (1979) 127 University of Pennsylvania Law Review 897
———, 'Lawyers, Judges, and the Making of a Transnational Constitution' (1981) 75 American Journal of International Law 1
Stone Sweet A and Mathews J, 'Proportionality Balancing and Global Constitutionalism' (2008) 47 *Columbia Journal of Transnational Law* 73
Storgaard LH, 'EU Law Autonomy versus European Fundamental Rights Protection – On *Opinion 2/13* on EU Accession to the ECHR' (2015) 15 Human Rights Law Review 485
Streinz T, 'The Evolution of European Data Law' in Paul Craig and Gráinne de Búrca (eds), *The Evolution of EU Law* (Oxford University Press 2021)
Sweet AS, 'The Juridical Coup d'État and the Problem of Authority' (2007) 8 German Law Journal 915
Szwed M, 'The Polish Constitutional Tribunal Crisis from the Perspective of the European Convention on Human Rights: ECtHR 7 May 2021, No. 4907/18, Xero Flor w Polsce Sp. z o.o. v Poland' (2022) European Constitutional Law Review 1
Tancredi A, 'Of Direct Effect, Primacy and Constitutional Identities: Rome and Luxembourg Enmeshed in the Taricco Case' (2017) Zoom in 37 QIL Questions of International Law 1
Taylor A, *American Revolutions – A Continental History, 1750–1804* (Norton 2016)
Tega D, 'The Italian Constitutional Court in Its Context: A Narrative' (2021) 17 European Constitutional Law Review 369

Teubner G, 'Breaking Frames: Economic Globalization and the Emergence of Lex Mercatoria' (2002) 5 European Journal of Social Theory 199
Thomson JJ, *The Realm of Rights* (Harvard University Press 1990)
Timmerman M, 'Balancing Effective Criminal Sanctions with Effective Fundamental Rights Protection in Cases of VAT Fraud: Taricco' (2016) 53 Common Market Law Review 779
Torres Pérez A, 'From Portugal to Poland: The Court of Justice of the European Union as Watchdog of Judicial Independence' (2020) 27 Maastricht Journal of European and Comparative Law 105
Troper M, 'Sovereignty' in Michel Rosenfeld and András Sajó (eds), *The Oxford Handbook of Comparative Constitutional Law* (Oxford University Press 2012)
Tucker A, 'Uncertainty in the Rule of Recognition and in the Doctrine of Parliamentary Sovereignty' (2011) 31 Oxford Journal of Legal Studies 61
Tuori K, *European Constitutionalism* (Cambridge University Press 2015)
Tushnet M, 'The Possibilities of Comparative Constitutional Law' (1999) 108 The Yale Law Journal 1225
———, 'Authoritarian Constitutionalism: Some Conceptual Issues' in Alberto Simpser and Tom Ginsburg (eds), *Constitutions in Authoritarian Regimes* (Cambridge University Press 2013)
———, *The Constitution of the United States of America* (Hart Publishing 2015)
———, 'Varieties of Liberal Constitutionalism' in Xenophon Contiades and Alkmene Fotiadou (eds), *Routledge Handbook of Comparative Constitutional Change* (Routledge 2020)
Uitz R and Sajó A, *The Constitution of Freedom: An Introduction to Legal Constitutionalism* (Oxford University Press 2017)
Van Elsuwege P and Gremmelprez F, 'Protecting the Rule of Law in the EU Legal Order: A Constitutional Role for the Court of Justice' (2020) 16 European Constitutional Law Review 8
Vauchez A, *Brokering Europe: Euro-Lawyers and the Making of a Transnational Polity* (Cambridge University Press 2015)
Vinx L, 'The Incoherence of Strong Popular Sovereignty' (2013) 11 International Journal of Constitutional Law 101
———, 'The Kelsen-Hart Debate: Hart's Critique of Kelsen's Legal Monism Reconsidered' in Jeremy Telman (ed), *Hans Kelsen in America – Selective Affinities and the Mysteries of Academic Influence* (Springer International Publishing 2016)
Violante T, 'Bring Back the Politics: The PSPP Ruling in Its Institutional Context' (2020) 21 German Law Journal 1045
von Bogdandy A and Paris D, 'Power Is Perfected in Weakness: On the Authority of the Italian Constitutional Court' in Vittoria Barsotti and others (eds), *Dialogues on Italian constitutional justice: a comparative perspective* (Routledge-Giappichelli 2021)
Waldron J, 'Introduction' in Jeremy Waldron (ed), *Theories of Rights* (Oxford University Press 1985)
———, 'The Core of the Case against Judicial Review' (2006) 115 The Yale Law Journal 1346
———, 'Who Needs Rules of Recognition?' in Matthew Adler and Kenneth Himma (eds), *The Rule of Recognition and the U.S. Constitution* (Oxford University Press 2009)
———, 'The Rule of Law and the Importance of Procedure' in James Fleming (ed), *Getting to the Rule of Law* (New York University Press 2011)
———, 'International Law: A Relatively Small and Unimportant Part of Jurisprudence?' in Luís Duarte d'Almeida, James Edwards and Andrea Dolcetti (eds), *Reading HLA Hart's 'The Concept of Law'* (Hart Publishing 2013)

Walker N, 'The Idea of Constitutional Pluralism' (2002) 65 Modern Law Review 317

Walker N, 'Legal Theory and the European Union: A 25th Anniversary Essay' (2005) 25 Oxford Journal of Legal Studies 581

Walker N, 'Reconciling MacCormick: Constitutional Pluralism and the Unity of Practical Reason' (2011) 24 Ratio Juris 369

———, 'Constitutional Pluralism Revisited' (2016) 22 European Law Journal 24

———, 'Legal and Constitutional Theory of the European Union' in Paul Craig and Gráinne de Búrca (eds), *The Evolution of EU Law* (Oxford University Press 2021)

Waluchow WJ, *Inclusive Legal Positivism* (Oxford University Press 1994)

Watkins WJ, *Reclaiming the American Revolution: The Kentucky and Virginia Resolutions and Their Legacy* (Palgrave Macmillan 2004)

Weiler JHH, 'Eurocracy and Distrust: Some Questions Concerning the Role of the European Court of Justice in the Protection of Fundamental Human Rights Within the Legal Order of the European Communities' (1986) 61 Washington Law Review 41

———, 'The Transformation of Europe' (1991) 100 The Yale Law Journal 2403

———, 'Does Europe Need a Constitution? Demos, Telos and the German Maastricht Decision' (1995) 1 European Law Journal 219

———, *The Constitution of Europe* (Cambridge University Press 1999)

———, 'In Defence of the Status Quo: Europe's Constitutional Sonderweg' in Joseph HH Weiler and Marlene Wind (eds), *European Constitutionalism beyond the State* (Cambridge University Press 2003)

Wendel M, 'Paradoxes of Ultra-Vires Review: A Critical Review of the PSPP Decision and Its Initial Reception' (2020) 21 German Law Journal 979

Williams B, *In the Beginning Was the Deed* (Princeton University Press 2005)

Wittgenstein L, *Philosophical Investigations* (Blackwell 1988)

Wohlfahrt C, 'The Lisbon Case: A Critical Summary' (2009) 10 German Law Journal 1277

Zucca L, 'A Genealogy of State Sovereignty' (2015) 16 Theoretical Inquiries in Law

INDEX

Notes: Page numbers followed by n represents notes.